Bazaar Politics

Stanford Studies in Middle Eastern and Islamic Societies and Cultures

Bazaar Politics

POWER AND POTTERY IN AN AFGHAN MARKET TOWN

Noah Coburn

Stanford University Press
Stanford, California

Stanford University Press
Stanford, California

Printed in the United States of America on acid-free, archival-quality paper

Library of Congress Cataloging-in-Publication Data

Coburn, Noah, author.
    Bazaar politics : power and pottery in an Afghan market town / Noah Coburn.
        pages cm
    Includes bibliographical references and index.
    ISBN 978-0-8047-7671-4 (cloth : alk. paper) — ISBN 978-0-8047-7672-1 (pbk. : alk. paper)
    1. Istalif (Afghanistan)—Politics and government. 2. Istalif (Afghanistan)—Social
conditions. 3. Potters—Afghanistan—Istalif. 4. Political culture—Afghanistan—Istalif.
5. Ethnology—Afghanistan—Istalif. I. Title.
    DS375.I88C63 2011
    958.1—dc22
                                    2011004859

Typeset by Bruce Lundquist in 10/14 Minion

For RBC and JBC
Who Led Me to the Bosphorus

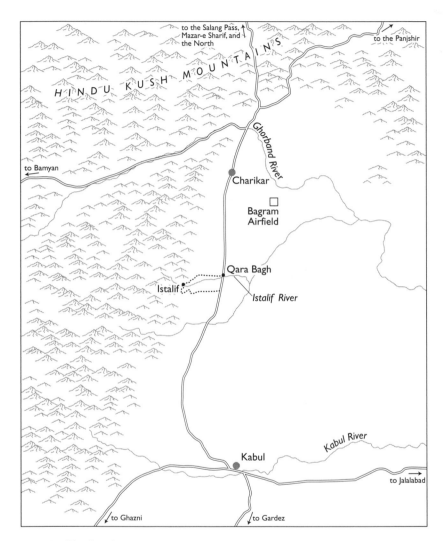

Map 1. Istalif and environs.

CONTENTS

PREFACE

I am fortunate to have conducted research in interesting, though also stressful, times, and this experience has done much to shape this book. The insurgency in southern Afghanistan was just beginning to spread as I started my study of Istalif, a small town north of Kabul. With instability growing in the region, questions arose for me and my informants: Would the area again turn violent? Could the international military forces guarantee security? Why had the Afghan government, despite massive amounts of international aid, failed to create a stable state capable of providing basic services? These questions, and uncertainty about the future, cast a pall over my conversations with Istalif residents about local politics. Thus, while this book is anthropological, beginning at the most local level, looking at politics in one community and within the families of that community, the individuals were always considering how their decisions fit into the politics of an increasingly unstable Afghanistan.

Because the tumult in Afghanistan is now more than thirty years old, what I present here is just a snapshot of life in one part of the region, during a time of relative stability, within a much longer period of political and military upheaval. While I argue that life in Istalif was stable and free of violence while I was there, I make no claims that it will stay that way, and sadly, I will be a little surprised if it does. Therefore, I have written this ethnography in the past tense.

Unlike other ethnographies, I include interludes between the chapters to convey some of the emotions of fieldwork that get lost in more formulaic writing. Istalif was a beautiful, mysterious, scary place, and leaving out these emotions would ignore both my own lack of certainty about much of what I saw and the uncertainty of my informants, none of whom was ever entirely sure which way the political winds were blowing. In addition, while Afghanistan has received an immense amount of international attention in the past ten years, the accounts coming out of the region (with a few notable exceptions) often rely on stereotypes and generalizations. Regardless of how they describe

Afghans—as unruly, ungovernable tribes or passive victims—these accounts miss the great human diversity that gets brushed over in casualty counts and tribal mappings. With the interludes I hope to provide a more human account of the people of Istalif—those who befriended me, protected me, told me fascinating stories and even more fascinating lies, tried to swindle me in the bazaar, and taught me a great deal about life.

The writing process also varied somewhat from the norm. I first visited Istalif in the summer of 2005 on an exploratory trip, visiting several towns with important bazaars across northern Afghanistan, but I collected most of the data from Istalif between August 2006 and February 2008. I then returned to Boston to begin the writing process. In the spring of 2009, with Afghan presidential elections looming, I returned to Kabul to conduct other, related research. The rest of this book was completed in Kabul between the spring and fall of 2009.

Being in Kabul and so close to my field site was both a blessing and a curse, because I could easily get on the phone with informants or go up to the town to check on specific details. This proximity led me to check and recheck facts, perhaps a little too much, while thinking through new angles. During this period I did little additional research. Instead, I looked at how Istalif had changed, asking whether the changes fit my theories, and exploring how I could apply what I had learned to understanding issues across Afghanistan. Ultimately, though this process slowed the writing, I hope it has made my work richer and more accurate.

During the long writing process I have been supported by, worked for, or worked with several institutions. First and foremost, the Anthropology Department at Boston University was always supportive, especially considering the issues around conducting research in Afghanistan. In Kabul, the American Institute of Afghanistan Studies provided me with my initial home in Afghanistan and colleagues with whom to think through many of my questions. I also spent time working with the Turquoise Mountain, the Aga Khan Trust for Culture, the Afghanistan Research and Evaluation Unit, and the United States Institute of Peace, all of which have helped me understand the community of Istalif and Afghan political life, even if my work with them was not specifically for this project.

Among the individuals who helped me, the most important was Sediq Seddiqi, who tutored me in Dari and accompanied me during much of my early research. Ester Svensson was immensely helpful, explaining many aspects of pottery production. Thomas Barfield, Charles Lindholm, John Dixon,

Shahmahmood Miakhel, Whitney Azoy, Omar Sharifi, Khadim Hussain, Anna Larson, Zaher Seddiqi, John Dempsey, Mohammad Hassan Wafaey, Zubair Ahmad, Kimberly Arkin, Robert Weller, Richard Norton, Rory Stewart, Alex Thier, and Jolyon Leslie all provided insights and encouragement along the way. I am also indebted to the anonymous reviewers who made numerous suggestions, which greatly aided the reworking of the text. Of course, any errors remaining are my own.

Finally, my family provided the grounding and support that made such a project possible.

.   .   .

All the names of informants, except recognizable, national-level political figures, have been changed.

Bazaar Politics

A Rocky Road

The district office was cool and dark, located in the basement of what had once been a Taliban post. Before that the *mujahideen* occupied it. Before that the communist government had its offices there. And before that it was a hotel, with rose gardens, for tourists passing through on their way to India.

An old man still tended the roses below the patio where the guests used to look out over the Shomali Plain, but the top floor of the hotel was mangled— walls collapsed, twisted steel jutting dangerously out of concrete. On the east side, the floor simply disappeared where a rocket had taken off an entire side of the building.

The basement, though, still bustled. Half a dozen policemen walked up and down the hall, and petitioners waited on a bench to see the district governor. On that warm summer afternoon, I sat in the governor's large office, which was filled with so many people that it felt small. In addition to the district governor and his deputy, there were four local elders, a former warlord, two businessmen from Kabul, three engineers from the Ministry of Rural Rehabilitation and Development, and a steady stream of subordinates and onlookers coming in and out. Five men had crammed onto the sofa I was sitting on, which was clearly designed for three. Assembled in this room, wearing clothes ranging from traditional robes and turbans to slick, imitation Armani suits, were a good number of the town's power brokers. Although they seemed to trickle in randomly, there was, of course, nothing random about it.

The engineers had just eaten a large meal at the house one of the elders— a potter; but instead of sitting comfortably, digesting their lunches, they were beginning to squirm. I had stopped by on other business and ended up staying for tea. Then the engineers arrived. At that point, with the tension building, I was sitting in the corner, more or less forgotten. One of the engineers did keep glancing at me with a weak, almost apologetic smile.

For the past week, people in town had been talking about the engineers and their surveying team. They had slowly been working their way up the winding road that climbs north from Kabul to the Istalif bazaar, taking careful measurements. The engineers had become something of an attraction for schoolchildren, who were mesmerized by the tripods, theodolite, and other surveying instruments as they walked home from school.

The rumor was that the Ministry of Rural Rehabilitation and Development had allocated money for paving the bumpy 10-mile stretch of road, and (according to the engineers) they simply had to submit the drawings and estimates and work would begin. Money had also been allocated the year before, but apparently, some member of Parliament had been able to convince the ministry to redirect the funds for paving the road to his much smaller village instead. Talk in the bazaar had been cautious, but optimistic, about the project.

The meeting was civil. Traditional greetings and pleasantries were exchanged as each new person entered the room.

Salam Alaykum—*Peace be upon you.*

Wa alaykum—*And upon you.*

Khub asteed?—*Are you well?*

Jur asteed?—*Are you healthy?*

Fameel-eton jur ast?—*Is your family well?*

Chetor asteed?—*How are you?*

Teshakur, al hamdallah—*Thanks be to God.*

Jur basheed—*May you be healthy.*

Zindah basheed—*May you have long life.*

The meeting began with leaders asking the engineers about their work and warmly wishing them success. The elders played their role well—poor rural townsmen who were impressed by the engineering jargon—but their questions gradually became more pointed: When would work start? How long would it take? Would the irrigation channels running along the road also be renovated? What type of materials would be used? How much money had been allocated? Who would be employed?

A couple of times, voices were raised slightly, but never in a very aggressive manner. In a few instances the men appeared bemused, but they certainly were not irate or offended. The only real sticking point seemed to be the shorter 6-mile stretch of road that passed through the bazaar and looped back to the highway, east of town. The engineers argued that this portion would be much more difficult and expensive to pave because it passed through several villages, close to boundary walls, and was much steeper. One of the elders from a neighborhood above this stretch of road was insistent.

"Why is it fair that those to the south get a new road while those to the east receive nothing? And haven't all the new government schools also been built to the south? Development should come equally to all Istalifis. Let's at least have the engineers survey this stretch of road as well."

One or two men agreed. Most muttered, shaking their heads, but nobody expressed dissent. Around this time someone came into the room and the district governor got up to talk to him, walking out quietly. More tea was brought in. The governor returned with some papers, which he studied intently at his desk.

The engineers tried to explain to the argumentative elder that surveying the additional stretch of road would delay the project, and that the ministry would not like a new, higher estimate, but the man seemed to have convinced enough of the people in the room. One elder on the far side of the room scowled fiercely, bowed politely, repeated the formalities, wished everyone a long life, and left with two other men.

I walked out about half an hour later with the son of one of the elders. The meeting had ended quietly and the district governor had moved on to other work. As we emerged from the office, my companion shook his head grimly and spat out a sunflower seed he had been chewing.

"Now the road will never be built."

And two years later, as I write this, the road remains rutted and unpaved.

· · ·

This book is the story of why the road to Istalif has not been paved, and why a major issue for the townspeople was resolved in such an undramatic, almost lethargic meeting. Deep political issues were discussed that day, and the failure to pave the road was a major setback for the Istalifi economy. Yet in the meeting, voices were never raised, violence was never threatened, only one man chose to opt out of the negotiations, and a veneer of civility was maintained throughout.

This book also tells the story of why, despite a long, violent history, in a country dealing with a growing insurgency, the town remained relatively free of violence during my time there. The two stories may seem unrelated. However, a close study of how political groups in Istalif formed, how individuals made political decisions, and how the political groups dictated the flow of power reveals a deep link between Istalif's lack of violence and Afghanistan's difficult search for peace.

1 GROUPS AND VIOLENCE

AFTER THE FALL OF THE TALIBAN IN ISTALIF, a small town west of the Shomali Plain, there was a high degree of political tension, as well as numerous disputes over land and water, a tendency toward factionalism and feuding, and a reluctance to cooperate. Simultaneously, local politics remained relatively peaceful and free of violence. What created this seemingly paradoxical situation?

It is inadequate to say that the low rate of violence was a consequence of government and international military intervention, because these forces had little presence in Istalif. Towns that were closer to urban centers, and thus more susceptible to intervention, experienced significant violence. At the same time, the region was deeply divided ethnically, and there was intense competition for limited resources, as well as a general disillusionment with the Afghan government and the international presence. An examination of why Istalif remained peaceful has implications not only for how local politics in Afghanistan have shifted in the post-Taliban period, but also, more generally, how group organization shapes the presence or absence of violence. In many ways, academics and policy makers have misunderstood the forces driving local disputes and insurgency in Afghanistan, and, as a result, these elements have not been addressed very effectively by either the Afghan government or the international community.

Political power in Istalif was fractured. It coalesced around groups and categories of authority, such as *maliks* (local elders),[1] who led patrilineal descent groups, and commanders (warlords),[2] who led former militias. Some of the men referred to as warlords committed countless crimes against humanity during the civil war and Taliban period, but others were instrumental in filling the void left by the lack of a central government, keeping schools open, and providing security. In fact, most "warlords" in Istalif who were active in town politics during my research fall into this second category.

All of these groups were produced, and reproduced, by social and economic processes. They were distinguished from one another and represented by symbols, ranging from the hats they wore to the language they used. I initially looked at several lineages of potters who formed a guild-like group that cooperated—politically and economically—using the idiom of kinship. Often, however, these ties broke apart, particularly when potters competed in the marketplace. Other sources of political power, job opportunities in Kabul, and economic resources offered by aid groups also caused young men to attempt to build personal, semi-covert networks of allies outside their group.

Although tribe–state relations were the central focus of many anthropological studies in Afghanistan during the 1960s and 1970s, my research shows that the next thirty years of war and reconstruction significantly complicated political relations. In attendance at the meeting with the engineers from the Ministry of Rural Rehabilitation and Development described in the interlude "A Rocky Road," for example, were the district governor representing the central government, traditional elders, a former warlord, and two wealthy businessmen. Others vying for power in town included the *mullah* (the town's chief religious leader), French forces that regularly patrolled the area, an assortment of mostly small-sized non-governmental organizations (NGOs), and a police chief. A more structural study of Istalif might focus on the differences between groups. However, by abandoning traditional categorical approaches that focus on kinship or political terms such as tribe, clan, or state, and by using a more Barthian model of social formation focusing on the maintenance of boundaries, it becomes apparent that these were flexible groups that created a coherent political system in which all struggled for power.[3] The system, in fact, created a struggle of "all versus all" that led not to a Hobbesian war and violence, but to temporary peace and stability.

My analysis focuses on patrilineal descent groups (qaums), religious leaders, a newly wealthy merchant class, former militia groups, the district government, the police, and international groups, including the military and NGOs. The chapters examine these models of social organization and cultural definitions of power, and explore how they shaped violence and local stability.

TIME AND PLACE

Istalif sits in the western foothills of the Shomali Plain. In older accounts this area was often referred to as *Koh-e Dahman*, skirt of the mountains. Occasionally it is included in the region called Kohistan, which more accurately refers to the mountains further north of Istalif.[4] Today most people simply refer to Istalif as part of the Shomali Plain that includes the northern districts of Kabul

Province and Parwan Province north to the Hindu Kush. People in Kabul often refer to Istalifis simply as Shomalis.

Istalif's green hills and cool breezes offer a respite from the dusty heat of the plains below. Its fertile orchards and thriving craft industries have been attracting visitors for hundreds of years. While there are few mentions of Istalif in academic accounts of the area, the name appears numerous times in travel accounts of the region by Westerners and non-Westerners alike.[5] In the 1958 travel classic *A Short Walk in the Hindu Kush*, Eric Newby's guide Ghulam Nabi told him, "He who has not seen Istalif has seen nothing"—a problematic observation since the two were speeding by on the road north.[6] Others, however, have lingered.

Emperor Babur was the most famous early visitor, and often when in Kabul he would visit and hunt in the area. In his 1504 autobiography he wrote:

> There are few places known to equal Istalif. A large torrent that runs through the middle of the village has orchards on both sides. Verdant, pleasant small garden plots abound, and the water is so pure and cold, there is no need for iced water. . . . When the trees blossom, no place in the world equals it.[7]

He goes on to praise the grapes and Judas trees of the area, both of which are still found in abundance. Babur also had several irrigation channels built using elaborate stonework to distribute water to other gardens, including some on ridges high above the village. The descendants of these channels continue to make Istalif a popular picnic spot.

Numerous visitors followed Babur to the area, often seeming to borrow from his prose as well as his itinerary. Notably, in the decade before the first Anglo-Afghan war, a series of British visitors wrote what were at the time immensely popular travelogues. Charles Masson, a British deserter, numismatist, and occasional spy, visited the town while doing archeological work in the area between 1826 and 1838; he wrote:

> Istalif is one of the most picturesque spots which can be conceived; all that a combination of natural beauties can achieve we behold here in perfection: their effect is not diminished, but rather augmented by the rude appearance of the houses of the town. The scenery of the country around is extensive and grand, in happy unison with the keeping of the whole picture.[8]

Masson's journals include a lithograph that is strikingly similar to today's view of Istalif.

Alexander Burnes, a British political agent and adventurer (later killed in the Kabul bazaar, days before the British Army's disastrous retreat from Kabul) followed Masson a few years later, exclaiming: "No written description can do justice to this lovely and delightful country." Burnes wrote: "We pitched our camp on one side of the valley, and directly opposite us, at a distance of about a thousand yards, rose the town of Istalif in the form of a pyramid, terrace on terrace, the whole crowned with a shrine embosomed among wide-spreading plane-trees."[9] From the description, Burnes undoubtedly camped on the present site of the district office described in the interlude "A Rocky Road," where Kabulis still come to enjoy the view and eat at the small teahouse.

Travelers did not remark exclusively on the beauty of the landscape. Nineteenth-century observers also described the instability of local political relations with Kabul, and a tendency toward feuding that set Istalifis apart from Tajiks in other parts of Afghanistan. Burnes lamented:

> It is a source of deep regret that this beautiful country should be inhabited by a race of men so turbulent and vindictive as the Tajiks have here proved themselves to be; and yet, throughout Afghanistan generally, these same Tajiks form the most peaceable classes of population. Here, however, their blood-feuds are endless: a week never passes without strife or assassination, and I have been assured, on the best authority, that a man frequently remains immured in his own tower for two and three years from the fear of his enemies. . . . It is rare to see a man go to bathe, hunt, or even ride out, without a part of his clan attending him as a guard. . . . These people have the reputation of being the best foot-soldiers in Afghanistan, and from all I could learn they merit the distinction.[10]

Many of these disputes revolved around land and women. The numerous gardens and orchards located some distance from the center of town became sites of conflict because the gardens, with shorter walls, exposed women to outside eyes and men to the rifles of their enemies. As Masson recounted, "Nearly every householder in Istalif has his garden or orchard. . . . The people themselves, Tajiks, are not very amiable . . . and the mulberry season, which draws them into the orchards . . . is generally marked by sanguinary conflicts and murders."[11] Beyond the Orientalist rhetoric of some of these accounts, Masson and Burnes do seem to have identified some trends in the local politics of the region.

Colonel Haughton noted in his account leading up to the siege of Charikar in 1841 that the areas around Charikar and Istalif were dominated by large, mud *qala* (fort) architecture that was more typical in eastern and southern Pashtun regions.[12] These large structures, some of which remain today in the eastern section of the district, have few exterior windows, many turrets, and often contain gardens—features that enabled their inhabitants to withstand long sieges during feuds or periods of unrest.

The tendency toward feuding can be explained, at least in part, by the high value of land and the ethnic and tribal diversity of the region, which meant villages were always in danger of losing land or water to their neighbors. In addition, Istalif and the entire region of Kohistan have a history of political volatility, during which Shomali leaders regularly renegotiated their relationship with Kabul. In contrast with many simple narratives of Afghan history, which describe the Pashtun government's dominance over other ethnicities, the Pashtun tribe in control of Kabul has almost always been forced to forge alliances with at least one major non-Pashtun group. This has given the Shomali area enormous importance at several stages in Afghan history. It also means that many of the revolts that have overthrown regimes in Kabul originated in the Shomali and Kohistan. The most notable of these was the overthrow of Amanullah Khan, in 1929, by Habibullah Kalakani, known pejoratively as *Bach-e Saqao* (son of the water carrier).

Istalif's political situation was even more complex because the town, located on the edge of the Shomali, was not socially or politically integrated into the region, as were areas further down in the valley. On several occasions the Istalifis broke politically with their neighbors. British accounts before the siege of Charikar noted that they had several allies in Istalif despite the near-universal contempt for the British occupation of the area.[13] Similarly, when describing the civil war and fighting with the Taliban, Istalifis claim to have supported Ahmed Shah Massoud, the Panjshiri leader who became one of the key figures during the resistance against the Soviets. However, they spoke of him with much less reverence than other Tajiks in the region, and his picture was not displayed with the same prominence as it was in towns closer to Kabul.

Istalif's location is not simply beautiful—it is strategic. The entire Kohistan area has always been a focal point for resistance to Kabul, and controlling the area has been key to holding the entire region around Kabul.[14] Over thousands of years, the Shomali Plain, with Bagram at its center, has been a tactical nexus. As historian Arnold Toynbee noted, "Plant yourself not in Europe but in Iraq, it will become evident that half the roads of the Old World lead to Aleppo and half to Bagram."[15] Sitting in the hills overlooking Bagram, Istalif has watched countless armies marching between India and Central Asia—sometimes assisting them, and sometimes drawing back and waiting for them to pass. In addition, at key points in Afghan history, opponents of rulers in Kabul gathered resistance forces in the mountain valley of Bamyan, to the west. For example, opposition forces regrouped in the valley at the end of the first Anglo-Afghan war in 1842, and almost ninety years later opponents of Habibullah Kalakani used Bamyan as a base from which to launch raids on Kabul in 1929.

Kabul is only a few days' march from Bamyan, but the narrow passes leading to the area made any group settled in Bamyan difficult to uproot. The Bamyan valley has two main passes leading east toward Kabul: a southern pass through Wardak, and a northern pass that follows the Ghorband River, parallel to the Istalif River just to the north and flowing toward Charikar. In times of peace, virtually all traffic along this northern route follows the Ghorband River. However, when the regime in Kabul wanted to seal off the Bamyan region, on several occasions it tried to block access to Kabul from the Ghorband valley by sending troops from Charikar as the British did during the first Anglo-Afghan war.[16] Once the main pass was blocked, one of the best alternative transport routes was across a few small mountain passes to the south of the Ghorband River, which took the traveler on a brief detour into the valley created by the Istalif River. It took about one long day's walk from the town of Ghorband to the center of Istalif for a man travelling lightly. Several men remembered making this trip on foot during the Soviet period, when it was an active route for those fighting against the communist regime. Townspeople blame the importance of the pass and its use by the *mujahideen*, Islamic resistance fighters, for the aerial bombardments Istalif was subjected to during this period. This, however, is just one of the tragedies from Istalif's troubled past.

ISTALIF'S BLOODY HISTORY

At the time he wrote his lyrical description of Istalif, Burnes was unaware that his fate had become inexorably linked with that of the town. Following Burnes' murder in November 1841 in the Kabul bazaar, there was a crisis of leadership among British officers leading the army that had recently occupied Afghanistan. Negotiations with Afghan leaders failed, but instead of immediate withdrawal, officers delayed until January 1, 1842. These decisions contributed to the disastrous retreat that resulted in the death of 16,000, with famously only one British survivor, Dr. William Brydon, completing the retreat to Jalalabad.[17] Eight months later the British sent an army of retribution back into Afghanistan to rescue 93 prisoners still held captive near Bamyan, and to attempt to restore some dignity to the British Empire.

Unlike the previous British presence in Kabul, this was not an occupying army. The main goal of this army, led by Major General Pollock, was a public display of force, with "the declared wish of the Governor General that the army should leave behind some decisive proof of its power."[18] The most notable display was the British destruction of the Kabul bazaar. Less well known, but central to our story, was an event that occurred earlier. A force taken from General Pollock's and General Nott's troops was sent to Istalif under Major General McCaskill. Istalif was said to have been chosen because Hazin Khan, one of the accused killers of Burnes, was hiding in the area. There were also material incentives; wealthy families in Kabul had moved many of their valuables from the capital to Istalif to protect them from the advancing army.[19] Just beyond Istalif, Akbar Khan, one of the central figures in the massacre of the retreating British, was also said to be in Ghorband, with his ally Aminullah Khan, amassing Barakzai troops.[20] If this was the case, however, the Afghan troops in Istalif offered only minimal resistance to the advancing British.

On September 29, 1842, British troops attacked the town.[21] Despite a position so defensive that McCaskill reported to Pollock it was "impossible to conceive ground naturally stronger,"[22] British losses were reported to be "trifling, for the advance of our officers and men was too rapid and decisive to allow the sharp fire of the enemy telling much upon them."[23] Hundreds of Afghans were killed, women were taken hostage, and McCaskill ordered the town burned. Eldred Pottinger, dubbed the "Hero of Herat" during the Persian siege of the city in 1837–1838 and one of two British survivors of the siege of Charikar, was an advisor during the assault. Clearly dismayed by the behavior of the troops, he later questioned the whole enterprise and left South Asia, where he had spent his entire career, shortly afterwards.

The brutality of the incident was later reported in the British press. It became an often-cited example in the debate, in Britain, about whether the excessive behavior of the British troops was warranted. Some five-hundred women and children were reportedly captured,[24] and multiple accounts even described two British soldiers flipping a coin to determine who would carry off a pretty girl.[25] When the two men were stopped by a political officer, one is said to have remarked, "By Jesus, it's a hard case, and I pledged not to offer her any violence till I married her."[26] The British army found so many valuables that it did not have enough carts to carry them, and left much of their plunder to burn with the town.[27] Many vigorously defended the action, arguing it was a legitimate response to the massacre of British troops, despite the fact that there was little evidence that Istalifis (or shop owners in the Kabul bazaar, for that matter) had been significant participants in the massacre.[28] General Pollock weakly defended himself in a letter to Lord Ellenborough, the governor general of India at the time: "If any excess has been committed which I have not noticed, I can only affirm that I recollect none."[29] The British Parliament even debated what had become known as "the excesses at Istalif."[30] For Istalifis, the point was moot; the British had already withdrawn from Afghanistan, leaving the town in ruins.

Far from being left in peace, however, Istalif would be destroyed repeatedly over the next century and a half. During the civil war that followed the overthrow of Amanullah Khan by Habibullah Kalakani, Istalif saw recurring fighting beginning in 1929. As some Pashtun and Hazara tribes that had initially supported Habibullah began to revolt, the Ghorband and Istalif valleys again became strategic areas. According to the journals of Fayz Mohammad, a scribe of the Amir's court and one of the only local chroniclers of the period, on April 20 Habibullah sent forces to block the Ghorband valley, again making Istalif an important access point into the Shomali Plain. The town was attacked a week later, first by Hazara tribes on their way to attack Kabul.[31] Some of the oldest local men claimed to remember hiding in the hills during these attacks, and most of them stated that the town in general supported Habibullah, a fellow Tajik, who was from Kalakan, a town in the Shomali Plain a few miles to the south. Habibullah was remembered in town as a pious figure, and men told stories about how he had tricked Amanullah. Amanullah was portrayed as a pawn of the West who had lost his Islamic beliefs and ties with the Afghan people.

Istalif would suffer on both ends of the conflict. As Nadir Shah, a Pashtun general who had served under Amanullah Khan, measured strategies for attacking Kabul from the north, he considered Istalif an important point of attack.[32] When he finally took the throne following Habibullah's brief reign, indebted to the Pashtun tribes who had supported him, he gave them rights to raid the Shomali Plain for booty, especially from Tajik supporters of Habibullah, such as the Istalifis. A year later the Mangals and several other Pashtun tribes again rode through the Shomali Plain, sent by Nadir Shah to put down an uprising in Kohistan, leading to similar results.[33] During this period Istalif was badly damaged, and eighty years later some Istalifis still spoke of the cruelty of the Mangals, the tribe from southeastern Afghanistan that had been most active in the area at the time.

A period of respite followed. Istalifis spoke of the 1960s and 1970s as the golden age of both Istalif and Afghanistan. During this period, Afghanistan experienced growth in the tourist industry, with visitors passing through Kabul on the "hippy trail" between Europe and India to sample the delights of the area, including easily accessible narcotics. The Ministry of Tourism built a hotel on one of the ridges, and buses of visitors from Kabul arrived routinely. Photographs by visitors during this time show smiling tourists in lush gardens. Istalifis still cite the Friday visits of prominent national figures, such as Zahir Shah, king from 1933 to 1973, and Daud Khan, president from 1973 to 1978, as evidence of the town's importance. During this period the craft industries thrived. But it was not to last.

ISTALIF AND THE TALIBAN

The most recent destruction of Istalif came under the Taliban, and this episode continued to shape many aspects of daily life during the period of this study. While much of the town had slowly been rebuilt, entire neighborhoods remained in ruins, serving as daily reminders of the presence of the Taliban.

During the first part of the last thirty years of conflict in Afghanistan, Istalif escaped serious damage. Early in the communist period, a government office was set up in the old Ministry of Tourism guesthouse, but officials rarely ventured into the bazaar, and the Istalifis were primarily left to govern themselves. The exception was the school; most of the teachers were from Kabul, and Istalifis claimed that many had communist ties. One local commander was even said to have initially earned his reputation by killing one of the schoolteachers. Many of the currently middle-aged men in Istalif did not go to school or went rarely during this period, because their families did not want them learning from those *be-din* (without religion). As the Soviet-backed regime began to lose its grip on rural areas, the military pulled back to urban areas. Mujahideen fighters began to emerge from the mountains, and the Istalifi bazaar catered to their needs, selling supplies and ammunition. Istalif became the victim of periodic Soviet air attacks to punish them for assisting the fighters.

After the withdrawal of Soviet troops, mujahideen forces began to fight among themselves, and in 1992 what is now referred to as the civil war period began. Interestingly, while Istalifis would speak for hours about the days under Zahir Shah and Daud Khan, and would often recount the period under the Taliban, it was much more difficult to collect details about the *jihad* against the Soviets and the period of interfactional fighting during the civil war.[34] This is partly explained by the fact that the period was very unstable, and some Istalifis traveled back and forth between Istalif and Pakistan or more peaceful areas of the north. More importantly, however, Istalifis were reluctant to discuss this period because historical narratives were so contested. Small-scale local fighting, driven by a series of mid-level commanders and political parties, caused political tumult. Land was stolen, water rights were renegotiated, and a series of militia leaders rose and fell quickly. A series of commanders from both the west and the east of the district became increasingly central to town politics (see Chapter 6). Istalifis hesitated discussing the role of these men before 2001, and had good reason to construct political narratives that ignored some of the unresolved tensions in the area. To discuss the period was to draw attention to, and potentially reignite, long-standing land feuds and conflicts between neighboring families. For many, the political history of the 1980s and 1990s was a topic best ignored.[35]

During this period, Kabul, which had been undamaged during much of the Soviet period, became divided along ethnic and party lines. Street fighting and regular rocket attacks occurred across most of the city. Istalif and other parts of the Shomali Plain, however, were relatively peaceful during this period and became home to many refugees from Kabul. This would all change with the arrival of the Taliban from the south.

In 1996 the Taliban took Kabul with alarming ease.[36] Various mujahideen factions had exhausted themselves fighting against each other, and many Kabulis were tentatively relieved as the Taliban brought stability to the area. The rapid retreat of mujahideen forces was partially a tactical ploy by Ahmad Shah Massoud, who withdrew all his troops from Kabul during the night of September 26. The Taliban, with a false sense of confidence, instead of reinforcing their position, quickly advanced north across the Shomali Plain, occupying Istalif and neighboring areas. They advanced all the way to the foothills of the mountains south of the Panjshir Valley, where Massoud had taken his men.

Istalifis spoke of the town's first occupation by the Taliban as a period of relative calm. Most Taliban fighters seemed content to remain within the district center and police the outposts, as the Soviets had for much of their time in Istalif. The greatest frustration many Istalifis had was that these new rulers were almost entirely Pashto speakers, who had trouble communicating with the local population. As a result, several mullahs who had been educated in Pakistan and spoke Pashto became important intermediaries. Some Istalifis even gave food and expressed pity for this first wave of Taliban fighters, who had few supplies and were ill-equipped to govern the area. The Taliban asked local leaders to choose a district governor to represent them and supervise daily affairs in the town.

This period of calm was brief. The next spring, mujahideen forces, led primarily by Massoud and his men, poured out of the Hindu Kush, and the Taliban found themselves overextended. Massoud pushed the Taliban quickly across the Shomali Plain to the mountain pass that separated Kabul from the Shomali. Massoud, however, was not able to reenter Kabul. Several months of fighting followed, as the Taliban pushed back and the front line dragged back and forth across the Shomali Plain. In Istalif, the fighting cut off supplies, and people spoke of how they were forced to mix sawdust with flour to conserve their limited food stock. Some young men in town joined resistance groups, and the Taliban began to indiscriminately arrest men of fighting age. Numerous Istalifi men were sent to Pul-e Charkhi, the main prison outside of Kabul, while others were sent to prisons as far off as Kandahar. One family still had a carefully disguised hole in the ground in their mulberry orchard where the young men of the family spent days at a time hiding after the Taliban arrested one of their brothers. The treatment of those who were captured varied, but some were regularly tortured and held in squalid conditions without food. Many of the men in town still had scars as evidence of this treatment.

The most serious fighting in Istalif itself took place over three days, as the Taliban attempted to retake the town—troops pushing up the southern ridge, while Massoud's troops positioned themselves on the northern ridge. With no place to escape to, the townspeople were subject to three days of heavy bombardment. Families hid in local mosques in the hope that neither side would attack religious sites. Massoud's troops finally withdrew, leaving the town unprotected. Most Istalifis claim that relatively few of their sons actually took part in the fighting, but once Massoud's men had vanished into the hills, the Taliban decided to take revenge against those who remained. They gave those left in town 24 hours' warning and then systematically burned everything that had not been destroyed in the bombardment.

Istalifis scattered. Immediate families tended to stay together, but most of the wider kin groups did not. Some headed north to the Panjshir Valley, others tried to cross the border into Pakistan, but most went to Kabul, where they lived as refugees, usually in small, crowded rental homes. The situation was further complicated by the massive displacements of the previous decade. Following the chaos of the civil war in Kabul starting in 1992, many Kabulis with relatives to the north fled to the Shomali, which was relatively peaceful. With the Taliban's arrival in the Shomali, this pattern reversed itself, and Shomalis and Kabuli refugees fled back to Kabul.[37] Istalif was left in ruins for the next four years. Wolves roamed the streets, and rain and snow slowly washed away the few earth buildings and walls the Taliban had not taken the time to knock down.

.   .   .

Since the arrival of allied forces in 2001, Istalifis quickly returned to reclaim their land. Despite the volatility in much of the rest of the country and unresolved conflicts over land and water, the town has remained remarkably peaceful. The rest of this book explores why.

Ethnography and Suspicion

The gentle tapping on the door was too urgent. During *Ramazan*, the month of religious fasting, Daud usually woke me before sunrise so we could eat before the day's fast began, but the knocking was more persistent than usual. In the dark I glanced at my watch and noticed it was just past 1:00 in the morning. Too early to be eating. I opened the door. Daud looked worried.

"The new police chief is downstairs. He wants to talk to you."

"Why?" I asked.

"What do I know?" He replied.

I had heard there was a new police chief in town, but I had not met him. The previous police chief spent most of his time in the Istalif police headquarters, and I had rarely interacted with him. It was odd that the new one had chosen this hour to announce himself.

As I walked downstairs, my eyes were blurry. I had been up late the night before, playing cards with some of the young potters who were my closest friends. These games lasted longer during Ramazan, when people stayed up late and then lounged through the day. I conducted formal and informal interviews and gathered data through several social and economic surveys, but these late-night sessions, beyond simply being relaxing, were often one of my best sources of gossip. Without elders around, the young men were more at ease and spoke more freely about happenings in the town.

As she often did, my wife sat with us, taking part in the conversations. The men enjoyed talking with her and often commented on how bringing my wife with me demonstrated my trust in the town. They criticized soldiers and other international men who left their wives at home. The men treated her much as they would have treated any foreign man, with a few differences. When one got up to pour more tea, her cup was always filled, but when the card game began, she could sit and talk with us, but they never considered dealing her a hand.

Despite her inability to penetrate certain aspects of the male world, my wife had a mobility that I lacked. When we went to visit friends, she could begin in the guestroom with the men, and then casually move between the female quarters and guestroom. This was a social mobility no one outside the members of that family possessed. *Purdah* was strictly respected in Istalif, and there were no male–female interactions outside the extended family. Women rarely appeared in public, and when they did, they were covered in a blue *burqa*. The entrances to homes were strictly guarded; protecting your home also meant protecting your women and the honor of your family.

With the police chief in the garden downstairs, I realized Daud was primarily upset because my wife was upstairs. The chief and about eight other policemen were standing around in the dark garden. Istalif occasionally had a couple of hours of electricity a day, but never in the middle of the night. The flashlights that a few of the men carried created a confusing mix of light and shadow.

The police chief immediately began interrogating me: "Why are you here? Who is in charge of your security? Where is your permission?"

Still drowsy, I stumbled through my responses, explaining the work I was doing, that I had been in town for over a year, and telling them I had discussed the project with the district governor, the former police chief, and several other officials, getting permission from all of them.

"I do not work for the district governor!" he spat.

"Please," I said, "can we discuss this tomorrow? I can go to your office. It is very late."

The police chief was not interested in discussing the issue the next day; the other policemen shuffled their feet, looking down and trying to melt deeper into the shadows of the garden. Daud stood defiantly in the doorway, but did not speak.

My initial contacts in town were the family of the Malik, or head potter, whom I met early in my research, and several of his cousins. While no truly hospitable Afghan would ever admit it, it was clear that my presence was something of a strain on them. They refused my offer to pay rent, and although they were not poor, my staying with any family in town for more than a night or two was an economic burden. I also disrupted the social patterns in the household because women would not enter the room I was in. In addition, any family I was with felt it necessary to guarantee my security, which placed an added burden on them. On several occasions, the previous police chief had encouraged me to sleep at the police station, which he claimed was the safest place in town. I had declined, because of how this would have shaped the Istalifis' interactions with me, and the option grew even less appealing as I glanced at the shadows the police in the garden were throwing.

My difficulty finding a place to stay was just one example of the trouble Istalifis had placing me within their understanding of Westerners. I did not fit into any familiar category. At the time there were few foreigners in the country, and most were either military personnel or NGO workers. I did not wear a uniform, so I was clearly not in the military, and most agreed that because the town was not that central, I was probably not a spy, either. Some assumed that I was an NGO worker, but they did not understand why I was not distributing aid. Even my closest informants eventually decided I was writing a book about Istalifi history, because that explained why I would ask them about genealogies, regardless of how often I tried to explain my project to them.

An opportunity presented itself when I found an NGO that was just beginning to work with the potters in Istalif. The NGO was interested in opening a visitors' center in the bazaar. I helped them set up their center, introducing visiting internationals to local crafts families and doing some historical research. This arrangement greatly facilitated my explorations. I was able to stay above the visitors' center, and, my work with the center gave Istalifis an easy social category in which to place me.

Politically speaking, having my own space was important. It allowed me to be a guest at the homes of informants, and it also enabled me to host people. In particular, this private space let young men come visit me and speak without worrying about their elders and the elaborate formalities of hospitality.

My association with the NGO did lead some locals to solicit aid from me, especially early on, and, like nearly all foreigners in Afghanistan, I did have limited redistributive powers. I hired a cook, a gardener, and two guards. In general, however, I had few concrete resources to offer.

Early in my study when I explained what I was hoping to learn about Istalif, many of my informants assumed I was conducting surveys for an NGO. Later, as it became clear that I was not distributing any significant aid, informants became less interested in trying to convince me of their need for assistance, and my data collection went much more smoothly. However, there were still a few people who were convinced I had access to funds and was a relief worker who was simply very bad at his job.

Standing in the garden with the police chief that night, it was clear that he was not happy with the category I had constructed for myself. I considered trying to call the district governor or one of the local leaders with whom I was friends with to see if either of them could help convince the man and his small militia to leave. But it was 1:00 in the morning. Besides, cell-phone coverage in Istalif was not good—the best place in our compound was on the northwest corner of the roof. That would mean bringing at least the police chief inside. Not only did I not trust him there in the middle of the night, but I knew that bringing him in with my wife inside could have serious repercussions. It could damage my reputation, or worse—it could cause one of my friends to feel the need to take revenge. So I tried to hurry through our conversation by telling him we could certainly figure everything out the next day. Although the police chief seemed to have lost some of his initial fervor, he was still intent on lecturing me about security and the dangers of Afghanistan before leaving.

To a certain extent, he had a valid point. During my time in Istalif the insurgency in the south grew steadily, spreading to provinces that bordered Kabul. There had been an increasing number of attacks in the city of Kabul on internationals, including the audacious attack on Kabul's one luxury hotel, when four gunmen stormed the building, firing indiscriminately. Everyone in the international community seemed to know someone who had been there that evening. As a result, the internationals in Kabul became more and more isolated, less willing to leave their walled compounds. The potters complained that in previous years many more international visitors, including a few tourists, had visited the bazaar in Istalif.

As one of my friends often stated, I was always safer in Istalif because in the town everyone knew everyone else, and people were immediately aware of visitors. In contrast, Kabul was a city of strangers, where it was always unclear who was dangerous and who was not. Over time, I came to agree with my friend. There were police checkpoints on both of the roads into town that were continuously, if slightly lackadaisically, manned. More effective were the shopkeepers who sat in their storefronts, staring suspiciously at any unknown car that came through town.

Despite the relative peacefulness of Istalif, security and general political and economic uncertainty clearly had a psychological impact on me and on my informants, and complicated the process of doing an ethnographic study of the town. Throughout the period of study, attacks increased in Kabul and other places closer to Istalif, including nearby Charikar and Bagram. These changes forced me always to think about motives. While most anthropologists want their informants to be eager to speak with them, for me the situation was more complicated. Did the informant believe I could access funds for him? Later during my study, the kidnapping of foreigners became more of a concern in Kabul, and there were rumors that the Taliban were paying local criminal groups to kidnap internationals. Kidnappers were suspected of staking out homes where internationals or wealthy Afghans lived, to track their movements. Was the man in the bazaar who was so eager to speak to me simply an Istalifi who I had not met before because he had been working in Kabul, or were his motives darker? There was a Pashtun town to the south whose townspeople regularly came to shop in Istalif. Shopkeepers in Istalif were wary of these outsiders, and they would sometimes warn me dramatically to stay away from certain people.

Suspicion, I learned, was not reserved for me as an outsider. As we will see, politics in Istalif were a murky business, and power was often intentionally disguised. It was not always clear who was in charge or what people's true motives were, and political actors used this ambiguity to their advantage. Moreover, there was a strong belief in conspiracies; people often rejected the simple answer to political questions when the complex answer would suffice.

The atmosphere of suspicion made it especially difficult to gather precise economic data. When I initially surveyed shopkeepers, almost everyone claimed to have been there for only a year or two. Later I realized that this was clearly wrong, and shopkeepers simply feared being taxed retroactively (as some businesses in Kabul had been).[1] However, I do not believe shopkeepers actually thought I would give the information I gathered to the Ministry of Finance. Instead, there was a sense that in such uncertain times, it was better to keep private any information that could be perceived as sensitive.

Even as I continued to encourage the police to leave my garden, I knew there were probably other political processes going on of which I was not yet aware. I began to make a list in my head of people I needed to talk to in the morning. Where was the new police chief from? Who were his enemies in town? Was he really concerned about my safety? Was he simply looking to flex his own political muscle? Why target me in the middle of the night?

By the next afternoon, the situation was resolved. Several community leaders had called the new police chief on my behalf, and it seemed that he was primarily trying to demonstrate his political clout to his officers by intimidating a foreigner. But that night, in the shadows of the grape trellis, political power was more difficult to define. Thankfully, the police chief, too, seemed to tire of the conversation. But he turned back once more with angry eyes—"Don't you know that there are Taliban!"—before storming out into the night, his retinue trailing slowly behind him.

2 SOCIAL ORGANIZATION IN ISTALIF

IN TIMES OF POLITICAL AMBIGUITY, knowledge has great value, which increases rumors, lies, and simply misconstrued facts. As a result, answering some of the more basic questions about Istalif and Istalifis was challenging, particularly given the lack of academic accounts about the town and the instability of the previous decades. For example, there were no reliable census figures for the district. Charles Masson estimated in the 1830s that there were between 15,000 and 18,000 people living in Istalif and the surrounding villages.[1] In April 2002, a report from the United Nations High Commissioner for Refugees (UNHCR) estimated that before the Soviet invasion, the population was 36,000. The report claims that by 1999 the population had swelled to 75,000,[2] but in 2002 it was only at 8,500, as refugees began slowly returning to their homes.[3]

Trends in these numbers were generally confirmed by informants, but they should also be questioned because of their political power. The UNHCR report, for example, notes that the "head of the district mentioned 75,000 (in 1999) as a correct number of inhabitants before the war."[4] The head of the district at this point had a strong incentive to make such a "correction," because he had a clear interest in directing as many rebuilding projects toward the area as possible. As a result the figure of 75,000 is probably exaggerated, as is the 45,000 that the UNHCR also estimated would return by the end of 2002. Such manipulation of population numbers is a common method for increasing funds from the government and international donors. More recently, district officials and elders similarly encouraged residents to vote in national elections so the population would appear as high as possible and they could ask for increases in aid.[5] This distortion of figures did not necessarily originate solely in Afghan sources. The United Nations and other development organizations had a reason to inflate some figures. NGOs looking to appeal to donors for more funds wanted to demonstrate that their programs were assisting as many beneficiaries as possible. Thus, population figures provided by the International Relief and Development Fund and other relief groups should be considered with some skepticism.

Almost all surveys since 2002 are sure to have similar biases. The Central Statistics Office in Kabul estimated in 2006 that Istalif had a population of 29,800, which, from the surveying I conducted, appeared to be the most accurate estimate of the actual population of the area.[6] This number, however, still did not take into account another significant demographic shift: the increased weekly migration between Kabul and Istalif by young men seeking work. The three-hour round-trip between Istalif and Kabul meant that some laborers made the commute every day. Many had relatives in Kabul, through marriage or Istalifis who had chosen not to return after the fall of the Taliban. As a result many Istalifis spent several days a week with these relatives, returning to Istalif on Fridays. Other families had relatives living abroad, particularly in Pakistan, and wages sent back in the form of remittances and the flow of people between these communities both had a limited, but still meaningful, impact on social and economic relationships in the town.

Thus, the actual number of residents living full-time in Istalif was significantly lower than the number who claimed to live there. Further complicating the matter was the fact that in Kabul there was an emphasis on original locality as an important identity marker. Many people in Kabul whose ancestors had left Istalif several generations earlier, even before the last three decades of conflict, still called themselves Istalifis. This presents some complex questions about identity and social organization in the area.

UNDERSTANDING TAJIK SOCIAL ORGANIZATION

Understanding social organization in Istalif is further complicated by the fact that although many ethnographers have touched on the Tajiks, and some short accounts focus on them exclusively, no major English-language ethnography of the Tajiks has been written, despite the fact that they are the second largest ethnic group in Afghanistan. This is partly due to the fact that Tajiks have long been considered a residual category. Mountstuart Elphinstone, in his classic early nineteenth-century account of ethnic groups in *The Kingdom of Caubul*, defines Tajiks as a term "applied to all people of Afghaunistan, whose vernacular language is Persian,"[7] and many scholars since have followed this lead.

Ethnographies from the 1960s and 1970s tend to focus on smaller ethnic groups, Pashtuns tribes, and Kuchis. As a result, much of what has been written about the Tajiks is viewed through the lens of another ethnic group and attempts to contextualize them in relation to others. Many discussions of Tajik lineages focus on how they are different from or influenced by Pashtun or Hazara tribes. Certainly there has been significant cultural diffusion between these groups, but the odd imbalance in academic literature, along with the fact that Tajiks are not organized into neat tribal divisions the way most Pashtuns are, has resulted in a tendency to describe Tajik social organization as a response to Pashtun organization, ignoring the fact that the Tajiks have their own coherent, if complicated, system.

Because Tajiks often live in proximity to strong Pashtun tribes, some ethnographies claim that the relationship between Tajiks and Pashtuns is primarily feudal. In some areas of Afghanistan, primarily the south and southeast of the country, such relationships do exist. Families that are not members of any of the local tribes are referred to as *hamsayah*, which translates as neighbor (literally, "of the same shade"). But in this context, it implies a lower status; by labeling a group as a neighbor, the speaker emphasizes that there are no kin relations. Part of Elphinstone's bias comes from the fact that he was based in Peshawar in 1808 and gathered information primarily from informants from the east of modern-day Afghanistan and those related to the Pashtun court. The result is this assessment: "The Taujiks, who inhabit the lands of Afghaun tribes, either live as Humsayehs to those tribes, or in separate villages of their own."[8]

This observation has led some to assume that Tajiks in Afghanistan, particularly those living outside traditional urban centers, define themselves solely in reaction to the groups that surround them, usually in a subservient role. Elphinstone concluded that "Taujiks are all peaceable and obedient to the government. Besides the employment of agriculture, they occupy those manufactures and trades which are renounced by the Afghauns[9]. . . . They are of an unmilitary turn. . . ."[10] Although in Istalif it was true that Tajiks were often involved in craft industries that included few Pashtuns, the history of the town suggests that many Tajiks were far from "unmilitary." In Istalif, the Tajiks were simply not economically or socially dominated by the Pashtuns. There were a handful of Pashtun families in town, and certain cultural elements had been borrowed from Pashtuns, such as the qalas, in the lower sections of town, but the few Pashtun families had very little economic or political influence. Instead, town politics were almost entirely controlled by Tajiks, and Tajik social organization was more dominant than any Pashtun tribal organization in the district. If anything, the Pashtun families had become more integrated into Tajik culture, rather than vice versa.

THE CONCEPT OF THE QAUM

Some of the confusion about the strength of Tajiks as political actors seems to stem from the complex way the Tajiks around Istalif organized themselves politically and socially. While it is often easy to describe Pashtun tribal structures, identity and political power among the Tajiks are more difficult to define.[11] Furthermore, Tajik groups vary significantly from region to region, with many in the west actually being Shiite and referred to as Farsiwan. Elphinstone attempted to categorize the 1.5 million Tajiks he estimated were living in the kingdom of Kabul during the time of his writing by describing them as "intermixed with Afghauns"[12] and divided into Cohistaunees, Sirdehees, Poormoolees, Fermoolees, and Burrukees. He acknowledged that the Tajiks were not subdivided into tribes as the Pashtuns were, but seemed unclear about how to label them. Like some Tajiks, he sometimes used locality as an identity marker. Kohistani, or "someone from the region of Kohistan," for example, is a term still widely used in Afghanistan and defines Tajik identity by region. Despite this, Elphinstone also used the terms "tribe," "class," and "division" to describe Tajik social organization.[13] Some have defined the difference between Pashtun and Tajik organization as the difference between lineage and location, but in reality, as Elphinstone suggested, locality is simply one of the identity markers on which Istalifis relied.

Tajik social structures are not based around tribes, by most definitions of the term. Tajiks have no fixed lineages, and lineages are not corporate groups. Instead, there are local groups based on *manteqa* (area), usually composed of several villages, as well as groups organized by status and even by profession. In Istalif, political groups were simultaneously arranged by profession, lineage, ethnicity, and locality—it was the context of each political situation that shaped the formation of political groupings. As many writers have pointed out, this system means political organizations among the Tajiks tend to cohere less than ethnic groups that are organized around the more clearly defined tribes or clans. This difference, however, should not be construed as a sign of political weakness on the part of the Tajiks. In fact, the long history of this flexible ordering shows that the strategy of multiple, shifting forms of identification is a successful social adaptation to the political conditions in Afghanistan. For Tajiks living in the Shomali, close to Kabul, this ability to call on multiple categories of loyalties and quickly shift categories has been useful in dealing with the Pashtun political elite in the capital.

In the context of town politics, the Istalifis themselves often used the term *qaum* to describe their basic political unit, defined most simply as a patrilineal descent group. In Afghanistan, particularly among Tajiks, the concept is much more complicated.[14] In Istalif the term is used in a surprising number of contexts, ranging from the extended family to the entire Tajik ethnicity. Various texts have defined qaum as tribe,[15] ethnic/tribal unit,[16] and "a loose political federation or community."[17] In Swat, among the Pashtuns, Fredrik Barth reported that qaums are "patrilineal, hereditary, ranked occupational groups, conceptually endogamous," which he then equated with "estates or castes,"[18] suggesting a relationship between qaum and profession that appears only in certain instances in Afghanistan.

For example, among the itinerant threshers, peddlers, and sieve makers studied by Asta Olesen, *kesb* (profession) and qaum "became practically indistinguishable in daily use." This, however, seems only to be the case in "small qwams [that] were directly associated with specific professions."[19] In many Tajik areas there is little connection between kesb and qaum; however, in several cases in Istalif the two overlapped. An individual was born into both the pottery qaum and the pottery profession (kesb), but this was not true of all professions in Istalif. The potters, the weavers, the *pustin duz* (skin sewers), who primarily made fur coats and carpets, and the barbers were all organized in qaums. Some professions were not qaums, such as the farmers and masons, and some qaums were not professions, such as the Sayeds, who all claimed descent from the Prophet Mohammad. This system was rare in Afghanistan, but not unique to Istalif. The guild system, studied by Pierre Centlivres in Tashqurghan, organized craftsmen in an even more formal manner than the qaum.[20] Guilds in Tashqurghan during the 1970s, however, appear to have been much more stable than Istalif's dynamic qaum.

Olesen attempted to find a more generalizable definition, arguing that one's qaum "refers to his ethnic/tribal unit and for non-tribals to their ethnic and locality characteristics." She added:

> Qwam affiliation is neither an absolute nor an unchanging category. . . . Since reference to qwam affiliation is used to define a person's identity in the social world, it may be invoked in a segmentary fashion either to stress the shared identity of two parties or, depending on circumstances, to stress their lack of common bonds.[21]

Christine Noelle's study of state and tribe in nineteenth-century Afghanistan took the argument a step further, claiming that in conceptualizing qaum, difference is more important than similarity and that qaum is "overwhelmingly used as a mark of distinction vis-à-vis outsider."[22] As Barth pointed out about ethnicity, a term that raises similar issues, qaum "depends on the maintenance of a boundary,"[23] and in Istalif it was these boundaries that were most important. Qaum boundaries provided a "we" that allowed a group to define itself in opposition to others, but these boundaries could be shifted and redrawn. Although it did not provide the overarching structure a segmentary system does, in Istalif the qaum did provide individuals with a means of categorizing and organizing their immediate social world.

Sometimes it is possible for boundaries to be imposed externally. Barnett Rubin's recent study of the jihad against the Soviets indicates that the construction of qaum is often solidified by the state through such practices as making qaum a line on each identity card.[24] This practice was similar to the Soviet strategy of creating nationalities in Central Asia. In Afghanistan, with its limited state penetration, such policies attempting to shape understandings of ethnicity, the highest level of understanding of qaum, did not generally affect local identities. Other external forces have continued to shape identity more locally, and international forces and NGOs in Afghanistan recently assisted in this process by attempting to define groups that receive aid or were allies, further solidifying the boundaries of qaums.[25]

Models that claim that a qaum is purely a construct of the state or colonial powers are difficult to apply in Afghanistan. Historically, the Afghan state's power has rarely extended very far beyond Kabul. During the twenty-two years of Soviet occupation, civil war, and Taliban rule, state penetration into Istalifi life was sporadic at best. Instead, the important point Rubin helps us understand is that the category of qaum may become more relevant and politically powerful when the qaum engages with the state, international groups, or, in fact, any outside group. The qaum is an elusive and adaptable category, but it tends to solidify when political pressure is applied. It is within these boundaries that we can begin to study qaums and understand local politics in Istalif.

THE POLITICS OF FLEXIBLE BOUNDARIES

In Istalif, many of the qaums were craft-based and tended to be united by profession, giving them an economic incentive to cooperate as a group.[26] Others, such as the Sayeds, were not craft-based, but were held together by a common belief in a shared religious descent and duty. Some qaums were lineage-based; these were usually smaller and named for a notable ancestor three or four generations removed. Typical among other Tajiks living in the region, in Istalif this type of qaum was rarer and existed primarily among those working in agriculture in the eastern part of the district. Generally, if a man was not a member of one of these groups (or some other qaum), if asked directly he would claim that his qaum was the Tajiks.

The boundaries of these groups were described as fixed, but in reality, there was movement both in and out of qaums in the town. Such a flexible term in a dynamic political setting meant that membership could not simply be declared. In many cases, membership was constantly negotiated through a series of lived practices. Thus, for the potters (see Chapters 3–4), being a member of the pottery qaum was marked by: (1) the production of pottery, (2) the marketing of pottery, (3) a shared social and political hierarchy, (4) descent and marriage practices, and (5) a shared mythology. Not all of these were necessary for qaum membership, but one of them alone was not sufficient. Some members of the pottery qaum, for example, did not make or sell pots, and married outside the group, but they would need to be cautious or risk being quietly ostracized. This variety of markers allowed the pottery qaum, and others as well, to break apart whenever there was serious internal discord. At times of such discord, however, it was important that no one drew attention to the fact that the qaum had vanished temporarily as a political power. Instead, most members ignored the weakness of the qaum until the reason for conflict had passed, thus creating a near-constant political theater.

In his study of *buzkashi*, the Central Asian sport in which men on horseback wrestle to secure a calf carcass, Whitney Azoy's description of the flexibility of qaums is similar to their shifting nature in Istalif: "In its narrower sense, qaum refers to the whole hierarchy of segmentary descent groups extending upwards from the nuclear family to the ethnic totality. The ultimate weakness of such descent groups for guaranteeing social relationships has led, however, to a wide range of usages." In this setting, among Uzbeks in the north, khans and other leaders had enough political and economic capital to dominate this more organized, clan-based system. Therefore, Azoy continues: "This vagueness of the definition reflects the inherently situational nature of qaum. Lacking truly corporate group structure, they are organized instead around central khan individuals."[27] These observations about qaums among the Uzbeks help us conceptualize the idea of "qaum" in Istalif, but also demonstrate how the term comes to have different meanings in different political and economic contexts. In Istalif the qaum, in Azoy's words, extended "upwards from the nuclear family to the ethnic totality," but this system was not as weak among the Istalifis as it is among the Uzbeks that Azoy describes, and tended to coalesce around certain identity nodes as opposed to being a pure spectrum of identity.

While the Uzbeks organized around central khans who were able to manipulate the system, thereby weakening the concept of qaum as its own entity, most saw maliks in Istalif more as representatives than as leaders. Neither the Malik of the potters, nor any other of the elders in the qaum, had consolidated enough political or social power to undermine the qaum's corporate group structure. While the qaum as a whole was able to control membership, create alliances, and mediate many disputes, there was no single figure with absolute control over these functions. Quams controlled their leaders at least as much as leaders controlled the qaums. Although, as mentioned, in Istalif the qaum took on several meanings—including ethnicity, profession, lineage, and family—during the period of my study, the word was most politically relevant when used to refer to descent groups, because it was these groups that were competing for resources in the town. Qaums were extremely difficult to mobilize at the level of ethnicity, and at the level of immediate or extended family, qaums had a limited amount of power. As a result, at the middle level, roughly corresponding with clan—in this case, a series of lineages, often with a founder to whom some, but not all, could trace descent—qaums were most meaningful as groupings in Istalifi political and social life.

The fact that the qaum retained various meanings essentially allowed the category to remain flexible, resulting in the possibility of mobilization on either a wider or a more limited level. This was especially true in response to threats from the outside—most notably, during the civil war when fighting broke out primarily along ethnic lines, but also during the presidential election of 2004. Differing usages of the term were rarer in common conversations, but this was due to the fact that, as we will see, most of the primary competition over resources during this period was between descent groups and neighborhoods in the town, and it was not as common as it had been during the jihad to see town-wide mobilization on issues. More commonly, the multiple levels of meaning of qaum allowed members to redefine membership frequently, often opting out when loyalty became too burdensome, thereby effectively weakening the qaum as a political unit. Particularly for young men in Istalif, the flexibility of group definitions gave them the ability to operate around a system that was often dominated by their wealthier and more powerful elders. Simultaneously, these leaders, aware of the difficulties of maintaining loyalty, were forced to lead in such a way that did not cause followers to abandon them. The result was a flexible political system, but one in which participants were led to behave as if the system were fixed.

BEYOND DESCENT GROUPS

Patrilineal descent groups and professional groups were not the only forms of social and political organization in Istalif. Other groups, ranging from patronage networks to groups formed around religious leaders, often functioned in a manner similar to qaums, and they had the same ability to cohere and break apart rapidly. Former militia leaders, frequently referred to as commanders, often had a group of men who continued to support them despite the relative stability in the region. This was not simply an inactive militia; the commander would often provide economic aid and help support his men's families, a system that has significant parallels with the "big man" model from New Guinea. Some of these men were still considered members of patrilineal descent-based qaums, but many had lost membership by pledging their loyalty to the commander. In practice, Istalifis did not use the term "qaum" except as a rhetorical device to describe the groups of men that organized themselves around a central commander, but these political groups, often linked through economic cooperation and intermarriage, functioned similarly to qaums in several ways.

Commanders, like maliks, held feasts on holidays and helped arrange marriages between families within their groups. These groups often found themselves in direct competition with qaums in town. For example, if a weaver were involved in a land dispute, he would assume that other weavers in general would support him. Likewise, a man associated with a commander could count on the other men associated with that commander to come to his aid. Belonging to a qaum or being loyal to a commander was rarely a straightforward decision; it came down to individual political decisions and loyalties, and it was difficult for most individuals to balance significant loyalty to both groups simultaneously (although, as we will see, young men were able to manipulate this flexible system).

Groups based primarily on patronage and shared loyalty emerged around other figures as well. The police chief, the district governor, religious figures, and even some NGO workers created a similar group of men who were politically loyal to the group. The number and influence of these men often determined the group's political strength in town. Like qaums in Istalif, these groupings could hold together a large number of political constituents, but they also tended to dissolve rapidly in the face of internal discord. Membership was tentative, with participants always seeking external allies, thereby undermining the group's strength. This meant that like many Tajik leaders in Afghanistan, all leaders in town were *primus inter pares*, or first among equals, and, as a result, cajoled more than they commanded.

Each group gave its members the ability to take limited individual political capital and scale it up through group mobilization. To analyze these groups "tribally" misses the point that kinship was only one of many elements that created cohesion. Similarly, any reference to these structures as "traditional" misses the point that many of the groups centered on commanders or NGOs were, in fact, very modern. Even those that Istalifis considered "traditional," such as lineage-based qaums, were constantly interacting and competing for followers with the "modern" groups.

·   ·   ·

Confronted with this variety of forms of social organization, individuals continuously made and remade political decisions about group membership. As in any form of civil society, membership had its benefits, but the success of a group also required members to toe the party line, to some extent. This was true of young men and others who lacked political capital. As a result, in any such group there were political incentives for memberships, but also costs. The potters of Istalif provide a glimpse into how these patterns shaped the town's political arena.

Making Pots

Potters often talk about making pottery as a tactile experience: the feeling of wet clay spinning between your fingers, smoothing the clay, pushing out to thin the walls, making them as delicate as possible but not so thin that they break. For me, as an anthropologist in Istalif, pottery making was more of an auditory experience. The sounds of the workshops where I spent my time remain with me: the smack of clay being centered on the wheel; the *thunk, thunk, thunk,* as the potter kicked the wheel up to speed, gradually smoothing into a soft whirl while the pot took shape; the laughter of brothers joking as they worked; the crackle of the wood burning in the kiln.

In Istalif, potters never really had to learn how to make pots—they simply knew. In fact, potters were so afraid of outsiders stealing their glaze recipes and other techniques that they avoided giving instruction to anyone. As a result, I never progressed beyond making a few crude cups.

Pottery making for most potters was a business—not an art or a craft, it was an industry. At the end of the workday, the potters wanted to go home and drink tea, not experiment on the wheel. They did not understand why someone would want to pass time making pots, so mostly I listened and watched.

The one workshop that violated this principle was undoubtedly my favorite to visit. Mohammad Seddiq, with a Santa Claus beard to match his belly, lived above the shrine and had a commanding view of the valley below. Unlike many other potters, the pleasure of making pots was visible on Mohammad Seddiq's face when he worked. He would tell jokes, laughing at them even when I did not understand them, and he sometimes played the radio as he sat at the kick-wheel, something that was not commonly done in the other workshops in the conservative town.

He had two sons, both of whom were employed. As a result, he had a little more money than most potters. Even though one of the sons ran his rather successful shop in the bazaar, Mohammad Seddiq seemed truly to disdain the business of selling pots. He would go to the bazaar to visit and pray at the central mosque, but rarely would he speak to customers. He seemed to take pleasure in ignoring whoever came into the shop, while his son ran around showing off wares.

Perhaps because he took so much pleasure in making pots, Mohammad Seddiq seemed always to understand, more than most of the other potters, why I was interested in the politics and economics of pottery making. Who wouldn't want to write a book about potters?—his answers seemed to imply.

Despite his obvious pleasure, Mohammad Seddiq's hands did not linger in the clay. Instead, he seemed faster than most other potters, his movements more graceful and carefree. When he was working the fastest, with one of his sons or grandsons handing him prepared clay, the pots seemed to grow mysteriously out of the lump of clay between his hands. Vases, bowls, cups, plates. The wheel never slowing.

As he cut the base off of a small cup, he would hold it up to me: "For wine. Not for me, for you!" he said with a roar of laughter and, without missing a swing of his rhythmic legs, he handed the cup to his son.

With the laughter and the whirling of the wheel seeming to follow the rhythm of the song coming from the beat-up radio behind him, his hands eased back into the clay, already searching for the next cup within, waiting to be shaped out of the mud.

3 HOW MAKING POTS
BOUND PEOPLE TOGETHER

IN THE TOWN OF ISTALIF, the potters were one of the most active and influential political groups. This was remarkable because the potters were not especially wealthy or well-armed, and their connections with local commanders and government officials were informal. On the surface, they seemed simply to be more adept at organizing. At the same time, their political solidarity broke down regularly, as the potters quarreled among themselves. Although they had the ability to mobilize rapidly, they demobilized just as quickly. The potters successfully lobbied NGOs for tens of thousands of dollars in aid, but failed to stop the Sayed quam from repossessing land whose ownership was disputed between the two groups. While the potters stymied an attempt by the weaving clan to take political control of their neighborhood, they could not organize large public works projects, even when government ministries had already allocated the funds. The potters helped the mujahideen drive out the Soviets, but divided and fled as separate families when the Taliban arrived.

The process of pottery production, and the work of maintaining the monopoly on ceramic production, encouraged a high level of intrafamilial cooperation. In addition, informal interfamilial cooperation motivated the potters to cooperate politically more than other groups in town. In attempting to sell their wares, however, individual interests came into conflict with group interests, and kinship and qaum ties broke down. Elements such as high levels of family cooperation, respect for hierarchy, and alternating group fusion and fission were found in all groups in Istalif, but due the economic constraints of making and selling pots, the potters are a rather extreme example of these tendencies. Production and marketing trends indoctrinated young men into a system that demanded loyalty to those closest to them, while encouraging them to seek out other alliances that undermined group unity. Pottery did not simply shape economic incentives for these men; the lived experience of production continually reproduced much of the political and moral order of the community. This created tension between group and individual—a combination of co-operation and conflict, trust and betrayal.

PRODUCTION: THE BIRTH OF A POT

The hills around Istalif are composed of decaying granite. This feature left several clay pits in the area, but the potters gathered most of their clay from a single hill, above a graveyard, just south of town. Over the years, they had exhausted a clay source closer to their homes that many of the eldest men used when they were younger. This clay had been of higher quality; pots made in the 1960s and 1970s had fewer imperfections. To reach the new clay pit, workers from smaller workshops used donkeys. One man in the bazaar owned a large truck, which he rented for various construction projects, and sometimes members of the larger workshops hired him to bring loads of clay. A load of clay would sometimes be split between two adjacent workshops. Young men then cleaned the clay, sieved and mixed it with *gul-e loch*, a plant similar to a bulrush or cat-o-nine-tails. Adding water, they used their feet to mix the clay for up to four hours. This slow, laborious task demanded a good deal of attention—too little gul-e loch and the clay was not pliable, too much and it burned in the kiln, creating imperfections in the pots.

Once the clay was properly mixed, the potter broke off 10-pound slabs. To prepare a slab for use on the wheel, he kneaded the clay first. Using a kickwheel, he threw from the hump, pressing outward with his hands. Swinging one leg rhythmically, faster as the pot started to take shape, slower as he perfected the details, the potter could make several pots from each lump of clay. It was in these moments that pottery became less an industry and more an art. For ornamental bowls, the potter pressed waves into the rim or added a base or handles, then smoothed the form and cut off the excess clay, using either a plastic strip or a small metal chisel.

Depending on the size and ornamentation of the pot, it could take about a minute or more than 15 minutes to complete one piece. In the most active workshops, one man worked on the wheel while one or two others prepared the clay. These assistants handed the clay to the potter on the wheel and took pieces away as he finished them. Using this system, a group of men could prepare as many as 50 small pots in an hour, though 20 or 30 was a more usual number. One potter working by himself could produce pots, but this was rarely done because it was inefficient; several steps, such as unloading clay from the donkey, were nearly impossible to perform alone.

Once the pots came off the wheel, they were left outside in the sun until they become leather-hard. This step took only an hour in the summer, but could take a couple of days in cold, damp weather. During the summer, the homes of potters were easy to recognize—their roofs and courtyards were often covered with pots awaiting decoration. Occasionally a potter would bring a pot back to the wheel and use a chisel to remove excess clay and smooth rougher edges, but this was only done on higher quality pots. The pots were then stacked until the family was ready to decorate them.

The weather and the seasons shaped the rhythm of pottery production. The potters were most active in the summer, though many workshops only operated in the early morning, from about 5:00 until 8:00 A.M. The younger men in the workshop then went off to work at other jobs or in their orchards, while the older men went inside to escape the heat of the day or to attend to other business. Production stopped almost entirely for three months during the winter, when it became difficult to dry the pots.[1] In the weeks before *Naw Ruz* (the Persian New Year in March) or *Eid-e Ramazan* (the festival at the end of Ramazan), when many visitors from Kabul come to Istalif, the potters worked particularly hard to make sure their stores were well stocked. Depending on the size of the workshop, it took several weeks to prepare an entire kiln full of pots, and families would carefully plan ahead for firings based on the season and any significant changes in demand created by large orders or holidays.

When the pots were dry, it was usually the women from the family who covered them with a slip (liquefied clay), decorated them, and glazed them, though the men sometimes helped. Women would often work on decorating pots as a group while watching the children. Preparing the glazes demanded a significant amount of grinding, generally done by hand by the women.[2] At this point designs were etched into the more decorative pots with a variety of sharp tools, ranging from sharp bits of metal to pieces of broken combs. The pots were wiped clean and dipped in an engobe, a type of slip often mixed with colorant. For turquoise and clear glazed pots, the potters used an engobe that was a mixture of clay and quartz; for green, yellow, or brown pots they used an engobe of only clay. The glaze was a sodium glass substance, imported from Pakistan, that the potters purchased in Kabul. They mixed the glaze with flour, water, and various colorants.

Copper oxide made turquoise. *Gowar sang*, a stone with a high concentration of iron, produced a yellow-brown. Magnesium oxide, imported from Pakistan or ground from car batteries, made a purple-black. In the past, the potters had used *ishkor*, a bush found in the hills of the Hindu Kush, to make the turquoise pots that were traditionally associated with Istalif. They would burn the root of the plant, mixing the ash with water. Some old men talked about walking through the hills looking for ishkor, but more recently the potters found it easier to buy all the ingredients for their glazes in the bazaar.

The decoration and glazing processes reveal the most variation among the techniques of different workshops, even though to the untrained eye the pots in the Istalif bazaar were startlingly uniform. Several workshops had recognizable styles. The Malik's family, for example, almost always used a basic floral design. The pattern reproduced a daisy-type flower with long swooping stems. Most other workshops produced pots with primarily geometric designs. Potters used these patterns to identify the workshop of origin, though most consumers would have been unable to do so.

A few families that specialized in producing large amounts of pottery did little to no decorating, although most potters made at least a few spiral patterns and a few decorated extensively. One young man had recently taken an art class in Kabul and used a paintbrush to paint portraits (usually figures from Afghan history) and landscapes on some of his pots. These pots, however, were very expensive and he had trouble selling them, so he continued producing most of his pots with only basic patterns similar to those of other workshops.

The techniques involved in pottery production were far from fixed. There had been a variety of changes over the previous decades, and innovations had reshaped the pottery production. According to the potters, turquoise was the only color they used until a French ceramist worked in the town for several years in the late 1960s. He introduced green, yellow, and brown (unfortunately primarily using lead-based glazes). During my stay, one of the older potters, whose workshop was known for being slower than most but also for producing high-quality wares, experimented extracting material from car batteries for colorants. Following these trials, he developed a beautiful purple-black glaze. Initially this color was found only in his shop, but as other potters learned the technique using car batteries, the glaze appeared in almost half the workshops in town.

The French potter also helped Istalifi potters improve the design of their kickwheels. Previously the wheel had no frame and spun freely, balanced between the potter's legs. The potter dug a shallow hole, sat on the edge of it, and rotated the kickwheel spindle in a small, hollowed-out section of the hole. One potter still had such a wheel, although he never used it. The French potter introduced a design found more commonly in American and European pottery workshops, composed of a fixed frame with an attached bench. With the stability of this frame, the spindle rotates on ball bearings and allows for much smoother and steadier wheel operation. These new, primarily metal wheels quickly replaced earlier wooden versions, though some potters created a hybrid of the two models by building earth walls on the sides of the wheels. For the most part, potters had stopped building kickwheels themselves; when it became necessary to replace one, they would bring an older wheel to an ironworker and ask him to reproduce it. Kickwheels were also one of the items donated by an international aid group to the potters following the fall of the Taliban, and many of the wheels in Istalif were from this group.[3]

Beyond some of these innovations, which all workshops had incorporated, there was a reluctance to experiment with any techniques that might create a serious economic risk. Occasionally, potters would experiment with new designs for ornamental pieces, but these pieces were placed at the very top of a kiln load and never made up a significant percentage of a firing. In particular, the use of new materials risked explosions in the kiln, and thus a potentially substantial economic loss. Similarly, potters were aware that their kilns were not the most efficient, but the risk and cost of experimenting and producing new kiln designs meant that no potter had attempted to incorporate new firing techniques into his daily production, despite encouragement from three NGOs that had been sending outside experts to the town since 2002. Instead, Istalifi potters preferred to produce less risky wares that they knew traditionally sold well in the market.

Finally, the pots were fired in large updraft wood-burning kilns. One kiln was approximately 12 feet tall, with a base 6 feet by 6 feet. Through a small opening on the front of the kiln, potters fed wood into the fire, while using one large hole and four smaller holes on the top for loading and to allow smoke to escape. Because of this design, the loading process required a lot of cooperation. Generally one man would climb into the kiln, while another handed him the pieces of pottery from above and another handed pots up to the second man. Some kilns were built into hillsides or had roofs aligned with the roof of the house, facilitating loading by only two men.

Each kiln had a large shelf that held all the pots near the base, about a foot and a half above the firebox. The potters stacked the pots upside-down on top of each other, with larger bowls toward the bottom. Often, small cups were placed near the top of the stack. The items were each separated by a clay tripod called a *say paye* (literally, three feet), which left three faint bare spots on the inside of each pot that the glaze did not cover. For higher-quality ware, the potters later sanded and painted over the bare spots using acrylic paint. Bowls and plates made up the majority of each kiln load, though some more decorative and intricate pieces, such as teapots, vases, and figurines, were also made and left between or on top of the bowls.

The potters fired the kiln using *archa* (cedar wood). During firing, the large hole on the top of the kiln was covered, and smoke was forced through the four smaller openings. The initial temperature was kept very low for about an hour, in order to heat the kiln gradually. The potters then added more wood, and the kiln fired at higher temperatures for another 4–6 hours. Many potters said that when the black smoke coming out of the chimney turned white, the kiln was ready. Other potters looked in the small opening above the firebox; when the inside of the kiln glowed red, they said, firing was complete.

The potter watching the firing would cover the firebox with a metal sheet so the kiln would not cool too quickly; the kiln then sat cooling slowly overnight. When the pieces were cool enough to handle, the potters removed them, studying each one. If the glaze had run during firing or the pot had some other small flaw, the potters attempted to paint over or sand down the imperfections. The potters loaded the pots into a car or onto a donkey, and they were transported to the bazaar.

THE FAMILY THAT POTS TOGETHER . . .

Pottery making shaped the rhythm of life for the potters; it integrated social and economic actions within the family and, to a lesser extent, the qaum. Collective labor, using skills that could only be acquired through apprenticeship, encouraged loyalty and hierarchy within each immediate family. This, along with the high startup costs and low returns associated with pottery production, ensured that the potters retained their monopoly on their industry and encouraged a social and moral order among themselves.

The demand for a level of familial cooperation and integration in the production of pottery was greater than it was for the production of most other crafts in town. Weavers and farming families had a high degree of cooperation within their extended families, but in contrast to potters, their patterns of production did not require the same integration of multiple family members. For example, an increase in the members of a family working as weavers tended to expand output in a fairly linear fashion, depending on the number of looms the family owned. Only in pottery was there a clearly optimal number of laborers per family. Furthermore, the monopoly of knowledge that potters possessed limited wage labor as a significant economic factor. This was untrue of other groups, such as the farmers who hired temporary help when their farms demanded additional workers.

A typical pottery workshop had as few as two and as many as eight men actively working at one time. Several steps required collaboration, and there were many other steps that benefitted from cooperation, with the result of increased efficiency and productivity. The marginal rise in productivity, however, decreased with more than about four workers, because the workshop became crowded and roles were less well defined. For example, during the shaping of pots on the kickwheel, the work moved much more smoothly when several men worked together. With two men it was possible for one man to prepare the clay and hand it to the potter working on the wheel. Using this cooperative system, a potter could make dozens of pots with his kickwheel rarely stopping. The flywheels on most kickwheels were rather heavy, and the more the wheel slowed down or stopped, the more energy the potter had to exert to keep it going and thus produce pots efficiently.

These forms of cooperation in pottery making created an informal division of labor, primarily among brothers, that augmented the typical hierarchy within families in Afghanistan. Often, the eldest brother was the most-skilled potter. He had been learning the craft the longest and was the first to use the wheel with his father. Younger brothers were initially relegated to clay preparation—mixing the clay, kneading it, and then handing it to their father or older brother on the wheel. Many younger brothers never became skilled as potters, and in some cases never learned how to make pots at all, because they were not as important to the family's pottery production when they were young. This pattern reinforced the traditional respect that Afghans gave to the father and the eldest brother, the family members who guided the production process.

In addition, there was an informal *ustad-shogard* (master-student) hierarchy. Young men were often referred to as shogards until around the age of 17. There was no formal ceremony for becoming an ustad, but it was generally acknowledged that a shogard could not run a workshop alone, and that he was responsible for tasks that demanded more physical labor. It was also the duty of the ustad to focus on more technical aspects, such as glazing, and to oversee the firing process.

Since not all stages in pottery production required the same number of workers, there was a strong incentive for economic flexibility within the immediate family. In most families, one or more of the younger men worked in a shop or as a laborer during the day, but he would also be available to help his father and older brothers in the pottery workshop in the mornings. This arrangement ensured a more steady income; men working in other jobs, particularly in Kabul, became increasingly important during the winter months when pottery production stopped. The result was that in a typical pottery family, only one or two men worked full-time making pots, while an additional two or three helped when the process demanded. When a family had more men in it, some did not take part in production at all.

These working patterns strongly influenced residency arrangements. With a few members of many families moving back and forth between Kabul and Istalif, it was difficult to precisely define a household in Istalif. The large compounds generally housed more than one household, and families cooperated on some things but not on others. In smaller compounds, multiple closely related immediate families would share a cooking area and perhaps a guestroom, while each family had their own private living quarters.[4] Further complicating matters because buildings had been so heavily damaged, by 2002 it was common for groups of brothers moving back to Istalif to first repair the building in which they had grown up; younger brothers would then move out of the compound as time and resources allowed.

Despite these definitional problems, my survey results, along with the accounts of the potters, indicated that there was a relatively lower rate of fission among the potters than among other families in Istalif. In many cases, brothers continued to live and work together after their father died. Even when brothers had separated, they tended to live in proximity and cooperate informally.

COOPERATION BETWEEN FAMILIES AND THE MONOPOLY OF KNOWLEDGE

While there was cooperation between potters beyond the extended family, it was not as systematic or as predictable as intrafamilial cooperation. When a workshop needed extra laborers, a neighbor or distant cousin occasionally came and helped for a small, informal payment. Potters sometimes shared materials or let other potters use their kilns. There was a high rate of intermarriage among the potters, so much of this mutual assistance was a form of reciprocity among kin, but it notably decreased once the labor or goods involved were more than nominal. Political cooperation, however, did not neatly follow kinship patterns; often, geographic proximity and friendship were just as important. As one common proverb states, "*Az sad qaum-e dur kardee, yek hamsayay nazdeek betar ast"*—"It is better to have one close neighbor than hundred distant relatives."

Friendships helped potters like Nabi Jan, a poor man, who ran out of wood halfway through the firing of his kiln. This could have resulted in a disastrous loss of money, because he had already invested cash and labor in the work and was indebted to some of the shopkeepers in the bazaar. Instead of losing the entire kiln load, however, Nabi Jan sold the kiln's contents to Daud, a young man known among the potters for his diligence and intelligence. Daud finished firing the pots, making a profit for himself and for Nabi Jan. Daud and Nabi Jan were distantly related though marriage, but they considered themselves *rafiq* (friends) rather than *bach-e kaka* (sons of paternal uncles; the general term for paternal cousins or more distant agnatic kin, related through patrilineal lines). When I asked Daud and Nabi Jan how they were related to each other, their distant kinship connection was clearly not the primary way they thought of their relationship.

This type of informal cooperation among friends helped create unity within the qaum, but even more significant was the way the potters worked together informally to maintain their qaum's monopoly on pottery production. The Istalifi potters were not the only potters in the area, but they were the only group producing the prestigious glazed pots found in the markets in and around Kabul. Another large group of potters in Laghman and Nangarhar produced other earthenware pots, generally used for domestic purposes like holding water or yogurt, but these were cheaper and easily broken. The Laghman and Nangarhar potters had previously been itinerant; as late as the 1960s, they had traveled through the Shomali making pots during the summer, but this practice had ceased over the course of the past thirty years.[5] In Kabul and around Istalif there was another group of *tandoor sazi* (tandoor oven makers). This group made large bowls as well as bread ovens, but they used much courser clay and fired at much lower temperatures, often using tires for fuel instead of wood. Production of the ovens required very different techniques, and the tandoor sazis used molds to make their wares, instead of kickwheels. Rather than competing with this group, the Istalifi potters produced pottery that was primarily in competition with Chinese and Iranian imports.

The potters maintained this domestic monopoly primarily by closely guarding their technical knowledge of the craft. While it was easy to visit the potters in their workshops and watch them work, they were intentionally vague about the specific details of production. They would gladly sit at a kickwheel and demonstrate their abilities, but they would not show all their techniques to strangers, especially their glazing techniques. At one point two Afghan ceramists from Kabul—who had worked at the Sani-e School, the Soviet-style fine arts academy, in the 1970s—visited some of the potters. After the typical formalities, they began talking about pottery production in Istalif. The potters were interested in these visitors and were polite to them. When the visitors began asking about glazes, however, the answers became nebulous. The oldest Istalifi potter in the room took over answering the questions, claiming that all their measurements were approximate, and that he was not exactly sure what materials they used. The younger potters next to him simply nodded in agreement. I knew his statements were lies, having watched the potters carefully measure materials for glaze mixtures in the past, but they maintained a narrative that described their work as imprecise and reliant on custom as opposed to technical skill. The potters consistently portrayed production to outsiders as a folk tradition that was inherited, rather than as a profession that might be mastered by outsiders. Once it was clear to the potters that I was not interested in stealing their glaze formulas, they became much more open about working in front of me and talking about the materials they were using.

The potters collectively struggled to find a balance between their desire to portray themselves as skilled artisans and their claim of knowing little about technical aspects of the process. Key in creating this narrative of pottery production as an inherited trait was the Malik While the Malik was considered primarily a political representative by the potters, when outsiders came to visit, particularly the representatives of development NGOs, he often presented himself as the head potter as well, even though he was not the most skilled of the older potters and his sons did most of the work in his workshop. This approach encouraged NGOs providing technical assistance to work with the potters collectively, thereby decreasing competition among the potters for aid.

For example, when a group funded by the Japanese government came to take Istalifi potters on an exchange program to Japan, the Malik and his son were the chief liaisons between the community and the Japanese group. They helped administer interviews and tests at the Malik's house as part of the selection process. Afterward, some potters complained that the Malik had been the one who had selected which potters would go to Japan, but he adamantly denied it. The Malik made sure that most outsiders working with the potters worked directly with him, even though NGO assistance was not great enough to alter notably the economics of production. The limited number of NGOs, however, that had distributed resources perceived the Malik to be a useful tool for reaching the community. His narrative about the unity of the potters and his own position as chief representative supported their hope that aid was being distributed equitably (even if it was not), and going through him was much easier than contacting all the potters individually. Other elders in the community were similarly able to manipulate sources of international aid (see Chapter 6), but the Malik of the potters was one of the most skilled at navigating these relationships. The result was that the Malik was often central in distributing technical and material assistance, further unifying the production process and providing incentive for at least outward loyalty to the Malik and cooperation among other qaum elders.

While other artisans in the area, such as the jewelry makers, had a more formal apprentice system, the ustad-shogard system was an important means of regulating pottery production. The vast majority of potters working in Istalif learned as shogards from their agnates, primarily their fathers, paternal uncles, or older brothers. If a man was born into a pottery family that had stopped making pottery, or if his close male relatives had died, the only way for him to learn the trade was by becoming a shogard for another ustad, often related maternally or through marriage. In one case, the father of a potter named Hedayatullah had died when he was young, and Hedayatullah became a shogard of his mother's two brothers, who were working together. This was a natural turn of events, because Hedayatullah's mother had returned to her natal home following the death of her husband. In general, however, family members were less inclined to accept apprentices. Nabi Jan, whose father also died when he was young, used to spend hours watching Mullah Mohammad, his mother's sister's husband, make pottery. Finally, after some time, his mother was able to convince Mullah Mohammad to take Nabi Jan on as a student, even though he was clearly not interested in teaching his nephew the craft. These social and economic patterns helped ensure that the secrets of pottery production remained within the qaum.

The tendency of the potters to marry both inside and outside the pottery quam is discussed in Chater 4. Here, it is relevant to note that the major reason most young potters gave for excluding young women from most phases of production was that they might marry outside the qaum. The potters usually said it would be a waste of time for women to learn pottery making if they would eventually marry into families that had other occupations. Embedded in this reasoning was the less-articulated fear that the women would teach their new families how to make pots.

Before the outbreak of fighting, some potters had hired young men from other qaums in town to help them in their workshops. This practice ceased as the demand for pots dropped below the pottery qaum's production capacity. In the 1960s and 1970s, however, several older men with large workshops described how demand had been so high that it was necessary to bring in labor from outside the qaum. When I asked about these students and whether they became potters, the old men laughed and said, "Of course not, we would never allow them to become ustads." Instead, the outsiders were responsible for cleaning and mixing the clay, moving pots, and cleaning the workshop. The potters would not let them learn to use the wheel or take part in the glazing process. The one old weaver I met who had worked as one of these outside laborers when he was young claimed he did understand most of the production process, but had returned to weaving because the potters had not "allowed" him to continue. This combination of guarding knowledge and social pressure was very effective; as a result, no one outside the qaum was producing pottery.

Some members of the qaum had chosen to leave the group or had been forced out by informal pressure. One poor metal worker who lived further down the valley described how his father and grandfather had been potters, but how no one taught him to make pots. The rest of the pottery qaum denied that his family had ever been part of the qaum. As an outsider, I found it difficult to determine which of these conflicting narratives to believe. What was clear, however, was that the narratives that maintained the boundaries of the qaum had significant political power. The political incentives for maintaining these boundaries are discussed in later chapters, but one point to note here is the fact that the potters were well aware that there was an ideal number of workshops in town—too many workshops meant a greater supply of pots, and less profit for everyone.

There was some self-regulation, because it was often only the oldest sons who continued potting, but there were a few examples of potters pushing out other families. It seems likely that this number was even higher than my data suggests, since all the individuals I found who had formally produced pots I met by chance; the potters, unsurprisingly, did not talk about former qaum members. This was not simply an attempt to conceal the truth from an outsider. Any discussion of the fluid nature of the qaum boundaries would have weakened the narrative of the potters as a unified group, thereby lessening their political influence in town. It was also likely that families forced out of the qaum had less incentive to return to Istalif after its destruction by the Taliban.

Thus, by collaborative efforts to maintain an appropriate number of work-shops, pressure on other potters to leave production, and less-orchestrated attempts to control knowledge, the potters maintained their privileged economic position in the town.

ECONOMIC RESTRICTIONS ON ENTERING THE INDUSTRY

While the potters' monopoly on knowledge had helped preserve their control of the industry, the economics of production also reinforced the potters' control of their economic niche. Pottery production had high start-up costs and many risks, especially compared to other economic opportunities available to young men in the area.[6] The building of a kickwheel and a kiln required buying metal and bricks, contracting a metalsmith to weld the kickwheel, and hiring a mason to build the kiln. These materials and labor cost more than $500, and the tasks required specialized knowledge.

Despite the destruction of most of their tools by the Taliban, start-up costs for potters returning to Istalif were greatly reduced by formal and informal international aid, which appears to have had a much greater impact in the earlier years than during my time in the town. The first returning potters described receiving small amounts of cash from international aid workers in Kabul to restart their workshops. Later, during the initial period of reconstruction in 2002 and 2003, several NGOs worked with the potters, one supplying new kilns and another kickwheels. Kilns were important in distinguishing the potters economically and geographically from others in town. They were a key architectural feature in Kulalan, the neighborhood where most of the potters lived, and they were often integrated into building design. Keeping kilns close to the home and workshops enabled women to more easily work around them without exposing themselves to anyone other than neighbors, who were generally related. Some potters grumbled that when they had built kilns in Kabul during the Taliban period, their neighbors complained of the smoke whenever they fired them. This may also have contributed to the fact that potters returning to Istalif had generally moved back into the same neighborhood, whereas other returning groups did not always return to their ancestral homes.

There were forty-nine kiln sites in Kulalan. Twenty-nine of the kilns were used fairly regularly, with about half of them being fired every month—standard for a small workshop. An additional six were usable or could have been made usable with a few repairs; the rest were in serious states of decay from weather or damage during the fighting with the Taliban. These kilns still represented some opportunity for economic expansion among the potters, because a family with an unused or damaged kiln could return to pottery production at a much lower cost than one that had no kiln at all.

Many kilns required substantial repairs following the fighting and years of neglect, but a French NGO that was active in the region provided support in this phase of rebuilding. Other than these repairs, however, it was rare for major work to be done on a kiln. Most were simply patched in the fall of each year, and they could function for several generations with only this annual maintenance. These elements, including the risk of kiln explosions and the careful guarding of knowledge, allowed the qaum to maintain their monopoly on pottery production.

REPRODUCING THE MORAL VALUES OF THE POTTERS

The production of pottery also created moral cohesion for the group. While potters generally referred to pottery making as their qaum or profession (kesb), they also referred to it as their *wazeefah*, often translated as "job" with a strong implication of "duty." When asked why they returned to potting after the Taliban destroyed their workshops, potters would often say it was their wazeefah as potters. Sometimes this was couched in religious terms. One *qari* (a religious figure who has memorized the Koran) instructed me on how all good Muslims must do whatever duty (wazeefah) they had been given by Allah. That, he argued, was why potters were required to make pots and be active members of the pottery qaum. Similarly, many potters living in Kabul lamented the fact that they were no longer producing pots and confided that, given the economic means, they would have preferred pottery making to other professions. Some of the men were earning larger incomes with other jobs, and there was a strong element of nostalgia in their statements. While such claims were not unique to the potters in Istalif, young potters were still brought up in a world where producing pots and loyalty to the qaum were highly valued.

Several prayers were associated with pottery production, and some older potters would recite them as they began to work on the wheel or fire a kiln. These prayers had some similarities with traditional Sufic elements in pottery production, as reported on in Pakistan by Clifford Evans and Owen Rye in their translation of the *Kulal Nama* or *Book of the Potters*, which lists a series of prayers potters were expected to recite at different points in production.[7] These, however, were no longer an important aspect of the transmission of knowledge about the production of pottery in Istalif.

The potters did incorporate other religious beliefs into their work. For example, the potters related a common myth about a religious potter who was struggling to keep his kiln fire going. He prayed to Allah and Allah then blessed his firing, making the flames grow stronger and stronger. When the potter unloaded the kiln, he saw that Allah had etched his name onto each pot. A few older potters claimed that all the designs on each pot were simply a modification of the name Allah that was first etched onto the pots of that first religious potter. As a result, some old men scowled whenever they saw a broken pottery shard on the ground (a fairly common occurrence in the potters' neighborhood), claiming that this was the equivalent of soiling the name of Allah. Most potters, however, continued the practice of throwing broken pots outside their workshops, where the rain and irrigation channels scattered them around the town below.

Such claims of moral authority were not simply rhetorical; they often translated into real decisions for the potters. For example, six months before my arrival, a European women's NGO that had already done some work in the area approached some of the potters about creating a workshop equipped with a state-of-the-art electric kiln. Discussions occurred primarily between several of the employees of the NGO and the son of the Malik. The potters acknowledged their interest, but were concerned with how such a kiln could be shared. At some point in these initial conversations, however, through either a mistranslation or a deliberate misunderstanding on one side or the other, the potters came to believe that this workshop would be for everyone to use, while the NGO had previously decided it would be in a location where only women were allowed to enter.[8]

This created a problem. Women, while involved in some aspects of production, never assisted in the firing process. When the kiln arrived and was installed in the women's center below the town, the NGO asked the potters to begin sending their women to the workshop. The potters had a community meeting and determined that sending their women out of the neighborhood would have been shameful. Once the group decision to boycott the center had been made, all potters adhered to the decision, and for my entire time in Istalif, no potter from the qaum used the $20,000 imported gas kiln. A few of the youngest and poorest potters lamented this lost opportunity to me, but they did not publicly challenge the group consensus. It was later rumored that the district governor's wife and two of her friends (all of whom were from Kabul) were taking classes and making figurines in the workshop, and the NGO clearly treated the workshop as a place for art classes more than genuine production.

When I discussed the program with the head of the NGO in Kabul, she seemed pleased that the program was functioning at all and was undisturbed by its ineffectiveness. This was fairly representative of how aid was distributed, particularly in areas outside Kabul, where it could not be closely monitored; for many international and Afghan employees of aid organizations, the most important goal was to ensure that they could check off certain tasks from a work plan. Since the kiln and workshop had been established, it was no longer as important to the donor and those working for the donor how effective the program actually was. Potters were not passive recipients, and when a program violated their moral order, they were afraid to turn down aid. A few potters complained about this highly visible, gross misuse of funds, but nobody seriously considered standing against the boycott, once the NGO had violated the social regulations in pottery production.

While the potters made informal agreements to adhere to practices and limit the access of outsiders to knowledge about the production process, the economic demands of production and the structure of international aid also helped ensure that outside penetration was difficult. The potters had discovered that the economics of production did not force them to be overt in protecting their industry. It was informal agreements, gossip, and quiet negotiation that held pottery families together as a productive unit. We will see the results of this solidarity in the local political arena, but first we must understand how marketing made the potters' incentive to compete almost as strong as their incentive to cooperate.

The Art of Finding a Bargain

The selling of pots among the Istalifis, particularly during the bargaining stage, often had a lighthearted quality to it, but questions of honor and prestige were never far below the surface.

One older potter, who walked with a heavy limp, liked to tell stories about selling pots in the days before there were numerous stores in Istalif. He and his friends would walk down to the market in Qara Bagh with the pots on their backs. Sometimes they took the bus, but the bus cost 2 afghanis; for that amount they could buy a bag of 100 grams of peanuts, and it was more fun to walk back reciting poems and munching. Times, however, had changed, he concluded with a sigh. Now these young people are only concerned about business—they take cars everywhere—even if it is just half a kilometer!

Some of these stories were an idealization of the past. But included in the competition of the marketplace were deep issues of honor that were tied into the selling of pots, and associated with a complex moral economy in all aspects of life in the bazaar.

Bargaining in the bazaar was challenging. Particularly when purchasing pots, I did not want to get ripped off, but Afghans are sometimes generous to a fault. For instance, I had learned quickly not to compliment a shopkeeper on his scarf or hat, or he would try to take it off and give it to me. If I bargained too strenuously, the seller might offer the item as a gift.

I learned instead to use the proverb, *"Baradar ba baradar hesabesh barabar"*—"Brothers keep their accounts even." This almost always elicited a smile and moved the negotiations along. I knew the prices for most things in the Istalif bazaar, but I also knew that there was a sliding scale. The price for a pot varied greatly, depending upon whether the customer was Afghan or foreign, a wholesaler or a one-time buyer, and how rich he appeared. The question at this point was not about price as much as it was about who the shopkeeper thought the customer was.

Beyond this, however, there were other layers. Certain things could be bargained for and certain things could not. Some of my friends would get angry with a grocer for charging me too much for dry goods, which generally had set prices; but when the same friends saw me emerge from the barbershop, they would ask: "How much did you pay?"

"Seventy afs," I responded, about $1.40. Then they would laugh and laugh.

"But a haircut is only fifty afs!"

Because of situations like this one, Istalifi men did not often bargain openly with people they knew, the way they could in Kabul where customers usually did not know the shop owners, and interactions were simply business. In small towns like Istalif, however, nothing was simply business. The man from whom a customer was buying load of bricks was the same man who might be trying to marry his brother's daughter, and the same man whose herd of sheep ate some of the customer's cousin's bushes last week. Reputation and honor were constantly at stake. If the brick seller could get an unreasonably high price for the bricks, he would have the upper hand, and the next thing you know, he would not have to pay for the bushes, and the bride-price offer would have dropped.

Customers and sellers paid each other lavish compliments, joked about how they were not really interested in a product, or maybe would return at some other time. Facial expressions let the other know exactly how ridiculous a price was. Hand gestures encouraged the lowering of the price, and ceaseless compliments were designed to eliminate the underlying tension. If one man didn't agree with the price, he said nothing about it, but let his disagreement be known by moving on to some other topic of conversation. By drinking tea and talking about things that seemed to have little to do with the price of bricks, the price seemed to settle naturally into a place that both the buyer and the seller agreed on. If they did not agree on a price, either one could have gotten up and left with no hard feelings, since after all they were not actually bargaining, they were just passing time and drinking tea.

Friends often went to great lengths to avoid creating tension, especially when money was involved. Once I was buying a millstone for my house from a friend of mine, Safi. Unsurprisingly, I had no experience purchasing millstones.

"How much, Safi?"

"For you, it is a gift. You are a friend. I cannot take your money."

"No really, I insist."

"No, please, you are a guest here."

There is something rhythmic and beautiful about this tug-of-war that one went through each time.

"OK Safi. If you were to go down to the bazaar to buy a new millstone, how much would it cost?"

"Well, that depends on the millstone."

"OK, a millstone, like this one."

"Maybe a new millstone would be 1000 afghanis."

That amount was about $20. It seemed a little steep to me, and this was a used millstone (I wasn't sure if that mattered, but I knew little about millstones), so I decided 500 afghanis was probably a good price.

"How about 500?" I asked.

"Please, whatever you give me will be more than enough."

"Here," I said, "I only have a 1000-afghani note, do you have 500 as change?"

"Yes, yes, I have change" he said. He took the bill from me and put it in his pocket. He then pulled out a cigarette and offered me one. He began to wonder aloud when the grapes we were standing underneath would be ripe. I thought about saying something about the 500 he owed me, but I figured he meant that he had it at home.

About a week later, he still hadn't given me the 500 change. I did not want to embarrass him or myself, so I asked my friend Abdul Jaleel about it.

Abdul Jaleel laughed at me. "Of course he didn't give you change. That is a good millstone. It is worth at least 1000 afghanis. He just did not want to argue with you about the price."

By quarrelling with me about the price Safi would have dishonored himself as a good host and a friend, and would have dishonored me, by making me a greedy guest. But, of course, he didn't want to get ripped off and he clearly knew I had the money. So he tried to diffuse the entire situation by walking away with the 1000-afghani note. His plan worked well. I got my millstone, he got his money, and neither of us lost any honor.

4 HOW SELLING POTS TORE PEOPLE APART

ISTALIFI POTTERY WAS SOLD IN SEVERAL PLACES: the Istalif bazaar, several stores in the old city of Kabul, and a variety of shops in the region, mostly along the Kabul-Charikar highway. In all the shops, goods from Istalif were mixed in with Chinese and Pakistani imports of different levels of quality. Louis Dupree noted the lack of bazaars in Afghan towns in the 1970s,[1] but Istalif had long been an exception. Istalif served as a supply point for many of the villagers who lived in the mountains above town and could not make the round-trip to Kabul in a single day. Another reason for Istalif's sizable bazaar was the number of Afghan and foreign visitors who came to picnic there; on Fridays in the spring, the bumpy dirt road from Kabul was often clogged with cars, buses, minivans, donkeys, and bicycles. Istalif's bazaar had also thrived during the Soviet period, when mujahideen fighters would steal into town to restore their supplies before heading back into the hills.

All twenty-five of the pottery shops in Istalif's bazaar were scattered along the street running east-to-west between the boys' school and the town mosque. Several potters also rented storerooms, unrenovated enclosures shuttered with wooden planks, which were often adjacent to their primary shops. The other street in the bazaar, running north-to-south between the boys' school and the river, was home to the small grocery stores where most Istalifis did their daily shopping.

Shop owners in the pottery section usually sat outside their shops, talking and sharing lunch. They watched over others' shops when they had business elsewhere, and there was a tendency for relatives to have shops close together (though this was certainly not a rule). On a busy day, all the shopkeepers would be in the bazaar, while on quieter days, most of the shops were open but were tended by a smaller group. Fridays and Saturdays were by far the busiest days. On an average day in late spring and early summer, about 2,400 people passed through the relatively small bazaar, but that number swelled to 7,000 on a Friday.[2] The composition of visitors in the bazaar changed depending upon the day of the week; on weekdays, visitors were mostly men working and shopping in the bazaar; on Fridays, the number of women visiting the bazaar rose from 5 percent to 9 percent.[3]

In contrast with the hierarchy within the pottery workshops, it was often the younger sons who were in charge of running the shops in the bazaar; most of the older men looked down on being shopkeepers. Potters increasingly realized that they made their largest profits by selling to NGO workers, the occasional tourist, and other international visitors. Therefore, in several families one son learned basic English greetings, and these sons were the ones who usually ran the shops, especially on Fridays.

Not all of the pottery shop owners were potters, but about three-fourths of them were. Non-potters who ran pottery shops had established close relationships with the potters over the years. For example, one Sayed in the bazaar owned a pottery shop even though he came from a family of orchard owners.[4] His brother had married a potter's daughter, however, and this Sayed had begun to sell pots with his brother's father-in-law. Eventually, his business expanded and he sold from several different potters with whom he had good relationships. He occasionally joked that he had become an honorary potter.

Merchants in Kabul were another outlet for selling Istalifi pottery, particularly along the western end of the well-known Chaff Selling Street (also Kabul's central market for pigeons). Potters sold directly to merchants who came to the Istalif bazaar and occasionally took their wares to Kabul. Several potters had established ties with specific merchants, and some restaurant owners from Kabul regularly placed orders to supply their restaurants. Occasionally, a merchant purchased an entire kiln load of pottery before it was even fired. They did this for a greatly reduced price, but if the firing was poor or there was a problem with the glazes, the merchant was left with damaged pots. Families that produced more pots of lower quality favored this practice.

The potters realized that their profit dropped when they did not sell directly to customers, and in recent years they had worked to avoid selling to middlemen. Some of the oldest potters remembered a time (probably in the 1960s) when there were only three or four pottery shops in town, and most potters sold their wares in the surrounding area or in the weekly bazaar in nearby Qara Bagh. The potters described a later period (in the 1970s) when the number of pottery shops in the bazaar had climbed to a dozen, though it was only following the fall of the Taliban that the number had increased, so that twelve of the nineteen families with the largest pottery workshops also had shops in the Istalif bazaar (and those without a shop tended to have an arrangement with another shop). The number of pottery shops had increased not only within the Istalif bazaar; on the road between Kabul and Charikar, just north of Istalif, for example, there were twenty-two pottery shops in the summer of 2007.[5] This number increased while I was in Istalif as the area north of Kabul experienced economic growth. At first, local merchants had owned these shops exclusively, but potters had come to own at least a share of three of the shops. Young potters in particular spoke of their desire to set up shops outside Istalif; some talked of setting up shops on Chicken Street, the tourist-oriented market area in Kabul.

A few potters had even left pottery production entirely to focus on marketing. Two brothers, who had originally worked full-time as potters, had a shop in the bazaar, a bakery, and a basic goods store. They had also purchased a car and owned a 50-percent share in a pottery store about 5 miles south of Istalif, on the road to Kabul. They had established relationships with merchants in Kabul and sometimes drove pots to Kabul instead of waiting for the merchants to come to Istalif. Although they still had a workshop and a functioning kiln, for the most part they had decided to concentrate on marketing instead of producing pottery.

Pottery shops did not exclusively sell pottery; international customers also bought replica antique rifles, hats, cloaks, baskets, and other souvenirs. The shopkeepers purchased most of these goods from shops on Chicken Street and brought them to Istalif. They then raised the prices and led foreigners to believe that they were buying the goods directly from the source, making them seem more authentic. Most potters let the international visitors believe that everything in the shop was made in Istalif, but a couple of less scrupulous young men were accused of lying directly to the customers—a practice most older potters frowned on. During my two years in Istalif, there was something of a marketing revolution. When I first arrived, only one shop sold pottery and souvenirs. Over the next two years, more pottery shops purchased sizable stocks of "antiques." (Istalifis use the English word "antiques" to refer to all these items, even though few were truly antique.) By 2009, many pottery shops had as many "antiques" as pots, and several potters were becoming professional antique shop owners.

Despite these changes, most potters used similar methods to sell the same wares, creating competition in the process of marketing that contrasted with their cooperation during production. While competition was rarely overt, the economics of marketing fostered a system that instead of favoring collusion, favored a quiet, but intense, struggle for prime customers. In many cases, the divides between, and within, families that marketing created overlapped with the divides that appeared when potters fractured politically. Young men who spent more time competing to sell pots were less likely to cooperate than their fathers, who were focused on production. Despite the professed desire of many potters to cooperate more regularly, the economics of marketing meant that cooperation had limits.

THE ECONOMICS OF MARKETING

A precise cost analysis of the pottery industry in Istalif was difficult because of the many variables. Depending on how many unemployed men a family had and whether they owned a donkey, some gathered the clay at no cost (other than the time they spent). In most workshops, however, they found it more efficient to spend about $20 to bring in a truck full of clay at once. Similarly, large workshops purchased glazes in bulk from Kabul, while smaller, poorer workshops purchased small amounts, at higher rates, from their relatives or neighbors. (I have converted costs to U.S. dollars in this section, partly to make them easier for the reader to contextualize, but also because most Istalifis used dollars in a high percentage of economic transactions. The potters paid for almost all large purchases in dollars, and most shopkeepers kept the majority of their money in dollars, though they generally had a small supply of euros and British pounds at all times as well.)

In addition to these variables, there were hazards attached to gathering economic data. In my first months in Istalif, I found that many potters would lie about numbers; some assumed I would be more likely to assist them if they portrayed themselves as poor; other young men inflated numbers to boast about their business skills. Gathering economic data from shopkeepers in the bazaar, with whom I had few connections, was problematic, and I treated the data with skepticism until I could verify it from multiple sources. Potters rarely studied their own budgets, although they had a fairly acute sense about when they were making a profit or taking a loss. All the numbers below are averages from a half-dozen cost analyses of specific workshops, weighted according to whether I felt a workshop was representative of other workshops or not.

Assuming a workshop already had major equipment, such as a kickwheel and a kiln, here are the general production costs for pottery in Istalif (Table 1). The greatest expense was fuel for firing the kiln, at approximately $200 (though this varied by season and cost of wood). Toward the end of my study, the cost

Table 1. Production costs

Cost of wood	$200
Cost of glaze clay and other items	$50
Total cost per kiln load	$250
Pots per kiln load	900
Approximate cost per pot	$0.30

of all commodities became increasingly volatile as world food prices went up sharply, thus affecting the price of other goods. Glazes, quartz, and paint for touching up pots added to the cost. Some potters occasionally paid for labor, but many would hire a car or a donkey to help transport goods from their workshops to the bazaar. The materials for most kiln loads cost approximately $250. However, it was possible to reduce the amount of cash spent on each kiln load by increasing the number of labor hours from collecting the clay without hiring a truck and not hiring outside labor.

The kilns I surveyed held between 550 and 1,400 pots, and most averaged about 900.[6] Thus, the cost per pot came to about $0.30 (a little more, because every firing lost some pots). The bulk of each kiln load consisted of fairly standard bowls and plates, but potters also included larger, more intricate pieces, such as candlesticks and vases.

Prices were flexible, and in general a price was more a reflection of the customer than of the quality of the pottery. Roughly speaking, there were three groups of customers: merchants, wealthy or semi-wealthy Kabuli visitors, and international visitors. Merchants usually purchased at least 50 pots at a time (and occasionally an entire kiln load), often paying only a little more than the production cost ($0.30 per piece). Potters were willing to give these merchants a volume discount since they were good long-term customers, and establishing relationships with several merchants was one of the best strategies for creating economic stability. In addition, merchants who bought in bulk were less fussy about the pots they purchased, and potters could include slightly damaged pots that would be harder to sell individually.

Most visitors from Kabul who were not merchants came to buy pottery as decorative objects for their homes. Istalifi pottery was well-known; some Kabulis bought these items to reflect interest in their country and show that they had enough wealth to go on Friday picnics outside of Kabul. These visitors often praised the pottery as traditional, but rarely used it functionally, prefer-ring imported plates and bowls. A typical visitor purchased about five pieces of pottery and paid around $1.00 per piece,[7] depending on the style, size, and number. Shopkeepers who targeted Kabuli visitors could sell almost half their wares to Kabuli and international visitors, although most relied on merchants. Shop owners I surveyed claimed to sell between 5 percent and 30 percent to in-ternationals, and up to 80 percent to merchants. These numbers, however, un-derstate the economic impact of a few sales to internationals.[8]

While international visitors accounted for the smallest percentage of sales, the profit margin from these sales was by far the greatest. On an average week-day, seventeen foreigners passed through the bazaar, though several of these were often Kabul-based development workers checking on projects in the area. On Friday, the weekend, the average rose to 44 international visitors a day. Al-though internationals made up less than 1 percent of the daily visitors, their presence shaped much of the marketing done by young shopkeepers. One shopkeeper was notorious for trying to charge $20 a pot (more than 6,000 per-cent of the approximate cost) whenever a foreigner visitor came to his shop. This practice was frowned upon, and some of the other shopkeepers called him *be-sharam* or shameless, yet most sellers still tried to charge $4–$8 per pot (1,300–2,600 percent of cost). This meant that selling one pot to a foreigner, even at a lower price, potentially created as much profit as selling five pots to a Kabuli visitor or 50 pots to a merchant. Potters were acutely aware of the com-plaint of many international visitors that they could not carry large pots home in their luggage, and they responded by producing more of the more portable small bowls, vases, and candlesticks.[9]

Internationals were generally the only ones who purchased the other "an-tiques" in the pottery shops. It was fairly common for shopkeepers to expect a 100-percent return on these items, and a 500-percent or 1,000-percent re-turn was not unheard of, mostly for the few products that actually were locally made, particularly baskets, *pustins* (leathers), and *patoos* (shawls).[10] A display of a variety of wares outside a shop often lured international customers inside, where the seller could then convince them to buy other small items. Even the pustin-selling shop acquired several dozen pieces of pottery, which the shop-keeper attempted to sell alongside the jackets and other antiques he had in stock. Thus, while merchants purchased the majority of pots, it was the wind-fall profits from selling a few pieces to foreigners that created unpredictability in the marketplace and fueled competition between families.

Although each workshop in Istalif combined flexible production and marketing approaches in response to numerous variables, it is possible to examine
the differences in the extremes of various marketing strategies of three workshops (Table 2).

Workshop A sells exclusively to merchants.

Workshop B sells to merchants, heavily to Kabuli visitors, and regularly to
internationals.

Workshop C uses a mixed strategy, relying mostly on sales to merchants, but
also on regular sales to Kabuli visitors and occasional sales to international
visitors.

With an average kiln size of 900 pots, a price of around $0.30 per pot sold to
merchants, $0.70 per pot sold to Kabulis, and closer to $5.00 per pot sold to internationals; the average income based on a kiln load of 900 pieces was approximately $270 for strategy A, $1031 for strategy B, and $554 for strategy C (Table 3).

Based on a kiln cost of $250, a strategy of selling purely to merchants was not
truly viable because it yielded only $20 per kiln load. A couple of families still
used a strategy like this, raising income by cutting costs (avoiding the expense
of touching up pots or using outside labor). The workshops that used strategies
to target merchants also tended to fire more often, but even these shopkeepers
attempted to sell some higher-quality pots to Kabuli and international visitors.
This strategy was favored primarily by larger families having a healthy supply of
labor, the ability to streamline production, and frequent firings.

Table 2. Marketing strategies

Workshop	Percentage Sold to Merchants	Percentage Sold to Kabulis	Percentage Sold to Internationals
A	100	0	0
B	50	35	15
C	75	20	5

Table 3. Income from marketing strategies

Strategy	Income from Selling to Merchants	Income from Selling to Kabuli Visitors	Income from Selling to International Visitors	Income	Profit
A	900 x $0.30 = $270	0	0	$270	$20
B	450 x $0.30 = $135	315 x $0.70 = $221	135 x $5 = $675	$1031	$781
C	675 x $0.30 = $203	180 x $0.70 = $126	45 x $5 = $225	$554	$304

The most lucrative marketing strategy was B, which yielded a profit of $781 per kiln load. This strategy was also the most risky—purchases by internationals were the least predictable. It was possible for a shop to sell 15 percent of its pots to international visitors, but it was difficult to rely on such numbers. In addition, producing the higher-quality, decorated pottery that internationals preferred required more attention to detail and additional time spent to complete each piece. This reduced a workshop's ability to produce in bulk for more reliable merchants. Moreover, because foreigners were often fussy about which pots they bought, small imperfections could prevent a sale. An explosion in the kiln, or glaze running and ruining several pieces, was much more costly for a workshop aiming for the higher-end market.

The majority of potters favored the mixed strategy, strategy C, which yielded $304 per kiln load. This approach allowed workshops to balance their need to maintain a relationship with reliable merchants and their desire to seek the larger profits that outside visitors would guarantee. Similarly, shopkeepers preferred the mixed strategy because it combined the reliability of a stock of lower-quality pots for merchants and the possibility of enticing internationals with the higher-quality wares, which shop owners could display in the windows. Increased sales of antiques only contributed to this trend, making it more likely that an international's visit to a shop would be profitable for the seller.

COMPETITION AMONG POTTERS

Despite the competitive nature of selling pottery, most of the tensions in the marketplace were not immediately visible. As in many bazaars, there were unspoken agreements among the various shopkeepers. For example, they could call out to invite a passerby into a shop, which they did, especially if the person looked foreign or wealthy, but once a shopper had begun speaking with a shopkeeper or a potter, no other shopkeeper would interrupt. When the shopper left the first store, other shopkeepers again had the right to try to entice the potential customer into their stores.

It was generally considered a breach of etiquette to approach someone in the public area of the street, and most shopkeepers stayed within a small radius of the door to their shop. Older men spoke disapprovingly when young men acted in an undignified manner, pursuing customers out in the street, although because of the potential return from international customers, some of the young men still tried this approach. Obviously, the key to making a sale was to get a customer into the store, and some shopkeepers would steer shoppers off the sidewalks and into their stores, where the goods in neighboring shops were no longer visible.

Shopkeepers set up their wares so they spilled out onto the sidewalk and hung from the beams that supported the roof over the walkway. During the muddy spring, when the street was treacherous, visitors were forced to walk fairly slowly past each shop, picking their way through the wares. Pottery stores tended to have larger windows and doors than the entranceways to other shops; grocers, for example, already had a reliable client base and did not need to compete for customers walking in from the street.

Pottery shopkeepers knew that foreigners were often charmed by "traditional" Afghan hospitality, so they often offered foreigners tea and sweets to keep them in the shop, even though they rarely did more than make the ritualized offer to Afghan visitors as they were leaving. Occasionally an international visitor would actually accept the offer of tea, catching the shopkeeper off guard and forcing him to send a small boy running to the *chai khana* (teahouse) for boiling water.

Potters argued among themselves about different approaches to marketing, even within a single workshop, and competing strategies had both economic and moral implications. Some issues were especially contentious; many potters grumbled about the man who greatly inflated his prices for foreigners. This particular seller had a set of "Made in Istalif" stickers that he put on imports from China and Pakistan, as well as on the pieces from Istalif, catering to the desire of internationals for "authentic" goods. Although the potters did not try to stop him from asking $20 for a pot or lying about the origins of his products, they complained behind his back. Some potters felt it was slightly immoral to charge such prices, but more often they simply saw his approach as a poor long-term strategy that would drive foreign customers away from the bazaar.

Most shopkeepers competed not just to make sales, but to establish relationships with foreigners living in Kabul who (they hoped) would return several times over the course of a year, and bring colleagues or friends. Shopkeepers reduced prices and gave gifts to individuals they thought might return, a strategy that proved effective. Having friendships with foreigners also generated a new form of social capital for many of the younger potters who worked in shops and intensified rivalries between young men. Often, when I met a young potter for the first time, early in our conversation he would brag about all the foreigners he knew as evidence of his social connections and resulting economic status. ("Oh, you are from America. Do you know Mr. Bob? He is a friend of mine.")

The Malik used a similar approach with NGO workers from Kabul, cultivating individual relationships that he used to channel funds to the potters.

There was some competition among the potters for the business of merchants in the bazaar, although it was muted. Most merchants already had relationships with specific store owners. Often, they would call ahead to make sure the shopkeeper was working on a certain day, or to inquire about specific items. Such relationships were rarely exclusive, however, and some merchants would go to other shops to look at other goods while they were in town. Still, many potters would quickly pull merchants into their shops and try to secure their business, or tell them to come back toward the end of the day when other shops would be closed.

To gain a competitive advantage, some potters were willing to sell entire kiln loads to merchants before the pieces had been fired. The merchant assumed a greater risk, but the potter's profit was also greatly reduced. Potters who did not own shops favored this practice, because they did not like to be left with too much excess stock. As a result, few potters actually had many finished bowls in their homes. Potters often recited the proverb, "The potter drinks his tea from shards," interpreting it differently. Some said it implied that potters should sell all their wares, while others claimed it proved that potters did not appreciate the artistry of their craft, focusing too much on business aspects.

In addition to having connections with merchants, many potters without shops of their own sold their wares through one of the other pottery shops in the bazaar. In several cases this took the form of cooperation between blood relatives and relatives by marriage, but several of the larger shops bought from multiple smaller workshops and sold the stock collectively. For example, the Sayed shop owner discussed earlier sold pots from his brother's wife's family and from three other workshops, and had a history of purchasing pottery from others.

Some potters felt the competition between various pottery families should be eliminated. Mohammad Seddiq, one of the most talented potters I knew, felt this way. Mohammad Seddiq came from a fairly wealthy family and was an extreme example of a potter who focused on quality over quantity. His workshop produced fewer pots, but they were always delicate and beautifully colored. He had a store, but he claimed that keeping a shop was mostly a waste of his time. He often advocated among the potters for a collective shop from which they could all sell their pottery together; that way, fewer potters would have to operate shops, and they could all focus on production. Younger potters were especially opposed to this idea, because they felt they could make more profit by establishing direct relationships with customers. A few other older potters supported Mohammad Seddiq's idea, but a significant majority still preferred to control their own marketing, including the Malik, whose family had one of the most successful shops in the bazaar.

Competition, especially for foreign business, created factions. Close relatives helped each other in marketing, but most of the other potters constantly tried to steal customers from one another. Stores expanded in size, and some of them had ornate displays and signs designed to attract new customers. There were about five informal clusters of shops along the main street of the bazaar. Neighboring owners helped each other and looked after each other's shops, creating a sense of solidarity within each cluster and a consistent, but not an overt, tension between the clusters. One cluster of shops near the mosque resented a group of shops located near the entrance of the bazaar (the man with the inflated prices for foreigners had a shop in this cluster). Those shops deeper in the bazaar claimed that the shops closer to the entrance intentionally stopped customers on their way down the street.

Similar to debates over a potential cooperative, the practice of stabilizing the pricing might have been an incentive for the potters to cooperate, and many sellers of other goods in the bazaar had benefitted from informally fixing their prices. The potential for windfall profits from foreign visitors, however, prevented this from happening for the potters, and they subsequently lowered their prices for Afghan customers. If the number of foreign visitors to Istalif continued to decrease—as happened during 2008, 2009, and 2010 while the security situation in Kabul continued to worsen —competition seemed likely to continue increasing among the potters in the bazaar.

COMPETITION WITHIN FAMILIES

The matter of whether to form a collective was simply one area of disagreement between the younger and older generations. Cooperation during production had contributed to family unity, but intergenerational tensions appeared to be growing among the potters. Older men knew the most about making pottery, but the younger men were often better businessmen, and the ones who sat in the bazaar and had forged ties with foreigners and merchants from Kabul, resulting in much of the family's income. In addition, most older men knew little about selling "antiques" and tended to frown on the practice, despite realizing that there was a profit to be made. Selling antiques was not considered part of the wazeefah (duty) that potters alluded to when discussing the production of pottery.

Varying education levels were another source of tension that contributed to competition within pottery families. The literacy rate in Afghanistan was 24 percent,[11] but this number masks some significant trends. People in cities tended to be more literate than those in rural areas (49 percent versus 20 percent), with a rate of 31 percent for rural areas in Kabul Province. More importantly, the history of the past 20 years had greatly shaped literacy patterns. Nationally, youths between the ages of 15 and 24 tended to be more literate (35 percent in rural areas of Kabul Province). However, older men also tended to be more literate, and in Istalif it was common to find older men who could read and write. In contrast, far fewer men between the ages of 25 and 40 were literate, because they came of age during the Soviet and civil war periods. Men in this age bracket were required to leave school and fight; and even if they were too young to fight, their fathers often did not let them attend the communist schools in town. In several families, this caused tension between an older brother who was in charge of the family affairs and a younger brother who was better educated, but still expected to submit to his elder.

In many cases, specific roles for each family member were agreed upon by fathers and sons. The elders worked primarily in the workshop and the younger brothers in the bazaar. A few families, realizing the importance of establishing relationships with foreigners, had allowed younger sons to attend English classes in Kabul (thus far with limited success) and let them buy some Western-style clothes. In other cases, however, the tension remained unresolved, especially in poorer families with multiple unmarried young men. High bride-prices, and the fact that elder brothers almost always married before their younger brothers, caused resentment among the younger brothers, especially when they felt their marketing skills were contributing the most to the family's income.

The combination of support for the idea of a collective by some members of the older generation and the near-unanimous rejection by younger potters, illustrates the tension around economic and political incentives. Elders were already married, and for the most part many were economically secure, so they had time to worry about political and social issues, such as feuding between families and tensions in the qaum. Most elders were financially conservative and did not speak about economic mobility. Younger men, on the other hand, felt incredible pressure to raise money for marriage, so they worried somewhat less about political or social tensions within the group. Older men in the qaum claimed younger men did not understand the potential long-term repercussions of political relationships—they desired the stability that the collective would foster among the potters. The young men aspired to becoming rich and potentially moving to Kabul or abroad, and the collective would have eliminated the potential for windfall profits that would enable them to realize these goals.

An important consequence was that alliances among young potters, particularly those working in the bazaar, did not always overlap with the alliances their fathers had established. Young sellers were most likely to work with friends or the shopkeepers around them, while the older generation relied more strictly on kinship and marriage ties. The tendency for young potters to form alliances with friends who were not kin was reinforced by the fact that when Istalifis fled the town following the arrival of the Taliban, they did not always do so with their own families. Perhaps there was nothing new about this phenomenon, and the friendships of the younger generations would eventually result in alliances as they marry each other's sisters and cousins. However, the result was that older and younger generations had different views on alliances in town; the elders were much more intent on preserving unity and political balance within the qaum, while the younger men were more concerned with establishing personal relationships. These opposing outlooks meant that different generations within a family could have different networks of allies and friends, which naturally caused periodic tension within the family.

It could be argued that these trends are due to the intrusion of modernity in Istalif. Was this simply a process of social ties being eroded and replaced with economic and personal ties, and respect for elders being replaced with respect for economic capital? In actuality, Istalif and most of Afghanistan do not fit well into the linear narratives that often characterize discussions of modernity. There has not been a steady process of urbanization across the country; instead, cities have swelled and then emptied on several occasions during the past half-century, because of fighting and changing economic conditions. Similarly, kin and tribal ties have not declined so much as responded to changing political conditions. In Istalif, even the most ambitious young men were not convinced that forsaking kinship and social ties for economic reasons was a wise strategy—a view that was even more apparent in groups who were loyal to commanders. The tension was a product of varying incentives and the different alliances to which each generation had access. This was most visible among middle-aged men, who had spent years focused on economics and were turning now to the consolidation of social and political power. The tensions between production and marketing, and between generations, in turn shaped marriage patterns, descent, and the political organization of the pottery clan.

THE POLITICS OF COMPETITION AND COOPERATION

Potters were one of several quams in Istalif, but their quam was particularly adept at mobilizing and cooperating economically and politically, partly because there were significant economic incentives in the production of pottery that were absent in other quams. Cooperation did not always follow simple kinship models. Friends were often just as important as kin, and business partners could become close political allies. The potters were not purely rational actors, but the economics of the production and marketing processes created social, economic, and moral patterning. Economic relationships became social or political, just as social relationships often encouraged economic cooperation. Families that did business together were more likely to form marriage alliances, and cooperation in the workshop in turn led to cooperation in the political arena. Young men were socialized in a production system that encouraged cooperation among the immediate family (and, to a lesser extent, the entire qaum). When it came time to market their wares, however, potters competed against one another. These economic incentives strengthened the tendency for competition outside the family and, to a lesser extent, within the family. This tension between unity and individual entrepreneurship dictated many of the qaum's political internal and external relationships.

Because production and marketing created such contrasting strategies of cooperation and competition, the potters were unique in Istalif, mobilizing more forcefully and fracturing more quickly than most groups in town. Orchard owners, for example, relied on cooperative labor to tend their trees, although they were more willing to use outside labor and had fewer incentives to cooperate outside the immediate family. Among orchard owners, social groups vacillated between cooperation and conflict, but not to the extremes of the pottery qaum.

These trends serve as a model for the political process of all Istalif groups, which also mobilized often, but always threatened to split apart. All of these groups used the manipulable idiom of kinship to justify mobilization. These terms were, in turn, reinforced through marriage alliances, friendships, and business arrangements. As a result, for all young men in Istalif, balancing the tensions created by cooperation and competition became deeply intertwined with the politics of marriage, descent, and leadership within each group.

Figure 1. The main street in the bazaar (photo by author).

Figure 2. Pottery shops with pots hanging on the doors (photo by author).

Figure 3. A young potter in his shop (photo by author).

Figure 4. Cleaning the clay with a sieve (photo by author).

Figure 5. A potter kneading the clay (photo by author).

Figure 6. The shrine above town (photo by author).

Telling Stories

Malik Abdul Hamid was a man of average size with sharp features, a weathered face, and piercing eyes. He spent most of his time greeting visitors at his house in Kulalan, the neighborhood where most of the potters lived, high above the bazaar. Several times a week he came down to walk around the mosque and the bazaar, where he owned a successful pottery shop run by one of his sons. The Malik always dressed in traditional robes, covered by a blazer, and was never without his turban. Due to his age, he walked slowly, but his grasp was still incredibly firm. Toward the end of my time in Istalif, Malik Abdul Hamid developed tuberculosis and was noticeably frailer. This did little to diminish his gravitas.

Like many Afghan leaders, Malik Hamid listened more than he spoke. During a visit, one of his sons often led the conversation while the Malik sat back and listened, clicking his prayer beads thoughtfully. Especially if the visitor was new, Malik Hamid would sit quietly, letting the visitor talk himself in circles, waiting to hear everything before entering the conversation. When he did speak, he quickly became animated and forceful. He liked to talk about the town and tell jokes, especially to foreign visitors, but his severity lay always just beneath the surface.

Malik Abdul Hamid was most animated when he told stories. He would lean forward on the cushions in his guestroom and stab with his finger to emphasize points, often asking "*me fameen*" (do you understand?) or "*fekre-ton ast*" (don't you agree?) to make sure the listener was paying attention. During my time in Istalif, I heard him tell his favorite stories half a dozen times, while talking with me as well as when I sat in on meetings with the occasional journalist who came to hear the Malik's stories.

His favorite stories to tell outsiders were about the origins of the potters in Istalif. He would make sure his sons had served tea, and then slide forward to get closer to his listeners:

"We potters do not have accounts of our past in books or in any type of written history. Instead what have comes to us from our *resh-e safeeds*, our white beards, our ancestors.

"Istalif was founded by potters 300 years ago.[1] Our pottery tradition originally came from Bukhara. During a time of fighting and instability in Bukhara, Sayed Mir Kulal[2] took his family and a few followers out of their land. They first went south and settled in Balkh, but were not happy there, though some potters stayed there and this is why pottery similar to Istalifi pottery may be found in Balkh. So they headed south, looking for the perfect site to start a village. Seeing the natural beauty and the clay of Istalif, our fathers decided to stay. One of the men who came with Sayed Mir was Eshan Sahib, a famous religious scholar. His shrine still stands today in Istalif on the hill above the bazaar.

"Shortly after the potters first arrived in Istalif, Bahodean, the son of an ancient king of Afghanistan, heard of the beauty of Istalifi pottery. Despite his high rank, he decided to learn how to make pottery. When he first came to Istalif, Sayed Mir was concerned that he was not really interested in making pots and would not work hard because he was the son of a king. So Sayed Mir attempted to give him a test so difficult that he would fail it and then not return. Sayed Mir asked him to bring him the innards of three sheep all at the same time, without any of them touching each other. So Bahodean went off to the bazaar and returned quickly with the innards of three sheep: one in each hand and one in his mouth. When Sayed Mir saw this, he realized that Bahodean was a bright man and would actually be a devoted student.

"Bahodean worked hard as a student and learned much, even though he was not from a family of potters. Eventually, other students became jealous of him. When he was assigned to do tasks, the other students refused to help him the way that they helped each other. One day, it was Bahodean's turn to fire the kiln, but Sayed Mir did not realize this and was far off working in his grape vineyards. Bahodean did not have enough wood for the kiln and the other students refused to collect more for him, hoping that he would be shamed if he had a poor firing. Having trouble keeping the fire up, Bahodean begins to repeat the name of Allah: 'Yallah, Yallah,' and the fire began to rise up, hotter and hotter. Sayed Mir sensed that Bahodean was in trouble, saw the smoke from the kiln, and came hurrying back. Sayed Mir began to rip off his shirt to throw it in the fire, but by this time the fire was so hot that there was no longer any problem.

"When the kiln cooled and Sayed Mir took the pots out of the kiln, on each one of them was etched with the name of Allah. Bahodean saw this and recited the poem:

> Etch my heart's carvings
> That they may call me a carver.
> Since then, we potters have been decorating our pots using etching.

"When Bahodean left Istalif he went to Bukhara, where he founded a new school of Islam called Naqshbandism. It is called this because the Dari word for etching is 'nach kardan,' and because it was Bahodean who first etched things on pots, his school became known as the Naqshbandi School. Today there are Muslims who practice the Naqshbandi way all over the world. They may not know it, but the way they practice Islam came from Istalif.[3]

"Bahodean and Sayed Mir traveled widely looking for students and followers, and when they died, they were both buried in Bukhara. They now have shrines there and we have visited them. There we spoke with Uzbek potters who all talked about the importance of Bahodean. They showed us some of the shards of his pots and told us how great Istalifi pottery is. They had his old kiln there and they gave us a piece of it, so we still have some of Bahodean's materials here with us.

"Also since this time of Bahodean, the results of a kiln firing have also always told us whether a potter is honest or not. If the pots come out of a firing and are discolored or ruined, this means that the potter has been lying or committing some other sin. To atone, he must provide a Koranic reading or a feast for the community. Only men who are pure and good will also produce pure and beautiful pots."[4]

The only story that Malik Abdul Hamid liked telling more than this one was his own story of how he became the head of the potters:

"When I was 18, I was chosen as malik—this was in the time of Daud Khan.[5] When my father died, the qaum was without malik. I did not really want to be selected, because I was young and not thinking about such things, so I did not put myself forward as a candidate. The elders went off and held a council meeting. The next day, however, the heads of all the families came to my house and put the turban on my head. They brought me to the district governor's and declared that I was now the bridge between the people and the government. . . . The turban is a sign of respect, not just for the malik, but for elders, mullahs, and qaris. Before I was malik I never wore a turban."

5 LEADERSHIP, DESCENT, AND MARRIAGE

MALIK ABDUL HAMID'S STORIES were almost always idealized accounts. The story of the potters' arrival in Istalif created a sense of unity, despite a history that was much more contested than the story implied. In particular, the tendency toward fusion and fission created a system where political groups and alliances were necessary, but never stable. This posed a dilemma for individuals: Remain loyal to the pottery qaum, or seek other alliances? Young men tried to do both. By solidifying their relationships with other qaum members and close kin, they increased the likelihood that they would be able to arrange a suitable marriage alliance, and thereby continue to take economic advantage of their positions as members of the qaum. But since the qaum was unstable, young men quietly sought allies outside the qaum, who would help them get ahead economically and provide a counterbalance to the qaum's power.

Of course, by seeking these alternate alliances, these young men further weakened the strength of the qaum, making it necessary for others to look outside the qaum for political support as well. Malik Hamid and other qaum elders strove to maintain the unity—or at least the perceived unity—of the group. While different social and economic positions helped shape the strategies an individual adopted, each person balanced internal and external alliances, further reinforcing the unreliability of a system that could never really be abandoned. This gave the pottery group the cohesiveness to be a force in town politics, but limited its capacity to mobilize consistently and forcefully once the political stakes increased.

Even at the most basic level, political relationships in Istalif were slippery, contributing to the ambiguity and theater that pervaded larger issues in the town's politics. Competition in the market hindered the sustainability of alliances among kin and between friends and neighbors, but social relationships—via leadership, descent, and marriage—also shaped the potters as a group. Malik Abdul Hamid, whose power came from his position as the qaum's traditional leader, was the individual most invested in preserving group unity, but even he had to seek support outside the group and form alternative alliances to maintain his status.[1] Other individuals also worked to solidify their position within the qaum while seeking alternative sources of power—especially through marriage arrangements and relationships between families. External alliances allowed individuals to shape the system, simultaneously reinforcing the group while assuring that each person had a network of allies when the group failed. The numerous ways an individual, including the Malik, could use his social and economic situation to shape his circumstances, despite established patterns and customs, created a political group that was simultaneously strong and tenuous.

THE KING OF THE POTTERS

A malik was often called the *pul*, or bridge, between the people and the government, and Malik Abdul Hamid was the chief representative of his qaum before the government. There were several other maliks in town, each in charge of at least one *gozar* (neighborhood). The potters' single qaum, primarily in one gozar with one malik, was an idealized structure that was simpler than the political situations in most other gozars. As the potters' main voice with the district governor and other outsiders, the Malik had a serious incentive to preserve group unity. Since his power came from the group, he was only as powerful as he could make the group appear. Yet to maintain his influence, he was often forced to provide resources that could only come from outside the group. To ensure his political position by providing those resources, he crafted alliances that extended beyond the traditional network of the potters. This meant serving as a liaison between the district governor and the potters, but also maintaining a relationship with local commanders and NGOs.

Malik Hamid's story of how he became the leader of the potters is a familiar Afghan tale. His narrative parallels the story of Ahmad Shah Baba (c. 1723–1773), commonly referred to as the "Father of Afghanistan." A popular story describes how, following the assassination of Nadir Shah Afshar in 1747, a *jirga* (tribal gathering) met to select a leader for the various tribes. After a nine-day deadlock, a holy man picked up a turban and two pieces of wheat (some versions say maize) and placed them on the head of Ahmad Abdali. Because he was young and from a relatively weak tribe, he had not been considered a serious contender for the throne. Ahmad Abdali became Ahmed Shah Durrani, and ruled for the next twenty-five years. In these stories, the leader makes no claim of superiority over others and leads only because he is asked to lead. This traditional tale of the reluctant leader whose people have thrust him forward still resonates in Afghanistan's local and national politics.[2]

Both stories, Malik Hamid's and the story of Ahmad Abdali, idealize a style of leadership that draws the strongest from among equals and values those that least covet the position (or seem least to covet it), giving the appearance of the rejection of status and hierarchy. Yet both stories at least partially mask the political machinations at work in establishing *primus inter pares* in Afghanistan.

In actuality, Ahmad Abdali's selection had a certain political logic to it despite the weakness of his tribe. At the time of Nadir Shah's death, Ahmad Abdali was considered a young, charismatic leader and in the resulting chaos, he and his men, who had been key bodyguards of Nadir Shah, had made off with most of the Shah's treasury. More important, however, was the fact that other Abdali tribal leaders perceived him as weak and manipulable.[3] Instead of fighting among themselves for the title, most leaders felt that by choosing a young weak ruler, each tribe could maintain its own power. This began a cycle of succession that has often repeated in Afghan history.

Similarly, while no one openly disputed the story of Malik Abdul Hamid's reluctance to claim the turban, his assertion that he "was not thinking about such things," seems unlikely. The position of malik was usually patrilineally inherited, though there was some flexibility in the system. It is likely that Malik Abdul Hamid's father, who was also the malik, had prepared him in some way to become malik. People often pointed out that if the eldest son of the previous malik was considered unworthy, another son or even a man from another family could assume the role. For the most part, however, this was simply a check on the power of the malik, and my research revealed few such cases in the area. As Malik Hamid aged, it was clear that his eldest son was being groomed to assume leadership. Whenever this son stepped out of line, though, others were quick to remind him of the vulnerability of his position. The rhetoric of the malik as a servant to the group helped ensure that the Malik and his son did little to offend the group—the story reminded everyone involved that the malik's power came directly from the group. On the other hand, the story allowed the Malik to continue leading the qaum despite the traditional Afghan reluctance to admit any man's superiority.

Malik was not the only title people used for Malik Abdul Hamid. I occasionally heard him called Mullah Saheb, especially by young boys, to emphasize his religious learning, although he had never studied in a religious school and left most religious duties to the neighborhood mullah. Despite the fact that he had not made the *hajj*, the pilgrimage to Mecca, he was also occasionally called Hajji Saheb. It was a common sign of respect in the area to assume that someone of his age and status had made the hajj, but when two individuals knew each other in Istalif, the title of Hajji was never used unless the individual had actually performed the hajj. Among the potters, the hajj was a symbol of political and economic status and carried a prestige that was not simply religious.[4] Those who used the title Hajji, but had not made the pilgrimage, tended to be disparaged behind their backs.

Some treated the term malik as a general way of referring to a powerful individual. (It could also be a first name; Malik Hamid's second cousin was named Malik Ibraheem, confusing things somewhat.) I visited an old weaver of patoos, who lived about two hours' walk down the valley from Kulalan, with Malik Abdul Hamid's son, Abdul Gul. The entire time we were there the weaver called Abdul Gul "Malik Saheb" as a sign of respect, even though he clearly knew that Abdul Gul's father was the Malik.

Context here was important. The weaver was not a member of the pottery qaum, lived a good distance away, and had little to lose by showing respect to Abdul Gul. In fact, the only political dealings the weaver and Abdul Gul would probably have was if the weaver came to Abdul Gul with a favor or needed Abdul Gul to intercede on his behalf, if the head of his own qaum could not or would not help him. On the other hand, members of the pottery qaum would never have called Abdul Gul "Malik"; in fact, they always emphasized that there was no guarantee that Abdul Gul would be malik. This ensured that Abdul Gul had to work constantly to maintain the support of the qaum, or risk losing their support when the time came to select a new malik. Similarly, while outsiders might have conferred extra respect on Malik Abdul Hamid by calling him Hajji, I never heard another potter do this. It would have meant conferring respect that he was not due. Most potters often referred to the instability of Malik Hamid's power, emphasizing that he must be beholden to the qaum first and foremost. The language of leadership thus gave members of the pottery qaum an important check on the malik's power, while the malik simultaneously used his title to foster links with government officials and other influential outsiders.

Malik Abdul Hamid was not simply a "traditional" Afghan leader, constantly providing subsidies to his followers to ensure a peaceful, continued reign. Such an assumption misses the dynamic conditions in which the Malik made political decisions, balancing the duties and social rituals that maintained the unity of the pottery qaum, while trying to establish an expanding network of political and economic support outside the qaum.

MAINTAINING THE QAUM AND ITS LIMITS

Malik Abdul Hamid had a series of formal and informal duties that reinforced his position and emphasized the unity of the qaum. These duties also tended to reinforce the traditional hierarchy among the potters. The malik's position was clearly visible especially on holidays, when all Istalif residents took part in the ritualized visiting of allies and kin. During this period, the position of the malik as host reinforced his status. During every visit there was an expression of a political relationship—the host demonstrating power, wealth, and benevolence through the offering of food and protection, and the guests reaffirming their loyalty to the host. Especially on Eid holidays at the end of Ramazan, the order of visiting was important. Everyone in a family always had to visit the eldest male in their family first. It was also important to visit the family of anyone who had died in the past year. After this there was some flexibility, but the order of visits clearly reflected the informal hierarchy within the family. Older men did little visiting themselves. Instead, they sent their sons or other representatives out to visit other figures around town and in the region, while they stayed home to receive visitors.

At the end of my second Ramazan in Istalif, on the first day of the Eid celebration, Malik Abdul Hamid stayed at home with most of his sons in the morning. In the afternoon, he sent all his sons except one to visit other elders in the village. On the second day of Eid, one of his sons went into Kabul to visit relatives, especially an influential family related to Malik Hamid maternally. At least one son was always with Malik Hamid to open the door, welcome guests, and pour tea. The son made sure each visitor had a glass of tea, and then a grandson was responsible for refilling the glasses, as well as other tasks, such as washing the hands of the guests.

At first only close kin visited Malik Hamid, while other potters began their visits at the homes of their own family members, but all the potters in Kulalan visited him or sent a representative at some point on the first day of Eid. At the Malik's house there was a lavish display. The normally simple guestroom had a tablecloth spread the length of the room with extra pillows on each side. The floor was set for thirty people, with a teacup marking the spot for each person. There were piles of candies, fruits, nuts, and other foods, decorated with heaps of plastic flowers. In other homes the display was a little less elaborate, but even the poorest families still had colorful trays of nuts and sweets prepared for visitors, which they would not have had on other days. People rotated through Malik Hamid's guestroom, most staying for a little less than an hour. Everyone repeated the elaborate Afghan greetings, adding wishes for a prosperous Eid. Outside, people strolled through the streets, greeting each other and chatting before entering the house of another relative.

On the second day, more distant kin and friends arrived. Many of the Istalifis with whom Malik Abdul Hamid had connections came on the second day, as did relatives who lived in Kabul. The third day was more peaceful, with a small assortment of visitors who had been busy on the first two days. For example, the major commander of the town, who was related distantly by marriage, came to visit the Malik's family. The commander, who rarely came to Istalif, had spent the first two days in Kabul receiving his own guests, visiting his major allies in town on the third day. The festive spirit continued for several days, and one especially jolly old man told me that although he had sent his sons as his representatives to visit kin in Kabul, he himself would go on the fourth day, because he did not want to miss out on the fun.

Visiting reinforced the political position of people within the pottery qaum and within extended families. Malik Hamid was obligated to provide food for all of his visitors. The expectations of such redistribution, however, also were a check on the power of the Malik, since this was a public test of his capacity to redistribute goods. The lavish displays of food in his house symbolically demonstrated the economic rewards and requirements of his authority; in turn, it was expected that each family in the pottery qaum and any other family allied with the potters would send a representative to wish the Malik a prosperous Eid. Even here relationships were never simple, and there was some flexibility for manipulating the politics of visiting. One of the other important families of potters prepared an elaborate guestroom for Eid that rivaled Malik Hamid's, and the numerous guests that lingered there expressed subtle dissent toward the Malik's leadership. Similarly, sending a younger son, or visiting somewhat later in the holiday period, delivered a political message.

While all the potters took part in these visitations, younger potters tended to treat the ritual slightly differently. Elder men were the most solemn and systematic about the visits. They took the order of visits very seriously, and there was a sense of purpose to their visiting and greetings. Younger men were more carefree, celebrating the holiday and the fact that they were no longer fasting. They fulfilled their duties to their patrilineal kin, but also visited various friends and relaxed outdoors. As we will see, these unmarried men, in particular, had a strong incentive to nurture relationships with other families and friends, any of whom could assist in creating a marriage alliance.

Several other customs reaffirmed the Malik's status as head of the potters. He was seen by many as the possessor of the group's history. Most of the stories I collected about the history of the potters, such as the one in the interlude that precedes this chapter, came from him. Other old men told me similar stories, but they almost always began and concluded by saying: "This is the story I know, but Malik Abdul Hamid knows the story much better, so you should ask him about it." The younger men did not tell stories at all and would only direct me to the Malik. On several occasions, when I asked a potter about his genealogy, he would tell me to ask the Malik to fill in the parts he had forgotten.

It was not surprising that the Malik focused so much on these stories while others tended to ignore them. The myths, in particular, tended to emphasize the collective origins of the potters and their descent from Sayed Mir Kulal. Other stories focused on the sacred nature of the potters or the blessings and miracles earlier potters had performed. These all reaffirmed the unity of the pottery qaum. The Malik was also the potter who told the most stories from more recent history. Some of these stories discussed the way Istalif was visited by individuals, such as Daud Khan and Zahir Shah, who had been impressed by the work of the potters.

At other times, Malik Abdul Hamid used these same stories to reflect his own importance as the head of the potters. He often told the story of a visit to the town by Zahir Shah. He began by describing Zahir Shah's clothes and the cars in his entourage, reminding the listener of the monarch's former splendor. He said that while in town, Zahir Shah met him and was so impressed by the Malik that he issued him a formal invitation to the palace and addressed him as Engineer Saheb (a title used for an educated individual, but one not typically used for Malik Abdul Hamid). Malik Hamid then said Zahir Shah gave him some money, because "he knew that the people of Istalif were very poor"—not an entirely accurate statement. He told Malik Abdul Hamid to distribute the money. This element of the story was interesting because Malik Abdul Hamid now claimed that if any development organization distributed money or other aid to the potters, they should do so through him. Zahir Shah had given Malik Hamid a large ceramic stove made in East Germany; he still kept it in his guestroom during the winter, and fondly reminded visitors that it had been a gift from Zahir Shah.

Some of the Malik's duties were not as uncontested as holding the Eid feast at his house. For example, he was also in charge of collecting 50 afghanis (about $1) each month from every married man in the community, to pay for the upkeep of the mosque and the neighborhood mullah's salary. People's reluctance to pay made this task tedious, so Malik Hamid never collected the money himself; instead, he sent his son. Such an approach had logic. Denying money to the Malik's son was not that offensive, but if the Malik had demanded the money personally, the honor of both sides would be at stake. By sending his son, he defused the situation. The Malik also collected money for recitation of the Koran during Ramazan and occasionally for funerals. Perhaps because these were more solemn events, people seemed more willing to contribute.

Malik Abdul Hamid thus had power in collecting and redistributing funds, but this authority was limited. Individuals were often unwilling to part with money, lest it seem that the Malik had genuine power over them. This was not a case of simple economics, as in the resistance to paying the mullah's monthly salary. The mullah was widely respected in the community, and I never heard anyone complain about the salary he received. Instead, they complained specifically about giving the money to the Malik's son. There was also a rotation, and the mullah was regularly hosted by each household in the community. On these nights the family prepared a rather elaborate meal for him, at a cost that far exceeded the dollar each family was expected to pay each month, yet most potters took part in this tradition of hospitality. The resistance to handing the money to the Malik's son reflected a general reluctance to submit publicly to the Malik's authority, more than any genuine economic concern.

Five years after the fall of the Taliban and the return of most of the potters to Istalif, the neighborhood mosque had yet to be fully repaired. The structure had two levels, but the roof and one wall on the top floor had been destroyed during the fighting. In winter the men gathered in the rather dingy basement to pray. In better weather they prayed in the open air on the second floor. As I was leaving, Malik Hamid was in the process of petitioning an NGO to help with the repair, but he had been unable to collect funds from the potters, despite several attempts. In contrast, several Istalifi businessmen living in Kabul had arranged for a new mosque to be built in the bazaar. The community had also supported the reconstruction of a shrine in town and several other small projects. Even if the potters had sufficient funds, there was a fear that one man, Malik Abdul Hamid, would receive credit for the project. This would upset the balance of power among the pottery families.

Malik Hamid had been able to mobilize sufficient resources and establish enough influence that all the potters, grudgingly or not, acknowledged him as the leader of the group. Their fierce egalitarianism made his position as a primary link to the government and other outside groups all the more important. A considerable amount of the resources and influence he was able to mobilize came not from within the group, but from his ability to forge ties outside the group. By the end of 2009, a Kabul-based NGO, with the potters providing much of the labor, had renovated the mosque.

THE NEED FOR EXTERNAL NETWORKS AND OUTSIDE SUPPORT

The Malik had several methods of compensating for his limited authority. As the bridge with the government, he was usually the first person the district governor approached when he had an issue with any of the potters. A typical example is land disputes, though with such disagreements, people in town often tried to avoid the participation of the government. When the government did participate, it often relied heavily on a malik for information. I was in the district governor's office one day when two men and their kin came in to discuss a claim. The malik of a different gozar was also in the room. The district governor listened to them all make their case and then waved his hand distractedly, telling everyone that he needed to think for a few minutes. Everyone filed out of his office, except for the malik. The district governor then emerged a few minutes later and announced his decision. During the interval he had clearly consulted with the malik, but privately; doing so publicly would have undermined his authority. Everyone seemed fairly content with the decision, and I did not hear about that particular dispute again.

Malik Abdul Hamid made sure that he has good relationships with other influential people in town. In the interlude that precedes Chapter 1, "A Rocky Road," about the dispute over building a road into Istalif, the engineers from the Ministry of Rural Rehabilitation and Development had recently eaten lunch with Malik Hamid. This was typical of the way he used his hospitality to create allies. He had sent one of his sons to invite the engineers to his home and provided them with an extravagant meal (by Istalifi standards). During events like these, political issues were not generally discussed, and it was unclear that the relationship with the engineers could actually directly benefit Malik Hamid in any way. Despite this ambiguity, the streets of the gozar were narrow and gossip spread quickly. When other potters knew about the engineers' visit to the Malik, it reaffirmed his ability to forge relationships with the government. Such a meeting suggested he would be able to deliver goods in the future, and, had the road been built, would have let him claim at least some involvement in the project. Because the engineers were surveying the road through many gozars, Malik Hamid was far from the only elder with interest in their work. I often saw elders talking with the engineers, while subordinates ran around doing most of the surveying, and I imagine that they emerged from their month in Istalif well fed.

The money, goods, and employment NGOs brought were an even more lucrative, though less predictable, form of income. There was a long history of NGO aid to Istalif, and international assistance had been important to the potters at least since the late 1960s, when a French potter worked with the community. NGOs were interested in the potters as an artisan group with possible international marketing potential; visitors were drawn to Istalif for its beautiful setting and proximity to Kabul. However, the potters had been able to mobilize a disproportionate amount of NGO support because of the Malik's ability to portray them as a unified group in need.

Creating a coherent narrative of NGO aid in Istalif was surprisingly difficult, particularly following the chaotic rush to pour assistance into Afghanistan in 2002 and 2003. Large organizations worked in most parts of the country, but Istalif, being close to Kabul but not within the city itself, became a fairly popular place for smaller NGOs to work. The result of these numerous, mostly small-scale projects was some confusion among Istalifis as to what organizations had worked in the area and who was responsible for which projects. Confusion also resulted because most funders ran small projects that were rarely coordinated with other NGOs or integrated into government structures. The increasing belief that the Afghan government was corrupt and lacked capacity further fragmented programs. Some of the political motivations of NGO workers will be discussed further in Chapter 6, but the fact that most were primarily accountable to offices in Kabul or abroad meant it was more important to create programs that appealed to funders on paper, than programs that had a genuine economic impact. The result was that while there was significant funding from NGOs in Istalif, the money was distributed in a haphazard way, and the Malik and others took advantage.

Beyond these difficulties, some of the problems I encountered while piecing together a history of aid to Istalif involved the political implications of creating such a narrative. Many individuals I did not know personally would initially deny having received aid, probably hoping this account of their poverty might encourage me to assist them. Often, the narrative of who had provided aid seemed more important than the aid itself. Rarely could individuals re-member the jumbled English and French acronyms of the organizations that had worked in Istalif since 2002; however, they did know when the money had been channeled through Malik Abdul Hamid and when it had come through another individual or group.

Malik Abdul Hamid had several strategies for maintaining connections with NGOs. Although he rarely traveled to Kabul or solicited these groups di-rectly, he made a point of immediately approaching any group that came to town. His third son, Abdul Zia, who generally ran his shop in the bazaar, played a central role in initiating many of these relationships. Abdul Zia would jump up to introduce himself to any international visitors more aggressively than other shopkeepers. This served the dual purpose of potentially selling them some wares and, if they represented an NGO, of establishing a relationship with them. It was not simply an attempt to market aggressively—Abdul Zia often invited these internationals to lunch or gave them pots as gifts, both of which were transactions in which he probably lost money. (Other shopkeepers also gave gifts, but Abdul Zia's more substantial gifts targeted internationals with whom he thought he could establish lasting relationships.) If he felt the visitors were especially important, he called his father down to the bazaar, or took them to visit the Malik and his workshop.

NGOs provided employment as well as funding, both of which were impor-tant aspects of these external networks. During my time in Istalif, two NGOs employed eight potters. Other potters had relatives in Kabul who worked for NGOs. This practice was not limited to the potters; NGOs accounted for a sur-prisingly high percentage of the employment in and around Kabul. Two of Malik Abdul Hamid's sons had been employed by multiple NGOs, as commu-nity liaisons or distributors of aid. In these cases, the benefits to Malik Hamid far exceeded his sons' salaries; the potters sometimes saw the aid being distrib-uted come directly from his sons' hands, and saw the Malik's family walking around town with these international aid workers.

Connections with NGOs were not the only relationships the Malik used to increase his prestige. Both Malik Abdul Hamid and his eldest son, Abdul Gul, spoke frequently about their connections with the international military. They discussed visits by a French commander who told them to call him if they had any problems with the district governor or the head of police. Despite these sto-ries, I never actually saw a military officer stop at the Malik's home. Most of the military remained in the bazaar, about a kilometer south of his house. The story remained powerful, however, because international military figures were seen as some of the few individuals who could directly confront local authorities.

A major factor frustrating Malik Hamid's attempts to establish personal relationships with the military was the high turnover rate among international military personnel. While I was in Istalif, although France was technically the International Security Assistance Force (ISAF) country assigned to the area that included the town, American, German, and Canadian forces all visited at some point, and the interrelationships of these foreign troops were never clear to the Istalifis. The international military also occasionally visited development projects, further up the valley, being run with the assistance of the Army Corps of Engineers. In a couple of instances, foreign troops even stopped in the bazaar, where they acted very much like tourists (though only in very small groups, and this behavior seemed to violate protocol). While traditional leaders in the area clearly had trouble establishing personal relationships with international military figures, Malik Hamid and other elders still gained political capital by suggesting that they were the most capable of establishing and maintaining these ties.

THE MALIK AND INTERNAL NETWORKS

Malik Abdul Hamid had several more traditional means of expanding his network of allies. Although marriage alliances were formed among all potters, marriages in Malik Hamid's family were in some respects unique. While I was in Istalif, Malik Hamid had two married sons and one who was engaged. The Malik had married his sister's husband's sister, and his eldest son was married to his sister's daughter (who was therefore also his wife's brother's daughter). The family with whom they had intermarried were also potters, but they were not active in the community. Most of them had moved into Kabul, and the rest lived in an orchard-filled area a little ways up the valley. This alliance helped Malik Hamid maintain his status, because his son's father-in-law was a schoolteacher, and the rest of the family were cosmopolitan figures who were respected by the community. The external alliance also increased the number of allies Malik Hamid could call upon when necessary. At the same time, because his father-in-law and his son's father-in-law were removed from daily affairs, they did not generally take part in any disputes that could threaten Malik Hamid's authority.

The Malik's second son, Abdul Yousef, was a different case. His marriage had taken place after his brother's, and his wife's family were not potters. When the potters explained his marriage, they said he had *girift* (taken) a woman from the family of Mohammad Zaher, the major commander in Istalif. It was unclear to me how Abdul Yousef's wife and Mohammad Zaher were related (they were not members of the same immediate family), but this ambiguity was common in Istalif. Precise kinship ties were often less important than the language used to define the social relationship. For Abdul Yousef's relationship with Mohammad Zaher, people used the phrase *bach-e mama* (son of his maternal uncle) for his wife, implying that his wife was Mohammad Zaher's mother's brother's daughter. This type of language, though, was flexible. For example, the more common phrase *bach-e kaka* technically translated as "son of the speaker's father's brother," but was used to refer to the speaker's father's father's brother's son's son, the speaker's father's father's father's brother's son's son (or his son), or multiple other patrilineally related males of a similar generation. More rarely, it also described matrilineal kin. Metaphorically it was used to refer to any close ally who had a relationship similar to that of a "father's brother's son." Taking all of this into account, Abdul Yousef could have been married to Mohammad Zaher's mother's brother's daughter's daughter—or some other equivalent relation. For the potters, more important than the actual relationship was the social status gained from the fact that Mohammad Zaher had "given" him a woman. This act created a clear bond between Mohammad Zaher and Malik Abdul Hamid's family.

Another important aspect of this relationship—one that inspired frequent comment—was Mohammad Zaher's status as a close confidant of Ahmed Shah Massoud, the former mujahideen fighter known as the "Lion of the Panjshir." In fact, there was some intermarriage between the two families. People said that Massoud called Mohammad Zaher *bach-e khala* (son of his mother's sister. While the relationship was probably not this close, there was an acknowledged marriage tie between Massoud's family and Mohammad Zaher's. This meant that Malik Abdul Hamid and Massoud were distantly related by marriage, and the Malik's son pointed this out to me on a couple of occasions. Most other potters, however, seemed to feel that the relationship was too distant to be meaningful, but despite their reticence, any claim one could make of a relationship with such a venerated individual was still respected, especially by the older generation.

At the end of my time in Istalif, the Malik's third son had become engaged, though his fiancée was a member of a family that was less influential than the families into which his brothers had married. His future father-in-law Najeeb was a simple donkey driver, and I would have been surprised to hear that the bride-price was very high. It was not clear to me whether this was an economic decision. Another possibility was that the arrangement was the Malik's attempt to quietly reinforce ties with other pottery families.

Najeeb was an interesting figure. Although poor, he had married his five daughters to increasingly influential members of the pottery community. All of his political capital seemed to come directly from his sons-in-law, who were all from various lineages of potters. The Malik's marrying his son into another pottery family created an alliance with serious political implications. Now that his son's wife-to-be was sister-in-law to several other young potters, Malik Hamid's had gently reinforced several less significant relationships (thus, with fewer obligations), instead of selecting one family with which creating political ties would have had more serious political implications.

Marriages, government connections, and links to international groups gave Malik Abdul Hamid two things: a manipulable network of allies independent of the potters, and a stock of internal political capital that enabled him to collect resources and influence and redistribute it among his followers. However, Malik Hamid was not the only potter who needed to balance loyalty to the group with attempts to ensure prosperity and political strength through alliances or other practices that potentially subverted the group.

DESCENT AMONG THE POTTERS

The potters were not simply an economic unit; they were also a patrilineal descent group, with a shared mythology that told the story of their arrival in Istalif approximately three hundred years before.[5] Across the several versions of this story, the central points were fairly consistent. As Malik Abdul Hamid described in "Telling Stories," the interlude preceding this chapter, the potters all descended from Sayed Mir Kulal from Bukhara. In Istalif, Sayed Mir had four sons, and all the potters were said to be descended from one of those sons (or according to one or two accounts, four of his followers).

In reality, descent groups were not so clearly defined among the potters. Malik Abdul Hamid could only remember the name of three of the lineages: the Merzaji, the Meraji, and the Sahji. Most other elders could list only these three at most, even while agreeing that there were in actuality four lineages. Finally, one old man told me the fourth group was the Dahji (perhaps because it rhymes with Sahji), but I could not find anyone else who claimed to know the name. Potters could recollect several generations of their genealogies, though few could recite more than four generations, with the occasional elder remembering six or seven and the younger generation remembering only two or three.

Despite difficulties remembering kin vertically, potters were all mindful of who their horizontal relations were. Members of the younger generation were acutely aware of their patrilineal kin, particularly their bach-e kaka. Among the potters, this was another common way of conceptualizing qaum. Even if they understood who was and was not in their qaum, potters had often forgotten the actual genealogical connection between two relatives. There was a sense, however, that one should remember one's paternal ancestors, and individuals were often interested when I collected genealogical data, occasionally arguing about some of the diagrams that I drew. I learned to wait until the end of a formal interview to ask young men about their ancestors, because on more than one occasion after being asked about a more distant relative, an interviewee realized he had forgotten the names of certain kin, and jumped up to ask his father or grandfather, effectively ending the interview.

Merzaji, the Malik's lineage, was the most cohesive branch and accounted for about one-third of all the potters in Istalif. Potters from this lineage occasionally referred to themselves as "from the Merzaji" without being asked directly. This was also the only lineage with a clear eponymous ancestor, the great-great-grandfather of most adult members of the lineage. Another third of the potters were from the two smaller lineages, the Sahji and the Meraji. These potters rarely referred to their lineage unless asked directly. Their genealogies could be traced back five generations, and there was a common understanding that their groups were distinct from the Merzaji. The rest of the potters were from scattered families who could rarely recount more than three generations of ancestors and did not claim to be members of a specific lineage. I found no genealogical evidence of the fourth lineage, the Dahji.

Lineage did have some impact on daily life, even when it was not clearly articulated. Families from the same lineage tended to live in the same area and usually cooperated economically. Cousins were sometimes, but not always, allies. In reality, lineages did not create strong social or political ties as much as they were used to explain the ties that were already there. This was true of one's bach-e kakas. Technically all bach-e kakas should have been in the speaker's lineage, but actually one only referred to a patrilineal cousin as a bach-e kaka if some other economic or social tie reinforced the relationship. The Merzaji were the only group that referred to their lineage directly because they were the only powerful group among the potters that coincided with the descent group. At the same time, members of the Merzaji who were not as politically integrated with their patrilineal kin tended not to refer to their lineage.

In practice, lineages were a means to describe and reinforce political and economic alliances. Descent terms were used to emphasize or de-emphasize such relationships. Lineages suggested relationship patterns, but had little impact unless they coincided with other ties. In many ways, residency patterns reflected local alliances more accurately than did lineage terms. For families from the same lineage living in the same area, proximity facilitated economic cooperation between workshops. Young men, in particular, tried to take advantage of the rights granted by such relationships, while trying to avoid many of the obligations associated with them. The flexibility of obligations to the group gave young men political opportunities that they would not have had in a more rigidly structured system. With these concerns in mind, for a young man, it was in a marriage alliance with another family that he could gain the allies that would help shape his political future.

ARRANGING MARRIAGES

While many potters did not describe their lineage as important, most of them explained that it was generally best to marry endogamously within the qaum. Because the concept of "we" in the qaum was not always simple or clear, the potters did not have a coherent set of marriage rules. They did have several clear preferences and tendencies that helped shape a young man's marriage options.

To a certain extent, all marriages were arranged in Istalif, but this was open to interpretation, as different generations described marriage arrangements in different ways. Younger men tended to emphasize that men could marry whom they chose, claiming that the elders were only in charge of the formal negotiations. Older potters tended to claim that they were the ones who made decisions about marriages between families, emphasizing the importance of endogamy more than their sons did.

There were clear political incentives for both generations. The older generation was more likely to have political debts that the father wished to fulfill by marrying off a daughter or reinforcing an alliance, whereas the younger generation tended to be more interested in creating new alliances.

Love was sometimes discussed privately, among friends, and men would describe falling in love with young women they had glanced in passing. These conversations, however, were almost always separate from conversations about marriage. In Istalif, there were no cases of "love matches" as there were among the upper class in Kabul.

Both older and younger men seemed to simplify things when they discussed how they created marriage alliances, and, according to many of the anecdotes I collected, women were more influential in the decision-making process than the men gave them credit for. In the end, marriages seemed to be compromises between all parties. Men with whom I was more intimate admitted that women had a significant but informal role in establishing marriage alliances, though this was rarely discussed openly. There were no professional intermediaries, but sisters often acted as go-betweens for young people of the opposite sex, and mothers could pressure the fathers to accept proposals for their daughters. Similarly, while a son could not publicly apply pressure on his father, a mother could intercede on her son's behalf.

Young men often feigned indifference to the entire arrangement phase, seemingly because they had few direct options. With friends, however, discussions were more open, and it was clear that young men often worked furtively to speed things along. In most cases older males, particularly fathers, made the final decisions and negotiated the formal arrangements, such as the *nikah* (wedding contract). In only one case did I ever hear a man—a visitor from Kabul—complain directly about his lack of agency in the decision-making process. In general fathers, like their sons, were interested in establishing the most effective political relationships possible through marriages. Older and younger men may have had slightly different goals, but they tended to discuss the process in similar terms. Both groups hoped to arrange successful marriages that also strengthened social, political, and economic ties between families; the tension was simply over the most expedient way to do this.

Despite the potters' emphasis on marrying other potters, many married into Istalifi families who were not potters. Occasionally, someone married into a family from one of the villages near Istalif, even from Kabul, although these families were usually ones that had once lived in Istalif. Elders often stressed that when they were young all marriages were within the qaum, and a few recollected a minor scandal about a young woman who had married a man from Qara Bagh, the town immediately to the east (though this practice had become much less shocking). Some claimed that in the past a male potter could marry outside the qaum, but a female could not. This was no longer a rule among the potters, but the Sayeds in town were still reluctant to marry their daughters into another qaum, although they accepted brides from many different groups.

Various relationship words distinguished social distance—thus, the likelihood of forming a marriage alliance with a group. *Az qaum-e maa* (from our qaum) was common and *az khud-e maa* (from ourselves) was also used to refer to very close extended family. *Khewsha* (relative) or the stronger *khewsha nazdeek* (close relative) referred to a family that was connected primarily through marriage. In contrast, a hamsayah implied someone who lived close by but did not "know our goods and evils," making a marriage alliance less likely. These terms were important because they established social distance, but also because they were malleable. Marriages, or the consideration of marriage, altered the language the potters used to describe different relationships.

The elders talked about the simplicity of marriage alliances and how strictly endogamous the potters had been when they were young. Although this seemed to be an idealization of the past, there was some direct evidence that marriage tendencies in Istalif had become increasingly complicated. The displacement of Istalifi residents during the fighting with the Taliban had seriously reshaped social alliances. Social and economic upheaval during the Taliban era had also led to a general drop in the marriage rate and an increase in the social distance considered acceptable for a marriage. Many families had not left Istalif together, and had created new alliances with refugees from other parts of the country who were their neighbors with in Kabul and Pakistan. As one man said, "We marry our neighbors. Because our neighbors in Kabul were from Wardak and Kandahar, we married them while we were living in Kabul." Despite these new practices, the majority of Istalifis still tended to marry each other, and there was little evidence of young Istalifis marrying families from distant regions while I lived in the town. The more lasting change was intermarriage between the contingent of Istalifis who had continued to live in Kabul and those who had returned to Istalif.

Young men were adamant that there were no fixed marriage rules, emphasizing that it was only important to marry a woman from a family with which they had a good relationship. The clearest marriage pattern was thus between families that already had a history of arranging marriages together. Often, this meant a man married his cousin (usually his mother's brother's daughter or his mother's sister's daughter). There was also a tendency for the eldest son in the family to marry the daughter of another potter, while his younger brothers were more likely to marry non-potters. This seemed to be a strategy of first solidifying relationships within the community, and then extending influence through alliances outside the qaum.

THE COSTS OF MARRIAGE

The period of arranging the marriage was drawn out and complicated, taking anywhere from six months to several years. Families performed a series of rituals that led up to the wedding, including announcing the engagement, giving sweets to the bride's family, and decorating the bride with henna the night before the wedding. Each ritual involved at least a small gathering. Throughout this process, however, the issue that seemed to slow the arrangement of a marriage most was the continual renegotiation of the bride-price.

The bride-price was almost always primarily cash, but it could involve jewelry as well, and the precise amount fluctuated widely, depending on status of the woman's family and the relationship with the groom's family. The general economic uncertainty of the previous twenty years seemed to have further destabilized bride-prices. During my research, I often heard stories about a woman from Istalif (not a potter) whose family had recently received $30,000 from the groom's family in Kabul. More typical bride-prices ranged from $1,000 to $8,000, though numbers alone do not reflect the complexity of calculating costs.[6]

I occasionally heard very different bride-price amounts for a given marriage, and there was a general lack of clarity and agreement in the community about the exact price. In many ways this inclination was not surprising. It was in the best interest of both families for people to assume that the price was high, because this rumor brought prestige to both families, implying that the bride's family was worthy of such a price and that the groom's family had the economic and political resources to raise a large amount of money. As a result, there was little incentive on either side to correct rumors that had inflated the bride-price. Similarly, there were many smaller costs that went into the celebration of the wedding: new clothes for those closely related to the bride and groom, hosting a henna night for the women, and several ritual exchanges of gifts and food between the two families. These costs were not considered part of the bride-price, but discussions of marriage sometimes included them in the calculation.

After the bride-price, the greatest expense was the wedding celebration, for which the groom's family was expected to pay. All the weddings I attended in Istalif had at least one hundred guests on the men's sides, with an equal number of women at a separate celebration, and children racing back and forth between the two. Even the wedding of one very poor potter I attended cost at least $500; more extravagant weddings in Kabul (for which the guests from Istalif were bused in) easily cost $10,000. Although the practice of having weddings in Kabul had become increasingly common for Istalifis, they were still much smaller than the incredible displays put on by middle-class and up-per-class Kabulis. One Istalifi who was helping arrange his brother's wedding grumbled to me that the wedding halls in Kabul charged 300 afghanis ($6) per guest for food, but the food was terrible, and really good food cost 500–600 afghanis per person. The high prices in Kabul caused a backlash against wed-dings there, and a couple of young men told me they preferred elaborate wed-dings in Istalif to simpler ones in Kabul. (Admittedly, some of the men who complained were already married and had younger, unmarried brothers, so they had a clear economic reason to avoid elaborate weddings.)

Another debate that arose during the negotiations between families was the use of music at wedding ceremonies. This issue had a significant history for the potters. The Taliban were notorious for their bans on music, and the fall of the Taliban was celebrated by a rapid return to music by many members of the younger generation.[7] The elders, however, had instituted a ban that was a source of contention among the young men. While it was permissible to have music at a wedding, it had to be from a single-unit stereo (such as a porta-ble cassette player,) and elaborate units, stand-alone speakers, or microphones were not allowed. The elders couched this restriction in religious language, even though it was unclear how a smaller tape player was more religiously acceptable than a large one. The young men were convinced that the reason for the ban was that louder music attracted more guests; when people heard music in the distance, they would come to see what was happening. It was dishonorable to turn away guests, but more guests required more food. They thus saw the ban as a money-saving technique for the elders whose sons were soon to marry.

The most stressful aspects of marriage preparation fell on the groom's fam-ily. The bride-price and the money for the wedding celebration were raised primarily by the groom's immediate family. The father and brothers were the most important sources of income, followed by close patrilineal kin, especially the father's brothers. More distant and matrilineal kin contributed as well, al-though men usually mentioned this only when a potential groom had a wealthy maternal relative who was contributing. Most potters claimed that these ex-penses were one of the reasons for the relatively few instances of polygyny in the town (although the more common reason was that women opposed it). Be-cause patrilineal kin raised money to pay the bride-price together, it was diffi-cult for a man to convince his relatives to help him raise money to take a second wife, especially when one of his younger brothers or sons was still unmarried.

POLITICAL TENSIONS AND MARRIAGE PATTERNS

Istalifis considered this period of negotiations just before marriage a time of tension and danger for the potential son-in-law and most of the other parties involved. This was especially true as both the cost and the timing of the wedding were debated. Once a couple was *nam zad* (engaged), the engagement could last several years as the families negotiated the bride-price, wedding arrangements, and other details. Patrilineal kin helped, but most of the pressure fell directly on the future son-in-law. Part of the reason for the length of this process was that the future son-in-law had to work to collect money, but it also seemed to be a way for the future father-in-law to express his power over the young suitor. Young men often complained about whimsical fathers-in-law who were unclear about the total bride-price or who constantly disputed other points. Theoretically, the groom's family set the wedding date, but in practice the father of the bride could slow down the entire marriage process. These tensions, however, were mostly below the surface. The groom's family would complain through intermediaries that the price was too high or the date was too distant, and the bride's family would respond using similar channels.

There was little public or direct involvement between the prospective families because, with so much honor at stake, differences of opinion between the parties could turn to violence. The young potters liked to recount the story of a feud in a neighborhood a couple of hours' walk up the valley. The Malik of that neighborhood, who was still feared as a lower-level warlord during my time in the town, had a maternal niece who had fallen in love with a young man fifteen years before. The two were engaged, but during the engagement period there was a dispute, and the girl's father killed the young man. (Some versions of the story implied that the couple acted "inappropriately" while they were engaged.) During the ensuing feud, thirty-one people from this relatively small area were killed. Young men claimed that that neighborhood's malik had become a feared man by killing so many people during that feud.

Despite the limited number of written accounts of Istalifi history, several early ones, including Charles Masson's, refer to political intrigue and the feuds produced by young lovers.[8] The extent to which the details of these tales and rumors were true was unclear, but these continued to be dangerous. If the father-in-law broke off negotiations, or if the prospective groom had trouble raising the bride- price, it could seriously damage the young man's reputation. Young men worked to win over their future in-laws (especially fathers-in-law) through informal bride service, trying to do odd jobs around the house. This led to an endless series of jokes about engaged men. This proverb, "The donkey brays [in pleasure] when the son-in-law arrives," was considered especially funny (the donkey is pleased because it knows the son-in-law will do all of its work). An alternate version suggested, "Sell your donkey when the son-in-law arrives." Young men occasionally teased their engaged friends, though they did this carefully and subtly, because it was easy to make him squirm.

The long engagement period, with potentially perilous negotiations, reinforced the notion that it was safest to arrange marriages with known quantities—groups with whom a family had negotiated before. There were likely to be fewer surprises and more people related to both groups who would mediate informally if problems arose—in particular, to pressure a father-in-law to accept a lower bride-price. In addition, in a society with such strict separation of the sexes, a man was much more likely to have associated with his maternal kin, or the women of families related closely by marriage, than with any other females. All these marriage tendencies reinforced social ties among specific families.

Another series of less ideal marriage patterns avoided some of the costs of traditional marriages. For men faced with real economic challenges, but who had sisters of marriageable age, it was possible to exchange sisters with another man. In such a case, money was sometimes ceremonially exchanged, but the bride-price was essentially zero. Occasionally the two weddings would occur at the same time, thereby reducing the cost of the celebration further. Similarly, some poor potters with no patrilineal relatives married their sisters to wealthier families and effectively joined the other family. Given that there was often a rather extreme age difference between the bride and groom, frequently the brother-in-law became something of an adopted son. Unlike other parts of Afghanistan, where such individuals were treated like servants, in Istalif they were simply considered slightly lower-status relatives.

In most cases, however, residence was patrilocal. Men went to live with their fathers-in-law only if they had serious economic problems, and usually worked for their fathers-in-law as well. Istalifis used the phrase *khana damad* (literally, "house son-in-law") derogatorily for any man who lived with his father-in-law, although it could also apply to any man who seemed overly subservient to his father-in-law. There were several other variations of this pattern, but these alternatives to tradition were universally considered imperfect.

Marriage patterns were not based strictly on the political alliances the marriage created. The woman's ability to cook and work in the house was often discussed as an important aspect in selecting a wife. Men sometimes gossiped about love matches, although the social implications of a match remained primary, even when emotions were discussed. I heard romantic tales about defying fathers to marry for love, but these stories tended to be associated more with the city life of Kabul. Among Istalifis the only true instances of men opting out of the system were those who lived in Kabul, with limited political or social ties to Istalif, and in this study of Istalif's politics, the role they played was minimal. In the end, every young man who wished to be politically active in the community had to risk the hazards of marriage.

MARRIAGES, ALLIANCES, AND INDIVIDUAL CHOICES

Lineages and endogamous marriage tendencies initially appeared to play the central role in organizing the potters. They lived close to other potters from the same lineages, cooperated with related families on economic matters, and often arranged marriages between individuals who shared a lineage. People regularly spoke of the importance of kin relations. But some of these tendencies were misleading. There was also a high rate of marriage outside of lineages, and similar descent did not guarantee economic or political cooperation. As discussed above, there were few set rules. Potters could choose to follow some patterns while ignoring others. Ultimately, most potters, especially young men, tended to form alliances that preserved loyalty to the qaum, while enabling them to establish networks among more distantly related members of the qaum or outside of it entirely. Rejecting the qaum and searching for marriage partners outside—a strategy chosen only by a few of the potters who had not returned to Istalif—meant forfeiting government and NGO assistance that was distributed through the qaum.

There was no precise way to achieve a balance between group solidarity and networks that extended outside the group, and individual social and economic circumstances could alter strategies drastically. The examples below represent two different approaches. Ideally, hierarchy, descent, and alliances were clearly defined: The potters were patrilineal, patrilocal, formed alliances with close kin, and tended to marry close cousins. As the examples illustrate, however, the extent to which a family or an individual conformed to these patterns varied—based on anything from a family's demographic composition to individual personalities—but did not lead to an infinite array of individual strategies. Rather, choices were finite, decisions were linked, and individual goals had a coherence that could be analyzed.

Three Brothers: Cooperation in the Immediate Family

In an extreme example of cooperation among close kin, three brothers had remained living and working together despite the fact that they were all well into
their mid-forties. The brothers—Mohammad Wakil, Mohammad Jabor, and
Qari Mohammad Rawuf—had been young men when the Taliban destroyed
Istalif; they lived together until they were forced to flee, and were among the
first to return to Istalif after the fall of the Taliban. Returning to find their house
almost completely destroyed, the three worked together to repair their home
and reconstruct it in such a way that the family of each brother had separate
quarters around a central courtyard.

In some ways this case was unique. The three brothers had found a way to
split duties fairly equitably. One brother was in charge of making the pots, the
other ran the store, and the third was a mullah and head of the local *madrassa*
(religious school). The mullah's duties prohibited him from working full-time
as a potter, but he could occasionally help the other brothers (though, one of
his brothers told me quietly, he did not make pots very well).

The three brothers had had an elder brother who died fighting the Soviets.
In most families the elder brother was the clear head of the household. This
often engendered low-level resentment and encouraged younger brothers to
leave the house after they married. In this case, the eldest brother was deceased
and the second-eldest was a rather quiet, easygoing man. Their egalitarianism
was further promoted by the fact that the mullah was the youngest brother and
was respected in the community for his piety, and because he had spent several
years at a madrassa in Pakistan. With his international connections, he was respected in a way many other youngest brothers were not.

The mother of Mohammad Wakil, Mohammad Jabor, and Qari Mohammad
Rawuf, still living, was an important member of the family. Two of the brothers
talked about her often, which was rare, since most men were generally hesitant
to speak of their female relatives. This was common only for women referred
to as *pech-e safeeds* (white hairs) or older, particularly respected women. The
mullah, telling the story of when the Taliban first occupied the town, described
how everyone had remained in their homes, too scared to leave, when the Pashtun fighters first arrived. The mullah had wanted to go out to speak with them,
partly because he was the mullah, but also because he was one of the few in town
who spoke Pashto well—but he was nervous. It was only after discussing it with
his mother and brothers that he went to meet with them. Similarly, after the cap-
ture of the Bagram Airfield by the Americans, the brothers brought their mother

with them when they returned to Istalif, "the day after the Taliban left." This unique move demonstrates a high degree of solidarity in the immediate family; after the fall of the Taliban, most Istalifi men returned first, leaving the female family members in Kabul until they had at least partially rebuilt their houses.

The three brothers also had a nephew, the son of the eldest brother who had died fighting the Soviets. The nephew was about 18 years old and had memorized the Koran, making him one of the youngest qaris in town. He worked with his uncles, occasionally minded one of their two shops, and did some day labor. This arrangement allowed the uncles to help support their nephew. If they had split up, it would have been unclear who would have supported him, thus making it impossible for the nephew to raise the money for a bride-price.

It was also significant that all three brothers were already married with fairly young sons, so there was no real competition for who would marry next, a problem that plagued many other families. The brothers did not have as many close patrilineal allies as some of the other important families in the village; however, with the mullah in the family, they were afforded more respect. The third brother came to be called Sufi Mohammad Jabor, as a sign of his religious piety. He was also one of the three men in Kulalan who was considered a talented cook, and he supervised the cooking at major feasts.

Mohammad Wakil and Mohammad Jabor, the brothers who focused on making and selling pottery, had done a good job establishing business connections outside the qaum. The brothers sold to merchants in Serai Khowja, on the road between Kabul and Istalif. They also had a relationship with one of the merchants in Kabul that stretched back before the Soviet invasion. Beyond business connections, the brothers had also established strong relationships with foreigners in Kabul. Upon their return to Istalif, the brothers lacked capital (a common hardship from this era, which many potters reported). A group of foreigners came to see what had happened to the town. Mohammad Wakil and his brothers were just about the only potters in Istalif. Observing that they did not have the materials to return to making pots, the visitors gave Mohammad Wakil $100 and asked him to make sixty pots and bring them to Kabul. With this capital, the three brothers began to rebuild their shop and continued to work together.

This example is a strong case of cooperation among closely related patrilineal kin who had only a few links to groups outside of the potters. It demonstrates that, even while there were forces and circumstances that tended to cause feuding within families, solidarity could create a basis for social and economic cooperation that minimized the need for external networks.

Nabi Jan: The Singing Potter

Mohammad Wakil, Mohammad Jabor, and Qari Mohammad Rawuf came from a family with some status in the community. Young men without strong patrilineal relatives, on the other hand, often had to find alternate means of establishing social alliances. Nabi Jan, the young potter whose kiln ran out of wood in the previous chapter, was one such example. Nabi Jan's father was a potter who had died when Nabi Jan was only 3 years old. His father had no brothers, and Nabi Jan, his mother, and two sisters were left with "no one" and "without remedy." (Nabi Jan's five brothers had all died during childhood.) When Nabi Jan was very young, his sister married another potter, Mohammad Islam, who took in Nabi Jan and his mother. Eventually, Nabi Jan's mother convinced Mohammad Islam to allow Nabi Jan to help him make pottery. It seems that although Nabi Jan lived in Mohammad Islam's house, he was not treated like a son.

Unlike most potters, Nabi Jan fled alone to the Panjshir Valley, and later to Pakistan, when the Taliban arrived—a somewhat surprising decision, since most potters fled as nuclear or extended families, and most went to Kabul. Nabi Jan says that he did not fight, as others who went to the Panjshir did, but lived in a refugee area protected by Massoud's men. After the fall of the Taliban, Mohammad Islam continued to live in Kabul with his wife and children, while Nabi Jan returned to Istalif.

Nabi Jan's other sister married Abdul Jalil, another potter. This relationship was not as beneficial for Nabi Jan, who claimed that Abdul Jalil had cheated his mother by convincing her to sell their house to him for less than it was worth. Nevertheless, Nabi Jan continued to live in a smaller house that he built next to Abdul Jalil's. Engaged to be married, Nabi Jan said he'd had to raise the bride-price money by himself. Though he was engaged before the Taliban came, he could not marry for several years, while he worked briefly in Pakistan and then as a day laborer in Kabul; apparently this is how he managed to raise most of the money for the bride-price.

Despite his poverty, Nabi Jan had been able to pay the bride-price, build a house, and feed his eight children, none of whom were yet old enough to contribute economically. Much of this was due to community support; Nabi Jan was a bit of a jokester and was widely liked by other young men. He had a reputation as the best singer among the potters (occasionally, they even listened to cassettes they had made of his voice), and he sometimes performed at weddings and other events. Although he did not appear to receive direct compensation, other potters clearly looked after him. When someone needed extra labor, such as for patching their roof, they often hired Nabi Jan, who had a reputation as a good mason. He always said, though, that he preferred making pottery.

As a man with few patrilineal ties who had to rely on the goodwill of many of the other potters, Nabi Jan tended to view lineage very differently than most. When I ask him what his qaum was, he said he did not know and that it did not really matter; they were all potters. The feuding Merzaji families would not have made this statement. Similarly, when speaking about families, I once asked Nabi Jan his grandfather's name. He produced the name eventually, but it took him a while to recall it. For many potters, remembering more than three or four generations back was a challenge, but Nabi Jan was the only one who struggled to remember just two generations.

Considering the strong way power and wealth were passed along patrilineal lines, a young man such as Nabi Jan, who had lost his father at a young age and had no paternal uncles, faced many challenges. Without relatives upon which to rely directly, he had been forced to develop a wider web of allies among the potters through economic cooperation and marriage. He also had cultivated a personality that endeared him to others in the community—and did not threaten the political hierarchy. Interestingly, although his network of allies within the pottery qaum was extensive, he had fewer allies outside the qaum than most potters. It seemed to be precisely because he was so dependent on the entire qaum for economic and social support that he could not jeopardize their aid by appearing to associate too much with outsiders.

． ． ．

As these examples suggest, while there were ideal forms of political and economic cooperation among the potters, there was also a great deal of variety. Most young men had to choose from a series of strategies that took into account concerns such as descent and the difficulties of arranging marriage alliances. The potters had a hierarchy with the Malik and other elders clearly in the key positions, but young men still had the ability to make certain choices within this setting. Decisions were often linked; making one choice meant limiting other options, as young men continually renegotiated their ties to their qaum. This was particularly important in the face of the complicated nature of town politics—the subject of the next chapter.

Dinner

At Basir's father's house, the dinner for the mullah was held in the formal guest-room. The family had done fairly well since returning to Istalif. Located on the hill west of the shrine, the house was made of cement, rather than the traditional earth-and-stone architecture used for other houses in the gozar. Basir ran a successful bakery, working all night long during Ramazan, preparing cookies and cakes. Now, about a week after the end of Ramazan, he was relaxing, smoking cigarettes, and listening to the radio with me in his father's guestroom.

Basir's father had three other middle-aged sons and about ten grandsons between the ages of 2 and 15. It was a Friday evening, and the crowd was rather boisterous before the mullah arrived. Basir, the youngest of the brothers, was leading the merriment, pushing off some of the younger boys trying to climb on him, and then sending them over to me with more tea and sweets. The older men sat on cushions against three walls of the room; the entire wall furthest from the door was reserved for honored guests. I sat next to one of the older brothers, close to the furthest wall, talking about the difficulties of working during Ramazan.

I found, early in my stay, that my own place in such situations was tricky. Whenever a group of men entered a room to sit, unless they were close friends, an elaborate dance would begin as each man tried to force his companions to sit in more honored positions. Each man would resist a few times, before all of them finally sat down according to the informal political hierarchy, based mostly on age and status. The ritual was also repeated when entering and leaving rooms, as the most senior figure was always pushed to cross the threshold first.

As a foreigner and an outsider, I was automatically considered something of an honored guest, yet most of my peers sat closer to the door, behind the elders. When I walked in, Basir's brother pushed me ahead:

"Please, go ahead."

"No, no, you."

"Excuse me."

I tried to force the older men ahead, but finding a balance was difficult. Too close to the honored position, and I was overstepping my bounds. Too close to the door, and it would seem like I did not understand the etiquette, making everyone uncomfortable.

That evening I tried my standard trick of sitting about halfway between, and then allowing Basir's brother to gently push me one or two positions away from the door. I found this most effective, because it meant that I would not offend those elders significantly above me, but the result was still that I sat in front of most of the men my own age, who were roughhousing with Basir by the door. As the evening progress, I would move a couple seats closer to those in my age group, but with the mullah visiting that evening, more formality was demanded. The dinner was part of an imprecise order among the potters, in which the mullah visited various families in the neighborhood on a rotating basis, and that evening it was Basir's family's turn to host the mullah.

When he arrived, the crowd quieted. A tall man, the mullah greeted the older men in a subdued manner and walked directly to the front of the room, not taking part in the traditional tug-of-war over where to sit, as others did. Most of the men in the room were wearing their best clothes, but they still contrasted with the bright white the mullah wore. The older men near the front of the room turned toward the mullah and again issued greetings. Conversations resumed in a more restrained manner. The younger boys sat silently or went off to the kitchen. The mullah listened to the conversations around him, nodding on occasion, intermittently adding his own view. He spoke a more formal style of Dari, and this, combined with the slight accent he had acquired in Pakistan, meant that I had more difficulty understanding him. I leaned in closer to hear what he was saying, and noticed that most of the other men in the room had similarly shifted their bodies toward him.

Shortly after his arrival, the young boys brought in steaming rice and mutton. Even the way the mullah ate contrasted with the others; he ate noticeably more slowly and deliberately. The host offered him more food, but he declined repeatedly. At the end of the meal, the mullah led the prayers and then talked briefly about the importance of fasting. A few of the men asked questions and one young man, a qari, added a few lines at the end of the mullah's speech. Tea was served, and the mullah and a few of the older men gradually left. At this point, Basir pulled out a cigarette and leaned over to turn the radio back on.

. . .

Unlike the mullah, Malik Abdul Hamid did not generally visit others, and his style of socializing was rather different. The Malik was expected to be hospitable and generous when people visited him, and although he was reserved and formal with new visitors, once he was familiar with his guests, his hospitality took on a vocal and emotional form. He relentlessly encouraged his guests to eat more, often piling the choicest pieces on the plate of whoever was his easiest target. He considered every bite further proof of his generosity, and I was caught off guard more than once when I thought the meal was over, only to watch another round of dishes brought in.

When the meal was over, the Malik led the conversation, retelling one of his favorite stories or asking me about life in America. The Malik, whose sons had traveled abroad to Japan, had been impressed with their stories about how terrible the food there had been. They used to send their driver off to the only Indian restaurant, an hour away. The Malik often asked about food in America, hoping to hear how much better the food in his house was by comparison. I would satisfy him by telling him that we did not eat bread with every meal, or another "appalling" habit of the West. When one of his sons interrupted a story, he would hold up his hand and silence him with a stern *"be-bakhsheen"* ("excuse me"), and then turn back to the conversation.

When the mullah and the Malik ate together, the Malik was less animated, but he still led the conversation and often asked the mullah specific questions. The mullah would answer patiently, maintaining his calm demeanor. He would refuse the Malik's insistence to eat more, frustrating his attempts to pile more food on his plate.

I always emerged exhausted from spending time with the mullah. But talking to both of them left me both tired and with a stomachache.

6 CULTURAL DEFINITIONS OF POWER IN ISTALIF

BEYOND THE CONTRASTING STYLES of leadership of the mullah and malik, one of the most striking aspects of trying to understand local politics in Istalif was the incredible number of different political actors. In the process of trying to open a pottery shop in the bazaar, a young potter drew on the support of his qaum; however, he potentially also found himself dealing with a wide range of actors, from local commanders and mullahs to NGO employees. A total of seven main categories of political actors, or roles, shaped daily politics in Istalif: qaums (patrilineal descent groups), religious leaders, a newly wealthy merchant class, former militia groups, the district government, the police, and international groups (particularly NGOs and the military).

Each group was active in certain political arenas and had followers that could be mobilized in specific political situations, but the way power was used and defined within each of these categories varied greatly. The result was a system in which power accumulated primarily within these seven categories. While each group defined power differently, they often relied on similar modes of creating and recreating power. The pottery qaum's internal politics (see Chapters 3–5) can also be applied, with slight variation, to other groups. Maliks in all qaums, for example, established alliances based on kinship and marriage, but they also relied on friends, business partners, and other less formal social relationships, as Malik Abdul Hamid did. Similarly, a commander had to distribute resources equitably to maintain influence; his position was only as strong as the consensus of his followers. The goods being redistributed and the language used to describe relationships varied, but each group depended on having followers it could mobilize—and was weakened by the need to rely on those followers. Expectations were often high, but there were few actual demands on the members of a group. Leaders had to motivate people, and they often tried to do so by portraying group strength and solidarity that did not exist. Similarities in the process of maintaining cohesive groups and competing for similar resources linked the groups to the wider field of Istalifi politics.

POLITICAL ROLES AND POWER

In Istalif, certain roles and expressions of power were clearly allocated—for example, the mullah always officiated at a wedding. Other roles, such as who resolved land disputes, were more complicated. Land disputes were often decided within a qaum, by a malik, but if the participants considered him to be biased, they brought the case before a local commander or asked a religious leader to observe the proceedings. As a last resort, the participants could bring such a case to the district governor.

Why did such divisions persist? Several authors have addressed the various forms of authority in Afghan political life.[1] In some ways this variety can be perceived as a complication of Barth's classic divide between religious and tribal authority among the Pashtuns.[2] More recently Antonio Giustozzi has closely examined how warlords and other local strongmen have maintained power outside the state.[3] In Istalif, however, the divides were even more persistent and important to daily politics than in these other cases, and they did not alternate, as suggested by Barth, as much as they co-existed in constant tension. Proponents of traditional tribe–state models argue that the state was not strong enough to consolidate power, but this view does not explain the complex way power remained divided, independent of government control. Why had no commander consolidated power, as others had in the south and southeast of the country? Why had the government been unable to take over the roles of traditional leaders, as it had in much of Kabul? Why, in Istalif, were there no commanders who were also mullahs, or mullahs who were also commanders? The answers to these questions lies in the ways political roles and authority were culturally defined, and how these definitions shaped the distribution and accumulation of power.

In much of my analysis I use Pierre Bourdieu's attempts to complicate Marx's notion of capital, particularly his use of symbolic and social capital.[4] As will become clear, however, the way power was accumulated and reproduced in Istalif does not fit overtly economic models. Most importantly, the forms of power were not freely convertible; religious authority did not translate easily into economic capital, and vice versa. In Istalif, several categories of authority created power and influence: simple economic capital, especially the control of land; honor, respectability, or what Istalifis often called "having a good name";

and religious capital. Finally, there was the power that came from the threat of violence. While there was some overlap in these categories, accumulating significant forms of one type of capital severely limited a person's ability to collect other types. Young men might possess limited amounts of multiple types of capital, but older men, the more important political individuals in town, only possessed substantial amounts of one type.

The networks of allies one could call upon established another type of power. In Istalif, these networks existed within the community and extended to Kabul and abroad. Along with Bourdieu's concept of social and symbolic capital, the networks help describe politics in Istalif. They also demonstrate that in the case of Istalif, there was serious difficulty converting various forms of capital as suggested by more economic models. In fact, it was the difficulty of converting and accumulating various forms of political capital in Istalif that allowed political life to continue in such a fragmented form.

Economic capital took various forms, such as money and land, but it also included other valuable goods, such as cars and cell phones. In turn, a type of economic capital could lead to cultural and social capital—for example, a video cell phone provided cultural capital among some young Istalifis. For the most part, though, these forms of economic capital were easily convertible and open to everyone who had the resources. With the high level of corruption in the Afghan government, economic capital could also buy political favors and influence. At the same time, and more important to this study, there were certain types of political capital in Istalif that could not be bought.

Economic power was often complemented by social power, in the form of allies, through internal and external networks. Internal social capital came through an individual's network of relationships (with kin, friends, and neighbors), primarily in the town. Istalifis expressed and maintained these connections through intermarriage and such practices as ritualized visiting. This contrasted with networks that produced and enacted external social capital through connections with other nodes of political power, in Kabul and further abroad. External networks included relationships with government officials in Kabul, international NGOs, and the military, but also friends, classmates, and business partners from time spent in Pakistan as refugees.

In Istalif, cultural capital was complex and generally took two key forms: religious cultural capital and cultural capital created by honor or reputation, often described as having a good name (*nam*). (A particularly respected individual was called a *namdar*, or one who has a good name.) Other types of cultural capital, such as educational capital (which Bourdieu analyzes), existed in Istalif, but it had much less effect than religious capital or honor.

Even something as central as literacy was considered to be a useful tool, but certainly not essential; many of the most powerful and respected men in Istalif were illiterate. The man most noted for his secular education was the principal of the central boys' school in town. Istalifis in the bazaar afforded the principal a certain amount of respect and deference when they met him in the street, but they only consulted him on matters concerning the school. His influence on town politics was minimal.

Finally, to any analysis of power in Istalif we must add the threat of violence. While violence was a very rare occurrence in Istalif during the period of my research, the threat of it was pervasive, and people were reminded regularly that the state did not possess a monopoly on that violence. All men wielded the threat of violence to some extent, but some groups were able to consistently threaten violence in a way that increased their political power. In Istalif, and even more so in Kabul, commanders with only informal ties with the government often traveled in heavily armed convoys of police trucks. In the adjacent district, a land dispute between two neighboring families turned into a gun battle. In Istalif, shotguns were commonplace in the bazaar. Despite these examples, the threat of violence was far more common than actual violence. Even in the heat of an argument, individuals rarely forgot politics, and the consequences of arguing with a man who was the close associate of a malik were very different from the consequences of arguing with a man who was closely allied with a former commander. With commanders—and, to a certain extent, the police—the potential for escalated violence shaped how individuals acted toward them.

As with religious capital and honor, the threat of violence was symbolized in several ways. Most obviously, men who wished to associate themselves with commanders wore flak jackets and other military gear. More subtle, however, was the *pakul*, a traditional Chitrali cap that Ahmad Shah Massoud had popularized. In Istalif, especially among young men, wearing the pakul had come to symbolize a willingness to resort to violence and a desire to ally oneself with, or show support for, former mujahideen. In contrast with the young pakul-wearing men, the school principal often wore a *karakul*, a lambskin hat similar to the one Hamid Karzai frequently wore. The hat referred back to the Kabuli and administrative elite, who had commonly worn it before the Soviet invasion. The only other figure in town to wear a karakul with any regularity was the district governor's assistant, another government bureaucrat.

With a basic understanding of the main types of political capital in Istalif, it is now possible to analyze how the town's political power was organized. The definitions of these forms of capital shaped how it was accumulated and converted. Accumulating various forms of power was difficult. As we will see, these cultural definitions, and the way resources were structured, helped define the seven main categories of political roles in the town. Qaum leaders derived most of their power from honor and claims of historical authenticity. Religious leaders relied on religious capital. The new merchant class had risen because of their wealth. Commanders still used the threat of violence to maintain influence. The district governor and the local police relied for power on their positions as representatives of the government and, to some extent, the threat of violence. Finally, international groups (NGOs and the military) used external networks, economic capital, and the threat of violence to reinforce their powerful positions.

QAUMS

The earlier discussion of the pottery qaum and its head, Malik Abdul Hamid, serves as an example of how patrilineal descent groups in Istalif exerted their influence. The potters described themselves as a unified group living in one gozar, with one political leader, but political divisions in Istalif were rarely that clearly delineated. In actuality, Kulalan had many residents who were not potters, though most still went to the Malik to ask him to intercede on their behalf. The situation in the rest of Istalif was more complex.

Each malik and qaum was generally associated with one gozar. Historically, Istalif had thirteen gozars,[5] though the geographic boundaries between these neighborhoods had blurred over the previous thirty years. Some gozars were not resettled after the Taliban were defeated, most notably the western side of the hill below the shrine, where the town's old bazaar had been located; the new bazaar was closer to the river. Other gozars swelled with returning refugees, expanding beyond their original boundaries. For example, several wealthy members of the pottery qaum built new compounds above the traditional edge of Kulalan. These homes were too high up the hill to have access to the main irrigation channel, but were significantly more spacious and modern than most of the homes below.

No gozar in Istalif was composed entirely of one qaum (though one qaum was often dominant), and not every individual in Istalif identified as a member of a qaum. (The very poor and the members of the new merchant class were the least likely to describe themselves as members of qaums.) Qaums in Istalif varied according to how members defined them, but many were craft-based, while others were composed of descendents of a recent historical figure.

Complicating the situation, there was some disagreement over what made a group a qaum. Istalif, with its long history of craft production and social organization around professions, had a more rigid qaum system than other Tajik areas in the region. It seemed that the history of defining a qaum in terms of a craft had encouraged the use of the word "qaum" as a name for a social organization, even for those who were not a member of a lineage that had a history of craft production. When I discussed qaums with a carpenter in the bazaar, he described how, although it was true that carpenters did not have their own qaum, they still organized in a similar manner. He was from the qaum of Nassir; his family had all descended from a man named Nassir Khan. Most Istalifis would not have listed the Nassir qaum among the standard Istalifi qaums, but this carpenter had been influenced by the way other qaums in the area described themselves. It is probable that, had he lived in an area where professional qaums had not made the notion of qaum such a salient feature of social organization, the carpenter would not have labeled his lineage as a qaum. My conversations with individuals in towns around Istalif indicated qaums in those areas were less important to daily politics and less rigidly defined than they were in Istalif.

During my time in Istalif, the district governor recognized eight individuals as maliks. A handful of other maliks, who were not recognized as maliks by the entire community, still had some influence. The authority and influence of each malik varied, but the eight men were universally acknowledged as representing their qaums and gozars. All maliks were associated with the gozars they represented to the district government, and several were associated with a specific qaum (e.g., the potters, the Sayeds, and, as we will see below, the skin sewers).[6] Istalifis spoke of maliks ideally as being honorable and having a good name. A good malik was said to be *fall* (active), out among the people. People showed respect for these men through rituals: extended formal greetings and addressing them as *sahib*. Possessing such a reputation, however, demanded the qaum elders to work to maintain their status.

This honor was primarily embodied cultural capital, but it was a form of cultural capital that both reinforced, and was reinforced by, social capital. A malik maintained a network of allies who respected him because of his honor, which in turn gave him wider political support. A malik was expected to provide feasts, raise money for the mosque, and mediate disputes between qaum members. Power, for a malik or an elder, was circular; such a figure's ability to wield influence came from his ability to perform these duties and to mobilize the resources and the respect of his community. The more honor a man had, the more men and resources he could mobilize. The more men and resources he could mobilize, the more he was considered a respected member of the community.[7]

Being considered a good Muslim helped a man's honor, but the two did not always correlate. The respect typically granted to a mullah was based on a different set of parameters. For example, an honorable man would respond violently to a serious insult, but a pious mullah would not answer violence with violence. Similarly, to maintain honor, most people were expected give feasts and be generous. A religious man, however, was expected to be so generous every day, handing out what little money he did have, that he could not accumulate the economic capital necessary to host regular feasts. The process of achieving and maintaining honor was also stressful. Negative rumors about powerful men circulated frequently, and men often worried about such talk. Several of Malik Abdul Hamid's chief rivals would often sit in the bazaar and discuss how inequitably NGO funds had been distributed. Simultaneously, whenever Abdul Hamid had a feast or gathering, he made sure that a representative of each member of the qaum was invited. The Malik's emphasis on strict equality aimed to prevent envy among other potters.

When Istalifis discussed the concept of maliks, they tended to describe the ideal case. This was politically useful, because it presented the appearance of a strong, unified front to the government and outsiders, generally increasing the status of the qaum. Qaums that were less well organized were spoken of disparagingly by their opponents, and individuals with few male relatives were often pitied. One of the traditions that best reflects the idealized structure of qaums and maliks as their leaders were the *melah-e barfis* (snow picnics). On the coldest afternoons of winter, many of the men and boys from the bazaar climbed the hill next to the graveyard, which was the steepest slope near town, and the men diverted the irrigation channel that ran along the ridge, flooding the hill. The water froze, creating a field of ice that the men slid down at suicidal speeds. Men from many different groups came to watch and chat. Often, they complained that this sledding was a poor substitute for the melah-e barfis of their youth.

They reported that the entire town took the several days off for these picnics. In addition to plenty of food, there was a general atmosphere of celebration.

The bazaar shut down, and people decorated the town with lights.[8] The central event was when the boys and young men from each gozar gathered together and built a dam of snow and ice across the irrigation channels in their part of town. A successful dam would create a large pond and, in turn, deny the gozar below water to create its own pool. The boys attacked the dams of the gozars above them, trying to destroy them and release the water, thus filling the pools below.[9] The maliks would then walk around and judge which gozar had the best dam that had not been destroyed by boys from other gozars. The maliks awarded prices and gave turbans—symbols of status—to the best group. One man from a neighborhood called *Bollah Deha* (literally, "above the village") reported that his gozar had this name not because it was above the center of Istalif, but because his gozar had won the snow fights with such frequency.

These stories reflect the ways many Istalifis continued to speak of an idealized political structure in which qaums, gozars, and maliks all overlap. Istalifis described gozars as precisely bounded entities with clearly defined membership and a single leader. In other conversations, Istalifis, and the maliks themselves, described the malik's formal position as the people's representative before the government—the pul (bridge)—although a malik's role extended beyond his connection with the government.

A malik and other qaum elders maintained influence through their ability to redistribute some economic capital, by hosting feasts for guests or on holidays, or loaning money to another member of the qaum, in a system that shared many characteristics with "big man" societies from New Guinea. In both systems, economic capital helped build social capital, but wealth was still a dangerous thing. While the qaum leader was necessarily rich in social capital, too much economic capital could damage his reputation. If a leader acquired significant capital without redistributing a great deal of it, his followers accused him of greed and he lost social capital, no longer able to claim that he was *primus inter pares*. This was most apparent in the disparaging comments people frequently made about commanders who had built new homes in Kabul. The emphasis, for qaum leaders, was on redistribution, and such practices in many ways served as a social leveling mechanism that prevented those with slightly more power than the rest of the qaum from acquiring too many resources. The system demanded that the more economic capital an influential member of the qaum had, the more he was required to give back to others in the group.

At the same time, a malik gained social capital through connections with the government and international groups, as his followers realized that these connections often resulted in development aid to the group. Yet, a malik who was too close to the government was viewed with suspicion about his potential to betray his people. This meant there was often an inverse relationship between internal and external networks. The more a leader associated with foreigners or the government, the less Istalifis trusted him. While many merchants, government officials, and young men from other qaums spent as much of their time in Kabul as in Istalif, maliks left Istalif much more rarely. Similarly, while a malik was expected to be able to petition the district governor successfully, no malik ever loitered around the district offices the way many others lounged on the benches outside his offices; this might have suggested subservience.

One of the elements that distinguished the malik's role from a commander's was the fact that the malik had limited ability to mobilize people and resources for violence. An interesting example was Malik Abdul Hamid's role in fighting. In several interviews, he discussed how his eldest son helped lead a small group of Istalifi fighters against the Soviets and the Taliban. During the Taliban era in particular, the Malik claimed to have been active in organizing weapons and planning attacks that his son then carried out. His eldest son talked of living in the hills above Istalif; he would sometimes point to the routes they had used. However, this was not a simple story.

Twice I was present when Western reporters interviewed Malik Abdul Hamid about the destruction of Istalif. In each interview, the Malik told the same story but with a different emphasis. He expanded the role both he and his son had played in the struggle and emphasized the atrocities the Taliban had committed. He claimed that the Taliban had beaten him and given him an assault rifle to publicly hand over to them, so the community would see he had submitted. In these interviews he portrayed his family as a group of freedom fighters opposed to the Taliban's gross violations of rights. In stark contrast, I never heard Malik Abdul Hamid discuss his role in fighting the Taliban with other Istalifis. In fact, though his son did fight, he seemed to have been a more minor participant in a community where the wounds of those who had fought were so visible—from the nearby shop owner who had lost an arm to the neighboring weaver, deaf from years spent firing artillery. It was only with outsiders that I ever heard the Malik complain about the Taliban's strict moral code, which in many ways conformed to traditional norms in Istalif. He paid careful attention to his audience when crafting his stories. The narrative of violence was not central to his position in the community, even though he did emphasize this role to certain outsiders.

Maliks were reluctant to use the threat of violence to gain power not just because they did not have the military resources, but because their power relied on honor. It was acceptable for an honorable man to respond violently to attempts to dishonor him, but he should not respond violently on other occasions. By resorting to violence too often, a qaum leader would lose his ability to achieve group consensus. As the leader, he could only threaten violence when the entire group sanctioned it—for example, the Malik's son loudly threatened a man for entering a house without permission, an act that all agreed was inappropriate. Such events were rare, and an ideal malik could not arbitrarily threaten violence the way commanders did.

Despite the idealization and simplification of the role of the malik in Istalifi discourse, maliks adapted rapidly to changing political conditions. Several groups used this flexibility to increase their political status. For example, the pustin duz (skin sewers), who tended to live east of the bazaar, were a fairly scattered group. Historically a pustin duz's work was not considered prestigious. However, as refugees in Pakistan during the civil war, many pustin duz found it was easier to find work than it was for other refugees, because tailors in Peshawar were willing to hire them. Following the fall of the Taliban, many pustin duz returned to Istalif with cash, and several still had business connections in Peshawar. The pustin duz qaum's status was somewhat higher than that of the weavers, and with their new capital they were able to create marriage alliances that gave them a degree of social capital. As a result, the group had recently gained economic and political stature.

Historically the pustin duz did not have a malik. Until recently, two elders had occasionally represented the group before the district governor, or individuals had asked another malik to intercede. This was possibly because many of the pustin duz lived in a gozar called Bagh-e Safed, which did not have well-defined geographic boundaries, and a number of the pustin duz lived in areas where they could claim the support of a neighboring malik. Eventually, they found it more expedient for one of their own to represent them. They initially asked one of the two main elders, but he felt he was too old to represent them, so they chose a younger, energetic man who regularly consulted with the elders. By choosing a malik, who the elders then presented to the district governor, the pustin duz gained better representation before the government and were better able to mobilize politically.

Maliks, and the entire qaum system, had lost some of their traditional power over the past thirty years, yet predictions of their demise from studies in the 1960s and 1970s have proven premature.[10] The political upheaval and lack of government presence created a space in which the qaum system continued to survive, though sometimes in an altered form. For example, many elders reported that maliks had once had the final say in all potential marriages within the qaum—a power they no longer possessed. Despite this loss of social power, several maliks in Istalif took advantage of the chaos following the withdrawal of the Soviet Union to expand their political influence in other ways. Since 2001, many maliks had negotiated with NGOs and international troops, and some had been able to disperse aid in a way that reaffirmed their power, incorporating development aid into the patronage system. NGOs were often very willing to partner with such figures, who could claim to be representatives of a group, but this, of course, was rarely so straightforward. The process was in some ways a self-fulfilling prophecy; if an elder could mobilize resources for a group, individuals were far more likely to acknowledge the political import of the group and the elder's ability to represent them. Similarly, others maliks established connections with parliamentary representatives in Kabul. Despite these new methods for accumulating power in Afghanistan's shifting political landscape, qaum leaders continued to influence town politics primarily through reputation and their ability to mobilize the qaum.

RELIGIOUS LEADERS

Religious leaders played an important role in many aspects of daily life—a role that complemented the maliks' social power in some ways. Mullahs presided over marriages, organized community prayers, and ran the mosque, but perhaps more important was their indirect influence on politics. When a man petitioned the district governor, he sometimes brought along the local mullah or another religious leader to support him. Similarly, mullahs served as mediators in sensitive disputes that required indirect negotiations, particularly between qaum members and their maliks. Unlike qaums, the groups over which religious figures had influence were less clearly defined. However, perhaps precisely for this reason, religious leaders were able to exert influence and mobilize individuals on a limited basis, and when they did this, they were less likely to be challenged than qaum leaders.

In contrast with how the maliks gained power, religious figures gained most of their authority through religious capital, which was embodied and institutionalized in a different way. Men who were considered religious had to display their piety, in the way they socialized at meals, the clothes they wore, and in other ways. Such figures included those with formal positions, such as mullahs and qaris, but the Sayeds and some men from other qaums were also known for being devout. Religious men were expected to possess—and demonstrate— serenity, keeping their voices calm and avoiding active roles in such practices as bargaining in the bazaar. Other symbols were linked to religious capital; mullahs often wore skullcaps, and prayer beads were popular among more pious men.

Religious capital could also be gained through institutionalized means. The most frequent example of this was going on the hajj, to earn the title Hajji. Many of the most important religious figures in Istalif had gained respect by receiving formal religious training, in madrassas abroad or, slightly less prestigiously, in Kabul. On a step below this were qaris, who memorized the Koran in the local madrassas. Some younger qaris were likely to become mullahs in the future, while others were simply acknowledged as being more religious than other Istalifis.

Religious capital made other forms of political capital difficult to gain. Most of the mullahs in town were not exceptionally poor, but they never displayed their wealth the way some religious leaders in Kabul did. Mullahs were rarely seen dealing with money in public; for example, the malik was expected to collect money for the mullah's salary. When the new mosque was built, religious figures were involved in the process, but a wealthy store owner who was considered a pious man but not a member of the religious establishment, organized the money. Religious figures were required to shun wealth or they would be perceived as "less Muslim." For the same reason, mullahs were rarely seen as threatening violence and usually did not associate themselves with commanders or the police.

The qaum elders and religious leaders were more closely allied than other groups in town, but there was still a divide between conceptions of honor and piety, and what made a religious man and an honorable one. This became clear to me one day when I was walking with the son of the Malik. We had recently heard one of the elders from the pottery qaum tell the story of how pottery had come to Istalif, brought from Bukhara by Sayed Mir Kulal. The story claimed that all the potters in Istalif were descended patrilineally from this man and his four sons. After walking some way with the Malik's son, I asked him why he was not considered a Sayed if he, like all potters, was descended from Sayed Mir Kulal. The question caught him off guard, and he thought about it for some time. Finally, he replied that being a Sayed was not simply about descent; it was also about acting in certain ways and, in particular, performing certain duties (here he was referring to the shrine we had just passed, which the Sayeds maintained). He continued that because he and his family had other duties in making pottery, they had given up the duties that could have made them Sayeds. As a result, they were not considered Sayeds, even if they were descended from the prophet. In the mind of the son of the Malik, the practices that made one a religious man were related, but still distinct, from the practices that made one a respected member of the pottery qaum.

The difference between qaum and religious leaders in Istalif was similar to the differences Barth described between Saints and chiefs in Swat:

> Many acts which would bring honour to a chief, such as the immoderate display of violence, would be regarded as most inappropriate in a Saint, and might seriously harm his reputation. . . . Truly "Saintly" behaviour implies moderation, piety, indifference to physical pleasure and withdrawal from the petty and sordid aspects of common life.[11]

In Istalif, the divide between religious leaders and qaum leaders had restricted the potential authority of religious leaders. There were several reasons for this, the most obvious being the relative and diverse power of other actors in town. Had the religious establishment declared maliks or government un-Islamic, authority in town would not have defaulted to them. Perhaps most importantly, Istalif still had strong memories the ways religious figures could misuse power. Istalifis often disparagingly referred to the leaders of the Taliban as "mullahs" and considered them both corrupt and impious. This tended to taint the popular opinion of the religious establishment, and it also seemed to shape the way religious leaders acted and discouraged them from stepping outside the realms where their religious authority was most clearly defined.

Even when there was some overlap in the roles of qaum leaders and religious figures, there were important differences in the way they carried out their duties. People pointed to both maliks and mullahs as important figures in resolving disputes, but how they intervened was different. As one mullah explained to me, he resolved disputes indirectly, often through Friday sermons with lessons that addressed the central issue in the local dispute. He quoted a *hadith* (a saying of the prophet Mohammad), which stated that there was no difference between black and white, implying that all men are equal under Islam and that it was his duty to remind people of that fact. He then expected the men to come to their own agreement. Sometimes the mullah would act as an impartial messenger, but there were few cases of such direct intervention.

In contrast, a malik took a more active role that resembled arbitration, often asking both sides to present their cases to him and announcing a resolution.

These contrasting roles in the community caused some tension. In particular, emphasis on Islam as the defining narrative by religious figures contradicted some of the stories qaums told. The mullah in charge of the mosque in the pottery gozar, who was a potter and whose brothers worked to produce pots, was the only potter I ever heard directly disparage the tales told by the Malik about the origins of the potters. He was not very adamant in his protestations, but he claimed any historian or outside expert could easily disprove the Malik's stories.

Finally, religious figures possessed social capital in the form of internal connections to qaums and other groups in town, but they did not cultivate external connections. Istalifis considered almost all outsiders to be less pious than they were, so fraternizing too much, even with people in Kabul, lessened a religious figure's cultural capital. On the other hand, merchants, whose power came from the ability to mobilize economic capital, often flaunted the personal connections they had with foreigners. As a result, while I knew several of the town mullahs well, as an outsider, and as a non-Muslim, my relationship with them was never as warm as it was with other members of the community.

There was one central religious leader, the *mawlawi*, who received his salary from the government. This man was head of the central bazaar mosque and was the most respected religious figure in town, addressed generally as "mawlawi sahib" or "mullah sahib." The mawlawi gained additional religious capital because he was considered the most religious of the Sayed qaum, though he was not considered the head of the Sayeds. He attended all weddings and other important events in town, leading the prayers that opened these gatherings. He was considered an unbiased judge, and members of the community often sought his counsel. While the mawlawi was the most respected religious figure, there was no formalized religious hierarchy below him. Instead each gozar tended to have its own mosque with at least one associated mullah. The mullahs had no formal gatherings, but often met informally with each other and with the mawlawi. Some talked of making an *ulema* council, or council of religious scholars, as there was in other districts. Some claimed there had been a more formal organization and hierarchy among religious figures in the past, but these accounts tended to be vague.

Like most religious figures in town, the mawlawi was from Istalif. Religious figures were often inactive members of the qaum system and owned land, sometimes working part-time with their brothers in their families' professions.

Still, religious figures were less important to internal qaum politics, despite their relative status in the community. This meant that in some ways they acted differently than other qaum members. One neighborhood mullah was married to a Pashtun woman, one of the rare instances of interethnic marriage in Istalif and something others pointed out to me on several occasions. As a religious figure, the mullah had less interest in establishing political ties through marriage and, as a result, had a different marriage strategy than his brothers, who were married to Tajik women.

Istalifis often said there were 111 mosques in the district, but the actual number was closer to 200, with 30 referred to as central mosques. Many of the mosques had been rebuilt recently, and several more were constructed while I was there. A UNHCR District Profile claims that only 18 were remaining in 2002,[12] though this number seems low because religious buildings seemed to be among the only structures in Istalif not directly targeted by the Taliban. In smaller mosques, many mullahs did not earn enough income working in the mosque to sustain themselves, and labored at least part-time as farmers or craftsmen. Others earned additional income by running small madrassas in their homes. Larger mosques had a caretaker and an assistant, in addition to the mullah.

One central mosque had been recently built in the bazaar. The old bazaar mosque was a more stately building 50 yards further down the road that had been heavily damaged during fighting with the Taliban. Unlike all the other buildings in the center of town, it had not been razed. The mosques were not the only important religious buildings; the shrine of Eshan Sahib atop the northern hill was the most striking building in town. The shrine was relatively well-known in the area, and older men often told stories about Daud Khan and other important national figures coming to pray at the shrine. Many Kabulis who came to Istalif for picnics in the spring stopped and prayed there. Directly above the shrine was a large pool that was pleasant to sit next to in the warm weather, and informal community gatherings were held here. This is also the place where Massoud was said to have met with Istalifi leaders on several occasions, once with the "minister of foreign affairs" from America.[13]

Despite the importance of the shrine, Istalifis were more conservative than many urban Kabulis who visited the town, often condemning the more unorthodox practices of those who visited the shrine the most regularly. One man claimed Eshan Sahib had called to him in a dream, but others scoffed at such remarks. The most common complaint about the shrine was that people went there to pray directly to Eshan, when they should have prayed to the saint to intercede with Allah. Women, in particular, were accused of this practice. As with many shrines in Afghanistan, a mountain goat's skull was nailed over the central gate. When I asked about this, the shrinekeeper and several older men dismissed it and told me it reflected the beliefs of some who misunderstood Islam. Nevertheless, it was apparent that no one dared take it down. Despite this grudging tolerance for more traditional practices, the shrinekeeper never used astrology or performed any of the fortune-telling practices that *faal bins* (omen-seers) used outside many shrines in Kabul.

Below the shrine was a grave that was known to cure headaches or tooth-aches if the petitioner placed a small stick in it. I rarely saw individuals putting sticks into the grave, but it was always covered with twigs, and yet there was some discomfort about the traditional beliefs this grave and the shrine pro-moted. While other shrines in the region and in Kabul often had *malangs* (wan-dering holy men) who would give blessings, ask for alms, and tell fortunes at them, only one malang appeared in Istalif during my research period, and peo-ple kept their distance from him.

I interviewed the malang during his short visit to Istalif in a young man's shop in the bazaar. After the interview, the malang left and I stayed and chat-ted with the young man, who repeatedly mentioned that he did not believe in the Sufi rituals and visions the malang had just described. The malang, who left town a few days later, did not fit easily into the town's social order. He claimed to be of the Sayed qaum in Istalif, but I could not find any Sayed family who ad-mitted being related to him. His claims to have received messages from Eshan, and his possession of specific knowledge about the shrine, must have also caused discomfort among the shrinekeeper and other religious figures in town.

The malang was originally from Istalif and had served at the shrine before moving to northern Afghanistan to attend other shrines in Mazar-e Sharif. He reported that there had once been large Sufi gatherings at the shrine. While this may have been an exaggeration, several Istalifis confirmed that the shrine had been a more active site in the past. This suggests that there had been some drift away from traditional practices when Istalifis, particularly as refugees, were ex-posed to increasingly fundamentalist doctrines in Kabul and Pakistan. In ad-dition, some of the mullahs in town had been educated in Salafi madrassas in Pakistan. There was no evidence that religious leaders from early generations had traveled very far for their education, and one mullah claimed there had been no need to travel far, because before the communists Kabul had had such good madrassas and religious institutions. Despite the growing adherence to a stricter interpretation of Islam, the shrine continued to be an active site for prayer, and most Istalifis quietly tolerated these practices. The Islam of Istalif was probably stricter than it was in the past, but still distant from the tenets the Taliban preached during their brief time there.

Religious sites in town also served important economic functions. Mosques brought in some income, but because the shrine was most often visited by outsiders, it was the biggest source of income for religious figures, and there was contention over who had the power to select the shrinekeepers. The shrine was on the border between the Sayed gozar and the pottery gozar, and members of both neighborhoods claimed to have historically served as the keepers of the shrine. There had been a struggle a few years before over who should serve as the shrinekeeper. The disagreement originated with a dispute over passage rights of a strip of land leading into the pottery gozar that passed near the shrine's graveyard, where several homes were being rebuilt. Tensions apparently grew until there were negotiations between the elders from both qaums, and a respected elder from the Sayed qaum from Kabul returned to Istalif to help mediate. As a result of the negotiations, the potters retained passage rights on the path by the graveyard, but the Sayeds solidified their control as keepers of the shrine. Despite the truce, there was still a coolness between members of the pottery and Sayed qaums.

There was said to be a rotation among the Sayed families who served as shrinekeepers. In practice, however, the families seemed to have agreed that one older member of the qaum should serve as the shrinekeeper. The shrinekeeper collected between 5 and 50 afghanis from each visitor. I assumed this money was then redistributed somehow among quam members, but no one admitted to such a practice—not surprising, considering the reluctance to discuss any economic function related to religious sites.[14]

In addition to mullahs, a series of other figures had accumulated considerable religious capital. This was especially true of young qaris. These boys studied in small village madrassas or attended madrassas in Kabul. Most of those who had completed their studies, however, had memorized the Koran while they were refugees either in Kabul or in Pakistan. Often, these were younger men who were expected to eventually become mullahs; they were frequently seen about town in the company of one of the mullahs. The mawlawi tended to travel with a small entourage of young men known for their piety. Although qaris had no official duties, they often performed at funerals and on other important occasions for a small payment. Elders treated qaris with much more deference than they treated their less religious peers.

When issues in town were clearly religious, religious leaders had the most influence, but they rarely entered political situations that were openly contentious, or when an issue had potential implications involving the district governor, a malik, or other leaders. Becoming involved in such situations might demand either economic capital or the threat of violence, both of which delegitimized religious authority. This further related to the way religiosity was embodied; a religious leader was not expected to act aggressively in town politics. Instead, he typically waited for others to seek his council.

As a result, religious leaders generally used their authority to exert influence indirectly, through their relationships with maliks and the district governor. In some ways this contradicts the traditional role of religious figures in the region, especially in the frontier area of Pakistan, where in the past religious leaders could unite previously divided groups by using the common rhetoric of Islam. Tribal structures in the frontier area are, of course, much stronger, thereby perhaps strengthening religious figures at certain points, simply because they offer the one legitimate counterpoint to the tribal hegemony. This limited role, however, also opposes the way religious justification had been used historically to rationalize uprisings in the Shomali Plain, such as Habibullah Kalakani's overthrow of Amanullah Khan in 1929. The influence of religious figures during such uprisings had less to do with their relative strengths; their influence was related to the tension between groups such as maliks, the local government, and commanders, all of whom were competing over resources.

In earlier times, religious figures in the region have been most influential when creating a counter-narrative to a government hegemony that they described as un-Islamic. This was the case with both Habibullah Kalakani and the jihad against the Soviets. During the relative stability of the post-Taliban period in Istalif, there was a certain logic to the politically marginalized position of Istalif's religious establishment. As politics and the distribution of resources continue to shift and Istalifis grow increasingly disillusioned with the internationally backed government in Kabul and the presence of international troops in the area, it is very possible that religious leaders could use their significant religious capital to resume a more central daily political position.

THE NEW MERCHANT CLASS

Another group in town shared some traits with maliks and mullahs, but this group was quite different. It consisted of a collection of families who had gained great economic wealth in the past thirty years, primarily as refugees working abroad, and whose political influence was derived almost solely from this economic capital.

These families came from a variety of qaums and professions in town. Many of them were weavers who, after selling carpets to merchants in Kabul for several years, had decided to open their own carpet shops. One man, Nur Agha, was acknowledged by most of the dealers as the first Istalifi weaver to open a carpet shop in Kabul, forty years earlier. His business expanded rapidly, and he developed a network of business associates in Pakistan, Europe, and the United States. Other young men from Istalif came to work in his shop and eventually opened their own shops on Chicken Street, the main street for tourists in Kabul. Serving as a broker between his international business connections and other weavers in the Istalif area, Nur Agha established a large patronage network. However, some spoke of him as selfish and claimed he had not given enough back to the community. Nur Agha's sons still ran his extensive shop just off Chicken Street, and a sizable percentage of all the shops on Chicken Street were owned by families of Istalifi origin; several of them had been started by men who had initially worked for Nur Agha.

Other families had set up basic goods stores in Kabul, and another Istalifi man owned one of the largest clothing stores in Shar-e Naw. Another supplier of goods to the international community in Kabul was Hajji Daud, an Istalifi who owned a large grocery store in the northern section of the city. His son previously had helped supply the United States military at the Bagram Airfield. Using these connections, his father and brothers sold everything from Starbucks frappuccinos to Victoria's Secret lotions to military Bibles at their shop.

These shop owners and merchants came from various parts of Istalif, but almost all of them had made their initial capital working abroad as refugees or as carpet merchants, shipping internationally through Pakistan. This group of newly wealthy merchants continued to own land and maintain informal relationships in Istalif, but most of them lived in Kabul, generally in the heavily Tajik northern areas of Kart-e Parwan, Khier Khana, and, increasingly, Sar-e Kutal, one of the last neighborhoods in Kabul on the road north to Istalif.

Despite this distance, many were still involved in Istalifi politics. Nur Agha and his son, using connections he had established with an American businessman, organized the rebuilding of the bazaar in Istalif, and Hajji Daud had organized the building of the new mosque in the bazaar. Several of these men had purchased the prime gardens between the bazaar and the river, which they used on weekends during warm weather. For the most part, however, since most of the merchants spent the majority of their time in Kabul, there was an odd silence in the neighborhood around these gardens. In contrast with the bustle of the rest of Istalif, the area was quiet, except for the occasional caretaker or springtime visits by the families.

While this new class achieved wealth and some of the associated status, in the volatile economic conditions of Afghanistan there was an aversion to any attempt to purchase honor, as well as skepticism among Istalifis about whether wealth would last. This attitude was apparent in the import/export industry, where the promise of large profits was always balanced with the risk of massive losses due to countless variables, such as changing regulations, corrupt officials, and falling prices. Stories about merchants who had lost vast sums supported these fears. One Istalifi carpet seller in Kabul was said to have given a Malaysian businessman $5,000 in carpets, on credit, for export. The businessman returned with an impressive profit. He then took $10,000 in carpets, again returning with a profit. Finally, the businessman took $50,000 in credit and was never seen again.

There were other, less impressive examples of the dangers of depending upon business deals. One respected, though not especially wealthy, merchant from Istalif was involved in a dispute with some of his financial backers. In the course of a few days, these men took back his stock and evicted him from his store, and he was forced to restart his business and acquire new stock for a much smaller store. As a result of such cautionary tales, many young men yearned for the wealth merchants possessed, but were weary of business deals. In a few instances, these merchants made loans to other Istalifis, but many were still cautious about taking such funds and were ambivalent about many of the merchants' dealings.

The individuals who made up this new merchant class had converted some of their wealth into land, but they had not been able to gain significant influence in town politics. For example, the carpet seller who convinced an American business partner to donate thousands of dollars to rebuild the bazaar in the center of town was treated with a certain amount of deference, but did not enjoy the same respect that qaum elders had. Whether true or not, rumors circulated that the man the carpet seller had selected to oversee the project kept much of the funds for himself, or at least favored the families closest to him when employing workers. In several interviews, his sons struggled to portray the work of their father and his associate as an act of selfless generosity, while clearly feeling disgruntled that Istalifis did not express their gratitude more clearly. At the same time, potters expressed their dismay that these merchants were taking their wares abroad and selling them for what they claimed were incredibly high sums, but returning little to the community. Because they had achieved such sudden wealth, it was inevitable that many others in the community would use this gossip to try to prevent them from gaining too much status.

As a part of this social-leveling process, the merchants' wealth hurt their ability to establish honor and influence in the manner qaum leaders did. It was a point of pride among Istalifis that they stayed until the final hour when the Taliban destroyed the town, and then returned as soon as the Taliban fled the Shomali Plain. The rich merchants, on the other hand, had made their money by leaving—an act that diminished them in the eyes of some Istalifis. The merchants did have, however, other means of attempting to increase their social capital. The new mosque in the center of town was financed by donations from several men, most of whom were from this emerging upper class. Yet some privately scoffed at these attempts to purchase religious capital, comparing it with rich, unreligious men who went on the hajj, attempting to make themselves look pious.

There are several more reasons the merchant class had only been able to exert a limited amount of power. First, work kept most of the newly wealthy merchants busy in Kabul and they often came to town only on weekends; they were therefore unable to participate in the routine social visits that reaffirmed many of the political networks in town (though in Kabul they visited each other's shops in a similarly ritualized social process). More importantly, many of the merchants were weavers, which was traditionally considered one of the lower qaums. Istalifis had an informally agreed upon, but imprecise, notion of hierarchy among crafts. Most agreed that crafts such as jewelry making were higher than those such as weaving and leather working. Some professions that were not craft-based also fit into this informal hierarchy; it was better to be a shopkeeper than a laborer, and among shopkeepers it was better to own a pharmacy than a grocery store. Weavers had always been one of the poorest groups in the area, and despite their recent economic success, members of many other qaums were still reluctant to marry weavers or forge other serious social ties with them. While many younger Istalifis claimed that such marriage traditions were no longer relevant, people still spoke hesitantly about marrying their daughters into qaums such as the weavers, while it was considered prestigious to marry into the Sayed qaum.

Much of this hierarchy remained largely unarticulated. While I spent a good deal of time talking about and trying to determine marriage alliances between families, my statistics on qaum intermarriage remain imprecise because of the taboo of speaking directly about women. (I learned quickly to ask an older man how many sons-in-law he had, not how many daughters he had.) I recorded about fifty marriages between and within qaums, but this number is biased because only informants with whom I had a fairly intimate relationship tended to discuss details as private as who their wives were. Similarly, young men were often more willing than older men to discuss such relationships, as were Istalifis who had moved to Kabul and considered themselves more Westernized; this meant most of my data came from marriages involving men my own age. These men also liked to talk about how they were more liberal than their fathers' generation had been, but it was difficult to determine how idealized this description was.

Furthermore, there were instances of families moving in and out of qaums over many years as a result of a series of marriage alliances. Thus, the marriage of an older man to a family within the qaum might have been seen as a marriage outside the qaum forty years before, and it might have been precisely this marriage, along with other alliances, that had brought the two families closer together. It is also likely that men were more willing to discuss a good marriage alliance than they were to discuss a marriage into a lower qaum. I could have been more aggressive in seeking information about marriage alliances, but during my fieldwork my first priority was always to maintain good relationships within the community—and, as mentioned above, this meant treading cautiously when it came to discussing women. Often, I could check with informants about the marriages of their friends and relatives, but even these questions were sensitive. These issues contributed to social tensions that were rarely discussed directly, but which created real political divides in town.

As a result of these marriage patterns, which were indicative of wider patterns of socializing, merchants did not command the respect generally afforded to maliks and mullahs. Instead, this newer class tended to rely on allies within the town when they wanted to address certain political issues. Hajji Daud's son, for example, was involved in the discussion about the new road with the district governor and the Ministry of Rural Rehabilitation and Development (see the interlude preceding Chapter 1). When he came to the district governor's office, he was with the malik of his father's original area, and allowed the malik to lead the discussion. The wealth of the new merchant class meant that other leaders in town could not dismiss them, but they were still kept at a social distance, and they encouraged this by focusing on economic and political networks that were often based in Kabul.

FORMER MILITIAS

The new merchant class was not the only group that had economic capital. Former warlords, or commanders, as they were more frequently called, also had a good deal of wealth. Both their wealth and their continued political influence were derived primarily from the threat of violence they possessed. The role of commanders had diminished significantly since the end of active fighting in the area. As one man described it, while some commanders still had much land in Istalif, others had lost everything—they were "tied to a donkey." The degree to which they still had the ability to threaten violence, and the extent to which Istalifis considered that violence legitimate, varied. Some of these figures remained influential, and a number of Istalifis believed they were waiting for international troops to withdraw before they reasserted themselves. Others had become increasingly involved in national politics, and had strong connections with government officials, especially in the Ministry of the Interior.

In 2003, as a result of the Disarmament, Demobilization and Reintegration Program (DDR), these commanders turned in most of their weapons. Located so close to Kabul, with a regular international military patrol through the center of town, the disarmament of militias in the Istalif area was more complete than in other parts of the country. The process was facilitated by the fact that in 2003 both the Ministry of the Interior and the Ministry of Defense were dominated by Panjshiri Tajiks, including Mohammad Fahim, a commander who was a close associate of Massoud. While he was not a very popular figure in Istalif, the perception of Mohammad Fahim as the heir of Massoud still made him a warily respected leader, so most people complied to some extent with the disarmament process.[15] Following the DDR, Istalifis were allowed only to possess shotguns or basic hunting rifles, which most men continued to own. It was rare to see Istalifis flout this law by carrying more lethal weapons, though a few of the most powerful commanders and the men that accompanied them still went around town armed with assault rifles and, occasionally, rocket-propelled grenades.

Despite having fewer weapons, commanders still possessed the threat of violence. At one point in an interview with a commander about the DDR, the commander was speaking about the handover of weapons when he noticed that I had glanced at the three bodyguards lounging by the door. They had Kalashnikovs (assault rifles) and flak jackets packed with more than a hundred additional rounds. He laughed, pointed at the men, and said, "Ah, but the government has left me with some weapons . . . only for self-defense, of course." This apparently also applied to the police pickup truck, with a mounted machine gun, parked in front of his house. Since the rest of the residents had turned in most of their arms, the commanders, even lightly armed, were much better equipped than any other group. The commanders possessed a potentially violent force that only the police came close to rivaling.

Beyond their potential threat of violence, many of the commanders had a strong economic interest in the town. The area's main commander, Mohammad Zaher, who had been banished from Istalif, lived in Kabul, where he owned one of the city's largest car dealerships.[16] One of the incidents leading up to his expulsion was his attempt to build on a large, prime piece of property in the bazaar, which he had acquired (some said confiscated) several years before, but which the government claimed. Mohammad Zaher was eventually forced to give up the land, but the government did not build on it or sell it, despite its prime location and the fact that Mohammad Zaher had already prepared it for building. This was indicative of the uneasy balance that had been struck. The commander was expected to remain in Kabul, yet he occasionally returned to Istalif to visit allies, especially on holidays. The pattern he followed suggested to his allies that the local government was impotent, but he did not openly defy the district governor. In a similar affront to the government's power, Mohammad Zaher's men continued to collect rent from a large number of shops in the bazaar, including several carts and the teahouse directly in front of the district governor's office, which were all clearly on public land.

Another commander in a village just east of Istalif had more clearly overstepped this boundary. He was collecting a tax on the water from a certain irrigation system, something he had begun doing during the Taliban period, despite the fact that he did not have the traditional right to collect such a tax. At first, the government did nothing, but the commander had a dispute with a man who had refused to pay the tax and killed him. Following this more blatant affront, several in the community complained to the district governor, and he was forced to act. During my time there, the commander's ultimate fate was undecided, but he remained imprisoned. It is important to note that this was a lower-level commander; it is unclear whether the government could have acted as decisively against one of the stronger commanders. (It also seems unlikely that one of the more powerful commanders would have been greedy enough to collect small sums from residents to use an irrigation channel.)

Most of the important commanders in town were from Istalifi families, but not from any one quam or profession. Commanders from outside the town had been active in the area during periods of greater upheaval, but following the fall of the Taliban, most had consolidated power in their original homes or in Kabul. This was particularly true of Panjshiri militias, which were influential in Kabul following the arrival of American forces. One of the key local commanders was from the Sayed qaum and had fairly close ties with the malik of the Sayeds. In general, however, the two had separate dealings, and each one's power simply reinforced the other's position—and the influence of Sayeds in town.

Similarly, Mohammad Zaher was not tied to one qaum. He was the son of a landowner who lived on the eastern side of Istalif, and had worked, in his youth, at his father's pharmacy in the bazaar. Mohammad Zaher was rumored to have killed a communist teacher during the Soviet period, when he was a young man, and forced to flee to Iran for some years. He spoke of this period in Iran as a formative and pleasurable part of his youth, and he apparently gained some influence among Afghan immigrants there, organizing laborers and negotiating on their behalf with Iranian business owners. After some time, his brother, who was doing logistics work for anti-Soviet groups in Pakistan, sent for him. Using his brother's connections and his reputation for violence and organizing Afghans from various groups, Mohammad Zaher rose in status among the jihadi groups and was generally linked with *Jamiat-e Islami*, the primarily Tajik mujahideen party. As this story suggests, some former commanders retained ties with qaums and certain maliks, though commanders acquired power in fairly different ways.

One malik on the western edge of town, who had been a mid-level commander, had used force to assume his position as malik about fifteen years before.[17] This, however, was an exception. The area he controlled was not one of the better-defined gozars, and there was no central qaum in the area. While he was a malik, unlike other maliks in town, he traveled with an armed entourage. Most of the men who accompanied him resembled the groups that accompanied other commanders; their loyalty was based more on weapons and money than on kinship ties. He also wore a pakul instead of the turban or skullcap favored by all the other maliks. He had a reputation of being corrupt, and I never heard of anyone taking a dispute to him. Thus, because this commander had used force to become a part of the qaum system, his power continued to come from the threat of violence, not from an honorable reputation. Though people called him "malik," he had no real qaum to lead. For all intents and purposes, he remained a commander.

In general, because commanders' strength came primarily from the weapons they were able to distribute (and thus, the men they were able to command), many formed ties outside of Istalif. Thus, the majority of their marriage alliances seemed to be with other commanders, who had been important during the jihad and the civil war. As discussed in the previous chapter, Mohammad Zaher did have a marriage tie with the son of Malik Abdul Hamid of the potters, but he had also formed a marriage alliance with Ahmed Shah Massoud that was more central to his influence.

The way young men discussed commanders emphasized the difference between commanders and qaum leaders. According to one young potter, if it were not for the government, the commanders would take all the aid that came to Istalif, even if there was "just one piece of candy." Commanders were also accused of telling lies, particularly of misrepresenting their positions in relation to the people, when aid was dispersed in town. Such open allegations of dishonesty, and a lack of generosity, would only be leveled at a qaum leader in the most extreme cases, and no malik's reputation would have withstood such accusations for long.

While Istalifis would speak in private against the commanders, for the most part they quietly tolerated them. Many commanders were respected by the older generation for the role they had had in fighting the Soviets and the Taliban. However, as discussed previously, many of the details about their role during this period remained hazy, and commanders were certainly aided by the tendency to idealize this period, ignoring the feuds and political divisions that remained from it. Despite this, it was clear that Mohammad Zaher and some of the other commanders in the area had provided important resources during the jihad and civil war periods when the Afghan state had not been a force in the town. They had maintained security within the district, kept the bazaar and schools open, and provided some other very basic services. At the same time, most Istalifis blamed the commanders for much of the inequitable distribution of aid in the years immediately following the collapse of the Taliban. Istalifis often observed that, in the period when there was effectively no national government in Istalif, especially toward the end of the Soviet occupation, the commanders had helped maintain stability and ensure that community services such as schools continued to function. Young Istalifi men were the most critical, principally those who had not been a part of the early jihad years, and who were attempting to raise money to start businesses and arrange weddings in an era when commanders controlled many of the town's resources. While most Istalifis quietly argued that the time for commanders had passed, the economic, military, and social power they continued to wield ensured that they remained a force in daily politics.

As a result, commanders continued to exert influence, but within narrower limits. These limits did not originate so much in the government or rule of law as from the fact that by using the threat of violence, commanders renounced other roles and forms of authority that had more relevance in the post-Taliban period. During the jihad, Istalifis thought of relying on violence as Islamic, but to continue to use unnecessary violence later was seen as an individual's acknowledgement that he could not mobilize other forms of political capital. In this sense, commanders were shackled by the very thing that had brought them to power.

THE DISTRICT GOVERNMENT

The main government representative in town was the district governor, whose office was in the crumbling, former hotel on the south hill of Istalif.[18] As the chief representative of the government, he was technically in charge of most matters concerning the national government; for example, he was supposed to sign national identification cards. In reality, he delegated much of this work to maliks, who were far more familiar with the local population. (During my research period, the district governor was from Shekar Darrah, a town about half an hour south; he had arrived in town shortly before I did.)

Since the ability of commanders to threaten violence meant that the state did not have a monopoly on violence, most of the district government's influence came not from its access to violence, but from its connections with Kabul. Beyond this, the district governor's cultural, social, and economic capital were minimal. Despite having the key governmental position in town, his power was limited and poorly defined. For example, he claimed to resolve land disputes, but most people in town preferred to take such a dispute to their local malik first, or possibly to a mullah. Only if the dispute involved multiple, irreconcilable parties would the district governor be asked to intervene.[19] Similarly, the government only became involved in disputes over rights to water access when the disagreement involved multiple districts.

The district governor himself was rarely visible in town. Unlike qaum elders or mullahs, he seldom appeared in the main mosque or walked through the bazaar. He lived in Kabul, came to town most days (but certainly not all), and usually remained in his office on the hill. The district governor had not been in town long, and this fit a general pattern in Afghanistan of rapid turnover among district officials.[20] There was a sense of impermanence about the role of many officials, whom the national government often transferred to new districts. More visible in the life of the town was his administrative assistant, re-ferred to by many as "the engineer," who did much of the day-to-day work of the district government.

Partially limiting the district governor's role was the fact that he had few of the financial resources the state traditionally possessed. The complex system in which aid was distributed and allocated in post-Taliban Afghanistan restricted the district governor's access to funds, and he did not have the redistributive powers that had created some patronage for government officials before the Soviet invasion. Much of the government's development aid in Afghanistan was distributed through the National Solidarity Program (NSP). The NSP aimed to support local development and governance by dividing Afghanistan into twenty-five to three-hundred family blocks that elected their own councils. The councils then determined which public works projects would be carried out in the area.

The NSP existed under the Ministry of Rural Rehabilitation and Development, but it was managed by a group of NGOs. As a result, the largest single source of aid money in Istalif completely bypassed the district government. The money for the public works projects, which came chiefly from the World Bank, was given to Istalifis by employees of the implementing NGOs, not government officials. In addition, the NSP's maximum per-community distribution of $60,000 was significant in rural areas, but in Istalif, where many of the men worked as day laborers in Kabul, such a sum divided among three-hundred families had a limited effect. Most of my informants tended to discuss the NSP dismissively.

This program was not the only one that bypassed the district governor. Other facilities that provided services in the town, such as the medical clinic next to the government offices, were also run by ministries in Kabul with NGO assistance. The clinic doctor was a recognized figure in town, but he did not openly associate with the district governor or any other official. As a result, the district government had little control over the distribution of medical services.[21]

The previous district governor, who was from Istalif, was said to have been a more effective representative.[22] He worked closely with the primary commander in town, and the two shared authority in the years before the transitional government became more assertive outside Kabul. Later, the Karzai regime attempted to centralize the government, taking advantage of the new, executive-oriented government the constitution had established. A large part of the approach was to assign governors and other officials to areas that were not their homes—a policy with a long history in Afghanistan—to ensure that the officials' primary loyalty was to the central government, not to local figures of power (maliks, religious leaders, and commanders).

Further complicating the role of the state, the legal framework for local governance was a confusing, at times contradictory, set of laws, including the constitution of 2004, the Provincial Council law of November 2005 and its amendments, the local administration law of 2000 (written by the Taliban), and the municipal laws of 1957.[23] This overlap of unclear regulations helped make the manipulation of local government possible. Little was done to clarify these laws, and the national government in Kabul used the confusion the laws created to reward those who were loyal and punish those that opposed it. Similarly, there was a national-level debate about when to hold district-level elections. The constitution called for them to occur immediately, but opponents claimed that because district borders were not finished, elections could not be held. Simultaneously, many in the international community were concerned about the great potential for corruption during the elections.[24] In Istalif, this created further ambiguity about the state's role at the local level. The result was a local government that was unpredictable and whose strength remained untested. In the face of this unpredictability, most Istalifis tried to avoid the government and its officials unless they had a close relationship with the district governor.

Most of the district governor's influence came instead from his perceived ties with other government officials in Kabul. He was seen as someone who could introduce a person to influential people in Kabul—for example, to help acquire permission to perform the hajj from the Ministry of Hajj and Religious Affairs. This social capital was based strictly upon external networks; the district governor had not been able to forge meaningful ties within the community because of his position as an outsider. The irony of this situation was that cultivating more local alliances would have weakened his ties to Kabul, and he would have lost the little power he did have.

In general the state was seen as the product of Kabul and modernization, which Istalifis perceived as suspiciously un-Islamic and intrusive.[25] Older Istalifis in particular tended to conflate the meanings of democracy, globalization, and liberal elements of development projects. Many times, older men told me they opposed this new "democracy"—they did not translate the term, but simply used the English word. As they elaborated, it became clear that they were referring to their opposition to programs that disturbed the traditional social order, such as those that tried to take women out of their traditional roles.[26]

Similarly, many of their concerns about the presence of international NGOs and the military were that programs were being designed to bring in external values. These fears further marginalized the government, but there was also an understanding that the state could create stability on a national level and encourage the flow of aid money into the area. People supported this aspect of the district government, while trying to avoid direct interaction with government officials. This distance, and the government's inability to mobilize funds or violence, made it impossible for the government to establish any sort of hegemony in the area, and the district governor was forced to compete with other political actors in town.

THE LOCAL POLICE

There were two successive chiefs of police in Istalif during my time there. They treated their positions rather differently. The first one lived in Kabul, was rarely seen in town, and seemed indifferent to local politics. During this period the police tended to stay in one of the four posts in the area, occasionally extorting small amounts of money or services from the residents. This police chief was from Shekar Darrah, just south of Istalif, as was the district governor, and the two were allies.

The replacement police chief was from Charikar to the north; he was the one who visited me in the middle of the night during Ramazan (see "Ethnography and Suspicion," the interlude preceding Chapter 2). Upon his arrival in Istalif, he immediately tried to establish a position of power independent of the district governor, bringing in new officers and trying to intervene more actively in local affairs. He was a much more visible presence and was often seen being driven around in a new green pickup truck on Istalif's bumpy roads, at breakneck speeds. This put him at odds with the district governor. The two had offices on opposite sides of the government building, where they competed for influence, rarely interacting with each other.[27]

The other police officers were a mixture of allies of the police chief, and several of the key commanders in Istalif. They had secured their positions through the various patronage networks of government officials in Kabul. As far as I could tell, however, most of these negotiations took place at the Ministry of the Interior in Kabul, and the process of assigning police officers to certain districts was completely untransparent to the people in Istalif.

Despite the upswing in activity after the new police chief's arrival, the police were still rarely proactive and continued to spend most of their time in one of the four posts. Soon after the new chief's arrival, officers at the post at the main entrance to town began writing down the license plate number of each car driving into Istalif, but stopped after a week or so. In his office, the police chief liked to pull out knives, brass knuckles, and other weapons that he said he had confiscated from Istalifis. In reality, crime in Istalif was limited; most community members preferred not to involve themselves with the police, even when incidents did occur. For example, the shopowners in the bazaar collectively paid for a night watchman, even though one of the police posts was near the center of the bazaar. The shopkeepers seemed to fear the police just as much as they feared criminals. After the incident when the chief of police entered my compound in the middle of the night, I discussed the situation with a usually jovial young friend of mine. When I tried to laugh about it at the end, he turned incredibly stern and said, "Noah, this is why you should live with me. I would like to see the police try to even cross my doorstep." He accompanied this with a violent gesture. His attitude—that it was an honorable man's job to defend his own home against intrusion from outsiders like the police—was common in Istalif.

In daily life, police officers were considered little more than meddlesome, but their ability to threaten violence ensured that they were still occasionally useful allies for other leaders in town. Maliks and qaum elders greeted the police chief respectfully when they met him in the bazaar. If nothing else, the police provided a useful counterweight to the commanders' continued presence. In addition to these roles, there were supposed to be coordinated talks between the police and the ISAF (International Security Assistance Force) troops that patrolled the area. I observed the two sides meeting occasionally, and sat in on one meeting, but no real cooperation seemed to emerge from the discussions. Rather, the two sides essentially gave each other increased legitimacy. The police chief in particular gained influence from his relationship with the military forces, but because a sharp increase in international military presence in the area would only have decreased his status, he had little incentive to cooperate more actively with them, and seemed happy to have them continue on their way.

Despite its ambiguous role, the police force remained a presence in town. The officers were well armed and owned several pickup trucks, which they occasionally parked in the bazaar or on one of the hills above town to make their presence felt. This equipment, purchased with assistance from the American and German militaries, were generally in good repair and gave them the appearance of the best-armed group residing in the town. This display of the police's ability to threaten violence was one of the few visible signs of government power in Istalif. The fact that this power was split between the district governor and the chief of police, however, helped ensure that actual government penetration in daily life in Istalif remained minimal.

INTERNATIONAL GROUPS

A final important political presence in town was that of international groups, both military forces and development agencies. In some ways, these groups presented an alternative to government structures (discussed in Chapter 7). NGOs had economic capital and supplied goods and services, the international military possessed the threat of violence, and both groups had access to wider political and economic networks outside of Kabul. Despite this potential, these groups rarely coordinated their work, and the effect of international presence seldom had its intended consequences. In some ways, the international community formed almost a parallel state. However, the goods and services the international community provided, and the stability they created, were never reliable enough to be perceived by residents to constitute a viable alternative to the state. In some ways, this last group was separate from the other categories in Istalif, because its goals were generally isolated from the goals of other political actors. Regardless, the international military and NGOs were a part of almost every serious political conversation in town. The economic and military resources they had meant that the other groups were constantly aware of their interests, even when their interests seemed out of place. As a result, the other groups treated them as significant political actors.

Officially, Istalif was in the zone around Kabul that was patrolled by French troops, and a convoy of three to five armored French transports usually came through town several times a week. Occasionally, other military groups visited, most notably the Americans and the Germans. These troops did not often stop, but would occasionally visit the office of the district governor or the chief of police.[28]

Istalifis were wary of foreign troops, and men pointed to their presence as one of the reasons women should not go to the bazaar. This distrust caused numerous conspiracy theories to circulate. For example, French troops were responsible for clearing any mines and unexploded ordinances (UXOs) in town, although most of Istalif had been cleared of mines, and there was no active demining work going on. One day, however, the fuselage of a rocket was found in the hills above town. It appeared that the rocket had failed to detonate, but then someone had removed the charges, leaving behind only the body. The French troops immediately went to remove it. After clearing the site, they left the fuselage sitting on the top of one of their troop transports for several hours, while they ate lunch on the hill above town. When they left town that afternoon, rumors spread that the troops had dug up several historical artifacts and stolen them. The general sentiment, however, was not anger at the looting of antiques, but at the thought that the French had kept the money for themselves.

In general, the policy of the international troops seemed to be to avoid the local population as much as possible. The translators they had with them were young men who rarely spoke with locals and did nothing to dispel any of the misinformation, such as the rumors of looting. All the translators were of Afghan descent, but many had been born, or at least raised, abroad.[29] Istalifis tended to resent the fact that these young translators often spoke condescendingly to town elders. This failure to create any serious dialogue meant that the international military's most significant role was as a constant, but inactive, threat of force.

NGOs had a more direct effect on the town, through a series of development programs. In the years immediately following the fall of the Taliban, these programs had been much larger; by 2006, most NGOs in Istalif ran rather limited programs. Several groups provided aid to various artisan groups, and a women's center had been established to train some of the women in literacy, health, and basic vocational skills. For the most part, however, the NGOs had limited budgets and limited goals.

Programs conceived in Kabul, or, more often, abroad, did not adapt easily to local conditions. For example, one NGO in Istalif supplied microloans, which had become popular in other parts of the developing world. Inflation and high prices in and around Kabul, however, meant that the amount of capital a person needed to start a small business often significantly exceeded the amount a microloan provided. In addition, with the presence of the emerging merchant class, Istalifis had access to other forms of credit that were much easier to secure than the time-consuming applications some NGOs demanded.

Particularly in 2002 and 2003, NGOs in Afghanistan were flush with funds and overwhelmed by the need to spend it, but lacked the staff to run multiple programs effectively. This led to a period in which many NGOs simply handed out tools, building supplies, and occasionally cash. Many Istalifis lamented that such distribution had ceased. When they heard about complicated business development schemes, which sometimes demanded a good deal of paperwork, they wanted to know why the NGOs no longer simply gave the money directly to them. Thus, there were a limited number of participants in the microcredit programs.

The greatest effect of the NGOs on the community was through employment. In Istalif, the NGOs primarily relied on local staff, with international staff visiting occasionally from Kabul. Afghan employees were paid higher-than-average salaries. They tended to be young, and many had been educated abroad. Many of them, such as those working in the clinic, drove out from Kabul each day. Some of the young men had connections in Istalif or the larger Shomali Plain area, but their current ties were all to Kabul. Most Istalifis who had stayed in Istalif during the years of fighting could not compete for technical NGO jobs with those who had fled to Pakistan and received more formal education and training. This was a group that had gained influence through connections with NGOs and the capital they distributed, despite the fact that they mostly lacked connections to other important town figures, such as religious leaders and maliks. This meant that while many NGO employees were literate and could communicate well with the development community, they were often not very effective at opening local lines of communication.

No group was less effective at accumulating influence than the international groups, whose various projects involved a mix of development, state-building, and stabilization goals. Despite the large amounts of money being spent in Istalif and the military might of the armed forces, neither NGOs nor the international military did much to influence local politics. Distrust of foreigners made it difficult to establish social connections, but even more significant were the ways both groups operated in Istalif. International contracts and tours in Afghanistan rarely lasted more than twelve months (in some cases, as with the British military, only six months), so there were always new officers to meet or development workers checking on projects. Such rapid turnover prevented any of these individuals from establishing the type of personal relationships that created trust in Istalif.

The Afghans working for NGOs based in Istalif used a similar approach. Looking to other NGOs and organizations in Kabul for new positions or opportunities, they had little incentive to develop political or social networks in Istalif. Another irony was that several NGOs in town had hiring practices that targeted "vulnerable" groups, such as widows or those who had been wounded by land mines. As a result, the NGO employees sometimes possessed the least amount of social capital, making it even more difficult for the NGOs to establish relationships. Similarly, most of the military's young Afghans translators looked down on rural Afghans and, at times, seemed barely able to disguise their disdain for local elders.

The contrasting goals of the international community and those of Istalif's residents made the creation of political power more challenging. The military seemed uninterested in any aspect of life other than security; they rarely visited with anyone other than the chief of police, and passed quickly through town except on the few occasions when there was a security concern. More surprisingly, the NGOs' goals often had little to do with a desire to improve life in Istalif. Most of the projects had been conceived abroad, and the goal of the development workers was to ensure that the programs ran as described in their funding documents, not in a way that created real change. The international community had so much economic capital to spend that it remained an aspect of many of the political conversations in town. However, because these groups had done little to translate their economic capital into political capital, they were only consulted on issues in which they were directly involved.

.   .   .

What explains the incredible number of local political actors during this period of relative stability in Istalif? Bourdieu's notion of various forms of capital provides a good framework for beginning to understand how politics were organized in this small town—but history had complicated the circumstances. One part of the answer is that Istalif's and Afghanistan's complex political history over the previous thirty years had created a situation that sustained a variety of forms of political capital and made their conversion challenging. Years of instability in Istalif had allowed different groups to emerge as the political and military landscape was radically altered. Thus, commanders during the jihad and the civil war came to possess more power (as the new merchant class had, more recently). Each group gained power at times when different types of capital were valued. As each period passed, certain forms of political capital were devalued, but rarely vanished entirely. In the post-Taliban period, the failure of the Afghan government to consolidate power, the disinterest of the international community in engaging with local politics, and the pervasive fear that Afghanistan had not really stabilized allowed these various forms of power to continue to shape daily life in Istalif.

The answer that history created these multiple categories, however, does not fully explain why they have persisted and why no one group has been able to establish anything resembling a hegemony in the town. There is an Afghan proverb, used whenever someone feels another person is receiving preferential treatment, and a frequent lamentation of younger sons: "*Yek bam wa du hawa*"—"There is one roof, but two weathers." Two people can be on the same roof, experiencing very different conditions. Why have different groups in Istalif allowed and, in fact, encouraged these multiple climates?

The next chapter suggests that the structure these conditions created encouraged groups to use political strategies that relied primarily on disengagement, allowing each group to horde power, but only within the boundaries of its realm. Istalifis tolerated this situation because the stagnation of political and economic conditions also ensured the suppression of violence. Politics in Istalif were an ineffective process in which it was in the best interest of most actors to conserve the resources they had and limit the access others had to these resources. This approach tended to lead toward inactivity, often against the best interests of the majority, but in a way that was generally stable and peaceful.

Election Day

The weeks preceding the elections in Istalif generated considerable excitement.[1] Even while most people felt Karzai would easily win the presidency and were convinced the Provincial Council was a powerless body, the elections still generated debates in the bazaar. Over the summer, it was difficult to have a conversation without the elections coming up at some point.

In many ways, the elections created a festive atmosphere. Men attended campaign rallies where they listened to speeches and enjoyed elaborate meals. Provincial Council candidates and campaign workers drove into town and handed out fliers in the bazaar. Supporters hung posters of candidates in shop windows, on walls, and on trees, and in the evenings boys ran around tearing down the posters of candidates who were not from Istalif. It was clear that although candidates from Istalif were competing with candidates from all across the province of Kabul, the real debate was about which local candidate the voters should support.

Men in town often spoke disparagingly about both the concept of democracy and the government in general, so it was somewhat surprising that the elections generated such high levels of participation. But in a political arena where competition was often muted, the elections presented an opportunity to make the debate public. The secrecy and intrigue that pervaded Istalifi politics remained, however; young men lowered their voices before discussing a candidate they knew their fathers might not support, and rumors ran rampant about certain elders and commanders who were publicly supporting one candidate while quietly telling their followers to vote for a different candidate.

On election day, the town was busy. There were several voting stations in the district, but the one in the boys' high school, in the center of the bazaar, was the busiest, with a line stretching down the path next to the soccer field that was almost a hundred men long for most of the morning. The men were frisked at the gate, turned in any weapons, and showed their ID cards. There was a formality to the process, and the men mostly stood silently in line, waiting their turns to enter the rooms with the ballots and boxes.

Outside the polling station, the mood was lighter and the crowd lingered. It was a beautiful end-of-summer day. A couple of young boys walked through the crowd selling snacks. One had a picture of one of the candidates pasted to his hat. Men greeted each other, lounged in the teahouse, and sat on steps in the sun. While on the surface this was informal socializing, I soon noticed that the observation and interaction going on was a little more systematic. Several maliks spent much of the morning standing outside the polling station, and voters stopped to pay their respects either on the way into the station or on the way out.

These men were joined at various times by commanders and the local candidates. At one point, Mohammad Zaher arrived in a convoy of four pickup trucks and SUVs, got out of his car, and shook hands with most of the men. After about fifteen minutes, he got back into his truck and sped off to visit other polling stations. Soon after he left, the district governor arrived and greeted people in a similar manner.

Although they did not apply overt pressure on the voters, everyone knew which candidates Mohammad Zaher and the district governor wanted voters to support. It was said that inside the polling station, election officials appointed by the candidates were quietly whispering to those coming into the voting area, and watching the names that were being marked. One commander outside kept saying, "Today is an important day for Hajji Mahmood," the candidate he was supporting. Then he would turn to another man, "Today is an important day for Hajji Mahmood."

Several of the elders worked more diligently to monitor who was coming and going. One malik spent most of the morning there, only leaving when his eldest son arrived. The son remained there until mid-afternoon, when his brother replaced him.

The voters were clearly aware of the importance of showing themselves at the polling station, and election day became an elaborate event for displaying loyalties. A group of men who lived in a village far up the valley walked for several hours to vote in the center of town, even though they walked past two other polling stations to get there. Similarly, many Istalifi families who lived in Kabul drove out to Istalif to vote and spend the day greeting friends and relatives, despite the fact that they could just as easily have cast their votes in Kabul.

As the morning progressed, the line grew shorter, though the crowd remained outside the polling station for much of the day. The polling station closed at 4:00, and by the time the sun went down, the only thing left to remind people of the election were a few torn campaign posters fluttering in the wind.

7 MASTERLY INACTIVITY: THE POLITICS OF STAGNATION

DURING THE ELECTIONS and throughout much of political life in Istalif, individuals were concerned with mobilizing support and resources. At many times, however, there was strong incentive to demobilize and avoid open conflict and engagement, leading to hushed conversations in the bazaar about candidates. These patterns and rhythms in politics helped avoid conflict, but they also discouraged cooperation and thus a wider marshalling of town resources. As a consequence, Istalifis missed out on key economic and political opportunities—namely, securing development money and electing parliamentary leaders. In some cases, particularly the parliamentary elections, the fractured nature of power ensured that no single group was able to build sufficient political capital. The result was a politics of stagnation. In most cases, however, the failure of any townwide political mobilization or cooperation appeared not as simple passivity, since the concept of passivity does not allow for the fact that such lack of activity was a deliberate and effective political strategy. It also does not take into account that, in many instances, political actors *worked* to make sure nothing happened by undermining the political plans or character of their opponents.[1] For this reason, I have chosen the phrase "masterly inactivity."[2]

In Istalif, masterly inactivity was the political practice of avoiding direct confrontation while simultaneously working inconspicuously to ensure that any competing group in town would have to mobilize followers directly in order to access resources—thus, forcing opponents to spend as much political capital as possible. Ideally, this would reflect the weaknesses of the competing group and its inability to maintain unity among its followers. The results were subdued political struggles and whispered conversations, rather than open confrontation. We have already seen this demonstrated on a micro level; sons quietly struggled to accumulate wealth and gain social independence without ever directly confronting their father or brothers, and the Malik tried to maintain solidarity in the pottery qaum while not ruling overtly and risking losing his status. Outside the kin group, however, there is more of an emphasis on directly undermining the ability of rivals to act.

Masterly inactivity was a product of the political landscape of the post-Taliban period. The fragmentation of power during this time meant the state had some power, but could not really penetrate society; commanders had been demobilized, but had not submitted all their arms; qaum leaders maintained much of their influence on neighborhood politics, but could not mobilize on more serious issues; and international military forces and NGOs had enough strength to upset this balance, but little interest in involving themselves in local politics. Because of the improbability of any of these groups being able to defeat the others, along with memories of violence and instability during the civil war and the Taliban period, no group seriously considered trying to establish hegemonic control over town politics.

Choosing inactivity preserved the status quo, while engaging in a public struggle risked defeat, which would result in the loss of honor. Such a loss would have further damaged the facade of political and social power each man attempted to create, thus ensuring more losses in the future. In a system where the potential cost of losing in a confrontation outweighed the potential gains from winning in most scenarios, individuals went out of their way to avoid the appearance of engagement.

Masterly inactivity was also about framing political issues, and individuals constructed narratives portraying themselves as stronger than their opponents, but simply disinclined to act. Therefore, while many political figures in town would confide their goals to uninvolved associates, once confronted with an opponent, they struggled to feign disinterest. The feeling of a sleepy town permeated the atmosphere, even while everyone was quietly struggling to make sure that nothing happened.

This chapter begins with two specific cases: a return to the story of attempts to pave the road to Istalif, and then a discussion of the Istalifi candidates in the parliamentary elections of 2005. In the case of the road, actors used masterly inactivity to block the paths of their opponents, while simultaneously compromising their own ability to secure resources. The chapter then discusses more general cases of competition within the bazaar, land disputes, and water rights. In each case, there was the potential for cooperation and also for violent competition, but by choosing strategies of masterly inactivity, Istalifis preserved the status quo, avoiding both change and violence.

A ROCKY ROAD, REVISITED

The story that began this book, an account of the meeting in the district governor's office to discuss paving the road from Kabul, embodies the competitive nature of Istalifi politics, leading most of the actors to use a strategy I call masterly inactivity. (See "A Rocky Road," the interlude preceding Chapter 1.) After the meeting, I spoke with various participants, trying to understand what had happened in the meeting itself, and why the project eventually failed, when there were clear benefits for all Istalifis. Why had there been no further discussion about the road? Why had no group publicly protested its defeat? Why had the project failed in such undramatic fashion? Although the story was complex and took time to unravel, it soon became apparent that the plan had not failed for lack of popular support. In fact, the state of the dirt road between Istalif and the main highway between Kabul and Charikar was one of the central topics of conversation in the bazaar; I remember hearing about it on my first day in Istalif. Why, then, had the men in the meeting chosen a self-defeating path?

The drive from Kabul to Istalif took at least an hour and a half; in some of the rickety minibuses that plied the route, it could take much longer. A traveler spent half the time climbing a rutted dirt road, only about 6 miles long, and the rest of the trip speeding along the newly paved highway into Kabul.[3] In late winter and early spring, mud slowed traffic to a crawl. In the worst conditions, the soft mud formed deep ruts that froze when the temperature dropped. Some people estimated that paving the road from the highway to Istalif would cut travel time in half (perhaps slightly exaggerating the road's impact), and the district governor said he supported the idea because it would lower the price everyone paid for a seat in one of the minibuses that commonly carried Istalifis and their goods to and from Kabul. In the meeting, he estimated that the current fare would decrease from 50 afghanis to 30 or 35 afghanis. It was difficult to find anyone who openly opposed the general idea of paving the road to Istalif, but the question was not that simple.

There were actually two roads that connected Istalif to the main Charikar–Kabul highway. The main road everyone took to and from Kabul ran south, from the bridge below the bazaar, and over the hill the district government building and clinic were on. The road then ran south for a short distance along a ridge before cutting east, down to the main highway. The other road ran through the bazaar and directly east to the highway, intersecting at the center of a town called Qara Bagh. This shorter road was the historic road to Istalif, but it was much less popular, twisting and turning through several villages where it was barely wide enough to accommodate a single large car. In other places, the road had a steep grade and was prone to washouts in the spring. Cars crawled at a tortuously slow pace, and the road could be closed by snow or mud for weeks at a time in the winter or spring.

Before it was more common to do business in Kabul, Istalifis had trekked down this road to the large weekly bazaar in Qara Bagh. Several older potters spoke nostalgically of traveling down the road with a stack of pots in their youth. Because it intersected with the highway several miles north, people still used this road, but generally only if they had a sturdy vehicle and were headed to Qara Bagh, north to Charikar, or over the Hindu Kush. The road south was in much better shape. It only became seriously rutted when the mud was at its worst, and, unlike the eastern road, there was space in most parts of the road to pass if a vehicle got stuck behind a truck or herd of animals.

Although the eastern road was rarely used, the difference between the two roads became the heart of the dispute over the Ministry of Rural Rehabilitation and Development's plan to pave the road to Istalif. Engineers had been under the impression that the ministry would only pave the road running south to Kabul, which had more traffic, but the way they discussed the plan implied that they had not received explicit instructions about this aspect of the project. They reasoned that paving only the first road was a sounder economic decision, and that paving just that road would still have reduced the travel time to points north, if one drove south to the highway and then turned north. It was clear that, before the meeting in the district governor's office, the engineers had not even considered paving the road to the east.

After I researched some of the background and conducted follow-up interviews, it became apparent that, while there were almost a dozen significant political figures in the room during the meeting, two maliks were at the center of the tension. Despite this fact, many others joined in the conversation, particularly a commander and businessman who had come with the malik who supported the road the most. This malik sat across from me and was fairly quiet, but scowled more and more as the meeting continued. He lived about a half a mile south of the bazaar, on the part of the road that was to be paved. He greeted the engineers and district governor warmly, but as the debate increased he became less vocal. Instead, several of his allies, including the businessman (who lived in Kabul), continued to defend the plan.

The other malik, sitting directly to my right, lived just east of the bazaar, in the first gozar one came to when taking the secondary road out of Istalif. He was the most vocal opponent of the plan. He repeatedly criticized the project, saying that paving only the road south of Istalif was not fair to those living on the east side of Istalif. At the time, I was confused by his criticism. Already the malik and anyone living in his gozar had to walk to the taxi stand in the bazaar and take a minibus on the road south. Few minibuses took the road east with any regularity. Even by paving only the road to the south, it was clear to me (and, I assumed, everyone else in the room) that the malik and the residents of his gozar would still save half an hour on each trip to Kabul—not to mention any reductions in fare and the economic opportunities that would arise from facilitating the transport of goods to and from Kabul.

Several others at the meeting, supported by the engineers, repeatedly mentioned that while paving the road south was a daunting task, paving the road east seemed nearly impossible. The malik who had been arguing in favor of also paving the road east ignored most of this reasoning, focusing on several other development projects that had already taken place in the town. He directed their attention to the fact that the major projects in Istalif were concentrated south of the river, pointing to the district government building, the new hydroelectric plant, and a high school. Several others in the room nodded in agreement at these examples, even though they were slight misrepresentations. The district office was in an abandoned hotel that had been built decades before—in fact, a new district office was planned for an area north of the river. The hydroelectric plant had been built south of the river because that hill was much steeper; the plant was meant to deliver electricity to both sides of the river. In other settings I had heard those on the south side of the river complaining that the plant had been built there. Finally, while there were two new schools south of the river, there were also two new schools built north of the river, along with the new town mosque and the rebuilt bazaar. No one, however, brought up any of these facts or disputed the malik's reasoning.

The argument seemed to have less to do with the validity of his claims than the themes he emphasized. His language focused on fairness and justice. Several times he used the term *rastkar*—correct work—to refer to the work the government and development organizations should do. The term recalled many of the conflicts that had arisen in 2002 and 2003, as aid money rapidly entered Istalif, and Afghanistan in general. The money came in a rushed and often disorganized manner. Several commanders in town had taken advantage of this situation, directing development projects to their own neighborhoods, or pilfering more directly. They were condemned for being *haq nashenoss*, those who do not know rights, and *be-iman*, without faith. The fact that the malik who sup-ported the road had come with a commander, and was from an area generally regarded as having received a disproportionate amount of aid, allowed the sec-ond malik to lead others in the room against this small group.

By the end of his speech, several of the other men were nodding in agree-ment. While some remained noncommittal, nobody openly defended the idea of paving only the southern road. The district governor, who had originally supported the idea and tended to repeat most of the engineers' arguments, grew increasingly quiet and distracted. As it became clear that reaching a con-sensus was going to be difficult, he began working on some papers on his desk, calling over his deputy to bring him other documents that seemed unrelated to the discussion. At one point he left the room to speak with someone in the hall, while the debate in his office continued without him.

The argument frustrated the engineers, but they seemed to realize there was little they could do. They emphasized that they were not from Istalif, and were merely there to help the town. At one point, one of them said, in exasperation, "I am from Ghazni and could be paving roads in Ghazni instead." The engi-neers admitted that they could also survey the road to the east and submit the estimate to the ministry to see if the ministry would approve the road, but they thought ministry officials would not agree to a higher cost. What remained un-stated, but seemed clear to everyone at the meeting, was that if the estimate ex-ceeded the amount budgeted for the road, the ministry would likely cancel the entire project.

THE TENSIONS BENEATH A CIVIL DEBATE

Why had the malik been able to convince other town leaders to oppose such a beneficial project? In my later research on the case, I learned that the two maliks who opposed each other at the meeting had a long-standing feud. I heard a couple of theories, but no one seemed exactly sure what had started the feud (this was not uncommon). Groups that directly opposed each other were re-ferred to as having *dushmani* (enmity). It was more typical, particularly when a feud had simmered for a long time, to say that two families had *khafagi* (sad-ness) between them. In such a relationship, there was no intermarriage or eco-nomic cooperation, but there was also no serious open conflict. The situation between the two maliks was more one of khafagi than dushmani. People said the malik who supported the road was responsible for convincing the ministry to survey it in the first place, using connections with a parliamentary member who had helped him submit a proposal. Money had also been allocated to pave the same road once before, a little more than a year earlier, but at the last minute another member of Parliament had used his influence to redirect the funds to pave the road to his smaller village, east of Istalif. While I could not confirm all the details of this story, most Istalifis believed that the best, and perhaps the only, way to secure funds from government ministries was through personal connections.

By the time the meeting occurred, it was clear to many that the malik's status in town would increase dramatically if the road were completed. The other malik's opposition was less about the logistics of paving the road than it was about this potential shift in power. He convinced others to support him by subtly alluding to the dangers of allowing this malik to form an alliance with the commander and businessman also present, couching his argument in phrases that reminded people of when power had been concentrated in the hands of a few commanders. Better to pass up this economic opportunity, his argument claimed, than risk returning to the inequitable distribution of resources from the days just after the fall of the Taliban. Although building the road was in everyone's best interest, it was also in everyone's best interest to keep the other malik from gaining prestige and unbalancing the distribution of power in town.

It was also significant that no one in the room stood to gain a considerable amount of economic or political capital by reducing the travel time to Kabul. Many (though not all) of the men at the meeting, such as the district governor, had private vehicles and already traveled to Kabul more comfortably than most Istalifis, who used shared taxes and minibuses. Similarly, most of the men would not have gained much from marginally lower prices in the bazaar or facility in moving goods to Kabul. Shopkeepers and orchard owners were more likely to gain from this aspect of the project. Paving the road would have been primarily a convenience for everyone in town, and would have generally helped Istalif's economic growth.

In the meeting, the result was a situation that encouraged masterly inactivity. The malik supporting the project did little to advocate for paving the road, relying primarily on the engineers and his associates to provide rather weak, obvious arguments supporting the project—and even these arguments were fairly limited. More importantly, no one, including the main supporter of the road, ever alluded to the feud between the two maliks, although it appeared to be the main issue in the debate. This omission helped reduce the overt tension in the room. In addition, anyone supporting the road more publicly would have lost honor when the project failed, and there was a good deal of skepticism about its prospects, especially since it had failed before. None of the other men in the room, including the district governor, wanted to risk supporting a losing cause that would have led, in turn, to increased tension between the men on each side of the debate.

The malik opposing the road used a more active strategy that undermined his opponent without ever directly confronting the key issues. He never openly opposed the road itself—if the road had been built, he would have lost honor, because he would have proved himself too weak to defeat his rival. Simultaneously, open opposition would have exposed his selfish motives and undermined his authority as a malik and a leader of the people. As his opponent did, he went out of his way to make it appear that their personal feud was not the issue at stake. Instead, by discussing the early post-Taliban period, he relied on arguments he knew fit into the public narrative of Istalif's history. He realized most of the men in the room could not openly dispute this narrative of injustice without exposing themselves as having been at least partially responsible for the imbalance of resources and power.

For me, at the time, all these points created an unexpected tone in the meeting. Despite the project's importance, everyone treated the meeting as if its consequences were minimal. The district governor reinforced this by leaving at one point, emphasizing his lack of investment in the outcome of the discussion and disguising his own lack of control over the direction of the debate. The most visible display of emotion came from the engineers, who were not as integrated into the town's political system, and could express their frustration at the lack of cooperation without potentially forfeiting political capital for the next major issue in local politics.

A final point, to dispel any notion that Istalifis simply have an aversion to development schemes, is the case of Bagh-e Mullah, a gozar about a mile and a half north of the bazaar. The neighborhood sat up in the hills, which were unirrigated, so there was a large stretch of barren land separating the gozar from the rest of Istalif. Until about a year before my arrival there had been no road to Bagh-e Mullah, just a steep dirt trail with several switchbacks. The people of the neighborhood had apparently decided to build a road together. One wealthy man gave half the money for the road, and the rest of the community distributed the labor and remaining costs among themselves. The road was not in very good condition, but a car could traverse it slowly, which was apparently a great improvement.

When I asked about the construction of the road (which cost several thousand dollars), people emphasized that the students had had a difficult journey down to the school in the bazaar (the gozar had no school of its own). They did not usually discuss any clear economic advantages of having a closer link with the bazaar. To have done so would have acknowledged the economic and political incentives involved in the project; instead, by pointing to the students' needs, they constructed a purely altruistic narrative. This case was simplified by the fact that it only involved one poorer gozar that was relatively isolated. None of the town's main political figures had been involved. The man responsible for much of the road's financing did not appear to have any major rivals in the area, and this mobilization of resources did not significantly reshape politics in the gozar, which was relatively small and primarily qaum-based.

A LACK OF REPRESENTATION

Another example of the limits of political mobilization in Istalif is the parliamentary elections of September 18, 2005, a year before I arrived in town. My data on the elections comes primarily from people's recollections of the elections, which often seemed to parallel the way Istalifis discussed other political issues (such as the paving of the road). The 2005 elections were for the Wolesi Jirga, the Lower House of Parliament, and the Provincial Council, but the campaign for Wolesi Jirga was perceived as the more important of the two.[4] The election was conducted through a single, nontransferable vote that outside observers often criticized.[5] This rather confusing system stifled political parties and encouraged an incredible number of candidates; voters across each province had to study long lists of candidates and choose only one. Each candidate was allowed to choose a basic symbol (from Microsoft Word) that would identify himself on the ballot. Istalif was the northernmost district in the province; those living just over the hill voted in Parwan Province elections. In Kabul, there were 390 candidates for 33 seats.[6] Due to this incredibly high number, there were not enough symbols, so many candidates were represented by multiples of the same symbol; for example, one pear represented one candidate, two pears represented another, and three pears represented a third candidate.

While several Istalifis ran for a seat in the Wolesi Jirga, none was successful. People expressed surprise at this failure, and some blamed corruption, although there was little evidence for that. Most were convinced the election had been shaped more by political deals between candidates and other leaders, as opposed to ballot-box tampering. Their surprise did not seem entirely un-founded. Istalifis pointed to the fact that a Qara Bagh representative had been elected in 2005, while Istalif's candidates had lost. In the past, Istalifis claimed, they had had a representative and Qara Bagh had been unrepresented. Qara Bagh, just to the east, had expanded rapidly in recent years due to its location along the highway. Based on informal surveys, a higher percentage of residents had moved there within the last two generations.[7] Perhaps because the area was more divided ethnically, qaum-based political organization was not as impor-tant there as it was in Istalif. Most Istalifis felt that those who were relatively newly arrived in Qara Bagh should have had more difficulty mobilizing, and yet it was the candidates in Istalif who struggled.

Despite their difficulty marshalling votes, several informants noted how political figures in town appeared, to a degree, to be cooperating, particularly the commanders. No major commander was a candidate—although candi-dates with militia backgrounds did stand for election in other areas for several reasons. While there were rumors that members of Parliament would receive general amnesty for all past crimes, this did not occur in the years immedi-ately following the 2005 election, and people seemed skeptical of this possibil-ity from early in the election process. Especially for the three or four leading commanders in town, it was difficult to see how possessing one of the 249 seats in Parliament could have expanded their already significant informal powers. More important, however, was probably the threat of standing and losing the election. Losing would have revealed to the public that the commander had weakened and could neither motivate voters nor leverage political connections with the election committee to win through fraud. In a heavily monitored elec-tion that was supposed to be conducted through secret ballots—particularly in Istalif, which was close to Kabul—it was, perhaps, difficult for a commander to assume he could win illegally.[8]

Had one commander stood, his rivals might have felt compelled to stand as well, rebuilding support for their groups and threatening government interven-tion. Instead, the commanders' strategy in Istalif was shaped by masterly inac-tivity. None of the commanders campaigned publicly for a candidate; they tried to keep a low profile during the entire election, only making it quietly known that they supported certain candidates. Their strategy seemed to be to sup-port an ally who was close enough that they would receive political favors if the ally was elected, but distant enough that a loss would not reflect on the com-manders. This led to a series of somewhat atypical alliances. Mohammad Zaher, the central commander in Istalif, joined forces with the town's central religious leaders and supported the mawlawi's son. The son of the mawlawi was associated with Burhanuddin Rabbani's branch of Jamiat-e Islami, which was generally considered the most effective and moderate of the mujahideen parties in the area. Most agreed that this candidate had received the most votes in Istalif.

Membership in Jamiat-e Islami may have helped the son of the mawlawi, since Rabbani's branch won an estimated ten seats, while affiliates of other branches won an additional twelve, making it one of the strongest parties in Parliament.[9] In Istalif, however, most people were utilitarian when it came to political parties, rarely discussing the political ideology of any party. During the jihad, they had supported the parties that had been most active in providing supplies and resources, either in Istalif or in refugee camps in Pakistan. Further complicating matters, Istalifis respected the charisma and effectiveness of the leaders of certain parties even when the party had little support in Istalif. Thus, they sometimes spoke highly of a figure such as Dostum, the Uzbek nationalist leader from the north, as a strong mujahideen leader, but no one would have joined his Uzbek nationalist party. In the post-Taliban period, NGOs and other organizations weakened the influence of political parties, because they were more effective suppliers of aid. On a national level, the election's single, nontransferable vote system further marginalized parties—there was no system of nomination, no mention of party on ballots, and no limit on the number of candidates who could run for office.[10] Thus, while the son of the mawlawi had the support of what was probably the most popular party in town, this did not guarantee success in the election.

Running against the son of the mawlawi were two main opponents. Qazi Ahmad was from Istalif, but had been a judge in Kabul before leaving his position to run for Parliament. He was associated with Ethad-e Islami, led by the former mujahideen Abdul Rasul Sayyaf and often referred to simply as "Sayyaf's party." Qazi Ahmad was not a Sayed, but his son and daughter had married into Sayed families, and he had close ties to the Sayed Atiqullah, the second most important Istalifi commander, who, like Mohammad Zaher, lived primarily in Kabul. Religious figures and former militia members had ties with both of the first two candidates (the son of the mawlawi and Qazi Ahmad), effectively splitting their votes. Agha Mohammad was the other opponent running against the son of he mawlawi. He was from a family that had been prominent in the government before the Soviet invasion. His father had been a malik who later became the Istalifi representative to the government (*wakil*).[11] His brother was the district governor of Kalakan, located between Kabul and Istalif; as a result, he had more active government connections in Kabul than the other candidates. Though people spoke respectfully of them, the family had not maintained enough active political interests in the town to convince enough Istalifis to support his candidacy. There were also some rumors, which I could never confirm, that Agha Mohammad's brother had fallen out with Mohammad Zaher, and this also hurt his appeal.

The town's votes were split among these three candidates. Allies of the primary commander or the mawlawi supported the mawlawi's son, those opposed to the commander and those supporting the Sayed qaum tended to vote for Qazi Ahmad, and those opposed to the commanders in general supported Agha Mohammad.[12] In discussing election tactics, some Istalifis felt the son of the mawlawi had really failed due to fraud, though most believed there was limited corruption in Istalif. Instead there were rumors of paying ballot counters in Kabul to change tallies. This conforms to some other accounts of the election, but certainly not all.[13] One young man from Qara Bagh told me he had been hired in Kabul to be an election monitor in the district where his uncle was a candidate. His uncle had expected him to stuff ballot boxes for him, which he refused to do. The circulation of stories such as these further delegitimized the political process among Istalifis. The young generation, in particular, treated the elections dismissively. In the province of Kabul, voter turnout was only 36 percent—24 percent lower than the turnout for the presidential elections just a year earlier.[14]

Among these candidates there was a degree of intercategory cooperation and mobilization that was often absent from politics in Istalif, but there were still sharp divisions, even within groups. The two commanders allied themselves with local religious figures for the election, thereby dividing the religious vote—no candidate successfully claimed more religious legitimacy than any other. Importantly, no major religious figure stepped forward to claim that one candidate had religious legitimacy, and no commander openly declared a candidate to be the heir to the jihad. Instead, support tended to be lukewarm and subtle. Competition between the commanders, the fractured nature of political categories in Istalif, and the failure of any political actor to fully endorse a candidate doomed the candidates to failure.

A look at the candidates throughout the province of Kabul reveals a similar pattern. Although candidates could not include party affiliation on the ballot, they could attach honorific titles to their names, and these had very different implications. For instance, numerous candidates included the honorifics "hajji" and "mawlawi" on the ballot. Some marked themselves as "engineer" or "doctor," and several female candidates used the term *bi bi*, a respectful endearment for grandmothers. In the absence of effective political parties, in a system that discouraged party affiliation, and faced with an overwhelming number of candidates, voters were forced to decide on the basis of categories, not on the political actors' actual beliefs. Across the province, usage of these categories and the single nontransferable vote system fractured potential voting blocks, allowing some candidates to win with few votes. This created a Parliament that was extremely splintered and legislators who were rarely effective.

THE POLITICAL LANDSCAPE OF THE BAZAAR

Masterly inactivity did not simply shape the decisions of the most powerful political actors in town; it was found in most public settings. The bazaar, situated in the middle of town, just above the river and between the hills where the shrine and government offices sat, was the most contested space in town. (See Map 2, page 187.) The bazaar had more than two-hundred shops along two streets that intersected to form an L. Although it had been entirely destroyed in the fighting with the Taliban, since 2002 it had been for the most part restored, with only a small section to the east still in a state of relative disrepair. Based on photographs from private collections, the bazaar's outward appearance had changed little, despite its destruction, except for the use of more metal and concrete in construction.[15] The center of the bazaar had also shifted somewhat to the west. The town mosque had been rebuilt at the eastern end of the new bazaar. The old mosque, highly damaged but not destroyed in the fighting, still stood another 100 yards to the east, in a section of the bazaar that had not been rebuilt. Correspondingly, many of the homes just above or below the western end of the bazaar were inhabited and at least partially restored, while most buildings on the eastern end remained in ruins, including the former town *hammam* (bathhouse).

All the pottery shops and most of the craft shops were on this east-west road, which was wide and easy to wander. The steeper street, which ran north-to-south between the boys' school and the river, was occupied primarily by small grocery shops and several teahouses (chai khanas). Set slightly back on the western side of the street was the central girls' school. Below the north-south road, the street opened up. The town's taxi and minibus stand was near the bridge, along with a series of more temporary pushcart and corrugated metal shops. On Fridays in good weather, this area became the animal bazaar.

The politics of space and ownership in the bazaar were complicated. Each of the political groups described in the previous chapter was present, in some form, in the bazaar. This was due partially to the economic importance of the bazaar, and partially to its symbolic significance as the religious, social, and political center of the town.[16] Despite the economic and symbolic capital available—the division of which was constantly renegotiated in the bazaar—competition was muted and tensions dulled by the fact that most of the economic and political competitors in the bazaar were influenced by masterly inactivity. This does not mean there was no tension in the bazaar, but the tension was rarely overt. I observed only one slightly violent incident, due to the collective strategies of those involved in the bazaar.

The bazaar was not a part of any one gozar, so no single qaum had significantly more influence there than any other. There was a slight tendency for similar stores to group together, such as pottery shops near other pottery shops and grocers close to grocers, but this was much less prevalent than in the Kabul bazaar or other Central Asian bazaars. Qaums with more shops, such as the pottery qaum, were more visible in the bazaar, and the malik of the potters visited the bazaar regularly. Several other qaums were also visible, including the pustin duz (skin sewers) and the Sayeds, who owned several grocery shops, while several larger qaums in town were generally underrepresented. For example, the weavers, one of the largest qaums in town, had only three members in the bazaar— one with a yarn shop and two who owned shops that they used primarily for storage space. Although a large part of Istalif's income came from carpets and other woven materials, merchants generally purchased them directly from the homes of the weavers, bypassing the bazaar entirely. This practice limited the diversity of businesses in the bazaar; several potters had branched out and owned bakery and craft shops, but this was not true of any of the weavers.

There was also some government presence in the bazaar. The boys' high school, though it had little involvement in the town's daily politics, was the most symbolically significant government building, after the district governor's office. The school stood at the intersection of the two main bazaar streets, with a commanding view of the area, and was the site of voting on election day. In addition, one of the town's police outposts was set back from the bazaar, with an entrance on the north-south road. Police presence in the bazaar was limited, although after the new police chief's arrival halfway through my time there, it became increasingly common to see young policemen squatting or sitting in metal folding chairs at the entrance to the compound. Even then, they rarely patrolled the streets and seemed content simply to mark the police post as government-controlled space.

Former militias were less visible, but their presence was still felt. As a group, their power was less spatially defined than that of the qaums, who tended to live in one neighborhood, or the government, which occupied a few key buildings. While the main commanders in town rarely visited the bazaar, only driving through on their way to meet with allies or praying at the mosque on holidays and funerals, several men who regularly visited the bazaar were known as important deputies to the commanders. One of them owned one of the main bakeries, though his family did not have a background in baking. He generally sat watching the activities in the street, talking with passersby, and only occasionally helping the men who worked for him. He came from a relatively poor family, and it was never clear how he had collected the money to open the bakery. The implication was that Mohammad Zaher had helped him in exchange for the man's active position in the bazaar. But he was not the only former militia fighter there; several other key figures maintained connections with commanders for whom they had previously fought. In addition, commanders maintained economic interest in the bazaar; several owned property and collected rent from various shopkeepers.

NGOs also maintained space in the bazaar. The women's center, established by a European NGO, had a shop where crafts were sold, although this shop had trouble competing with the pottery shops and other craft stores in town. It would have been difficult for a woman to run the shop, so the women's center hired a man who had been wounded during the wars. Unfortunately, he was rather lackadaisical in his attempts to bring in customers; if anything, the women's center shop inspired other shopkeepers to sell additional crafts. Other shops remained more competitive, because the NGO shop relied exclusively on local crafts produced by women and a fixed-price system that did not let the business optimize its prices for each type of customer, as the potters did. Unsurprisingly to most in the bazaar, the shop closed near the end of my time in Istalif.

Other NGOs made their presence felt in less overt ways. An Afghan NGO that had provided microloans to several small businesses stipulated that its name must appear on the signs of each shop that had received money. Another NGO that was conducting surveys and preparing the bazaar for electrification spray-painted numbers on the doors to all the shops, in an attempt to create an address system (which greatly facilitated some of my surveying). The NGO office where I stayed also served as a visitor's center, where occasional tourists would stop to watch a pottery demonstration or read about Istalif's history. As security worsened, however, the number of visitors declined.

International visitors passed through the bazaar as well, especially the military. In addition, international organizations came through the bazaar, such as a group that sponsored a mobile public library, which occasionally lumbered through town in a converted bus. The French troops in charge of patrolling the area often passed through, but they preferred to park their vehicles on the hill above the bazaar. Other military groups also visited the town and parked in the bazaar or by the river directly below the bazaar. Sometimes these groups would leave their vehicles and shop for pottery or crafts, although this was more common with small groups, such as the Special Forces or the Army Corps of Engineers who worked on a few dams in the area, than it was with larger patrols.

Religious leaders were perhaps the least active group in the bazaar, though they were still visible in the public space surrounding it. The central mosque was at the far end of the bazaar, and most shopkeepers went there to pray during the day. The potters went to the mosque in their gozar when they were at home making pots, but if they were spending the day in their shops, they prayed in the bazaar mosque. As a result, the head mullah, and other mullahs, were often visible in the bazaar, but due to the tension between economic and religious interests, they were far less a part of economic struggles of daily life there. It was out of place for a mullah to haggle over prices, for example, and considered bad form for a shopkeeper to overcharge a religious figure. In addition, *zakat* (alms giving) in Istalif was rarely formalized, and some shopkeepers refused to take any money from the more important mullahs, considering this a small act of charity.

TENSIONS AND COMPETITION IN THE MARKETPLACE

Despite the large number of political actors and the significant economic resources available in the bazaar, there was little overt competition. Instead, the bazaar generally had an air of sluggishness. Competing publicly for customers was taboo, and while owners of pottery shops occasionally approached foreigners, they never did so when a visitor was talking with another shopkeeper. In fact, approaching a customer at all was considered somewhat uncouth. More acceptable was to invite a potential customer in for tea and conversation, with the clear hope that this would eventually lead to business. Shopkeepers in other stores, especially grocery and fuel shops, which relied on a higher volume of customers and had lower per-transaction returns, did even less to directly solicit business. They never approached a customer, and waited disinterestedly to see what shop the shopper would choose. This quiet atmosphere contrasted sharply with the jostling and shouts of bazaars in Kabul, but the difference did not seem to be simply due to the volume of business.

For the most part, similar stores in the Istalif bazaar sold similar wares for similar prices, and for several items, such as cigarettes, soda, and bread, prices were absolutely fixed throughout the bazaar. Attempts to distinguish one's store were muted, and direct marketing initiatives, such as the installation of a new sign, were rare. Once a change had been made, however, other shops would quickly follow suit. For example, pottery shops increasingly sold other kinds of souvenirs, imitating the success of a few stores. Competition among pottery shops was more intense than it was between shops that catered strictly to Afghans, such as grocery shops and teahouses. Pottery shops were the only shops in the bazaar that regularly sold to foreigners, and the only ones that had the opportunity for the windfall profits that foreigners, unaccustomed to local prices, brought with them.

Attempts by other types of shops to distinguish themselves from competitors were even more subtle. For example, one bakery that had sold only baked goods began to sell candies and a few other dry goods usually purchased at grocery stores. This allowed customers to go to one shop, instead of visiting both the bakery and the grocer (which most families did daily). Within a couple of months, several other bakeries had adopted this practice. Notably, the bakery that had started the trend was run by two brothers who had been potters and were new to the baking business.

Perhaps the most interesting accusation of imitation was by an Istalifi whose father was a carpet merchant in Kabul. He claimed his father was the first to use the last name Istalifi.[17] It was fairly common to find merchants in Kabul, whose families had originated in Istalif, using the name Istalifi, particularly on Chicken Street. This was an effective strategy, as Istalif was known in Kabul as a beautiful area that made high-quality crafts. The man claimed that all his competitors using the name had taken it from him. Shopkeepers who claimed to have originated these ideas often grumbled about their peers' imitation, but there was no evidence of direct confrontation over any of the changes in marketing strategies. Instead, most of the competing shops eventually followed the lead of more successful businesses.

These examples are not to imply that consumers did not differentiate between shops; in fact, shops that looked superficially similar had different reputations. I asked one potter, who always bought groceries at the far end of the bazaar, why he bypassed several other shops on the walk from his shop. His answer spoke to the importance of social relationships and economics. He first said that he knew the grocer well and that he was a friend (rafiq), and went on to explain that the man generally had good fruits and vegetables there. This idea, that competition was primarily based on reputation, extended to other types of shops. Some butchers had reputations for having good meat or providing generous cuts, and local customers appeared to be fairly faithful customers of the butchers they frequented. The result was muted competition between these shops and little confrontation. Most shopkeepers used a strategy of masterly inactivity, in which they carefully guarded the reputation of their shops within their social network but did not directly challenge their neighbors. Instead, they gossiped about their rivals, in the hope that undermining their reputations would increase their own business.

The distribution of types of shops in the bazaar indirectly contributed to this strategy of competition. Almost every shop in the bazaar had a direct competitor. Of the twenty-eight types of shops in the bazaar, only a cosmetics shop, a cement store, and a jewelry shop were seemingly without rivals. These cases were unique; the jeweler had recently reopened his shop after being in Kabul for more than a decade. (His store did not seem to be very successful in the brief months he was open while I was in Istalif.) The cosmetics shop sold many goods that could be found in a pharmacy or household goods shop, so it was not entirely without competitors. Similarly, most large-scale construction sites purchased cement directly from Kabul; the cement store's main customers were Istalifis doing very small jobs.

The majority of shops in the bazaar dealt in high volumes with lower profit margins. This was true of seven of the top ten types of shops in the bazaar. The only exceptions were pottery shops and the metal workshops, both of which relied on relatively large purchases from a limited number of customers. The third category, tailors and cloth sellers, fell between the two extremes. Tailors and metalworkers relied heavily on their reputations among Istalifis; metalworkers had relationships with laborers who used them primarily for construction projects. As we have seen, potters were willing to be marginally more aggressive in their marketing, because the potential profit from each customer was higher than it was in other shops (see Chapter 4).

A large number of competitors opposed changing marketing strategies and breaking taboos about how to interact with customers. For most shopkeepers, the greater the potential profit, the more competition was shaped by rumors and malicious gossip. (For example, there were metalworkers and tailors with good and bad reputations, but it was rarer to find a grocer with a notable professional reputation, good or bad.) Further dampening competition was the tendency to imitate other shops; even small marketing shifts were countered by competing stores, ensuring a continuous return to the status quo. Particularly because the profit margins in most shops were minimal, the economic advantage of a confrontational strategy rarely outweighed the potential increase in customers and profit.

The lack of direct competition resulting from masterly inactivity contributed to an absence of violence in the bazaar. What made this even more interesting was the great deal of violence among children in public areas. Small children often wrestled rather aggressively in the streets around the bazaar, and high school boys regularly had brutal confrontations in front of the school. The shopkeepers and other adults in the area eventually broke these fights up, but there was no urgency in their actions, and they often allowed a fight to run its course. The only violent confrontation I observed among adults in the bazaar was between the bakery owner mentioned above and an engineer working for a French NGO. The two men shouted at each other and eventually there was some pushing, but other shopkeepers quickly pulled them apart. When I inquired about what had led to the fight, most people tried to dismiss it as the result of tension from fasting (it occurred during Ramazan). The incident ended remarkably quickly; afterward, observers went out of their way to tell me it had been insignificant.

Public violence in Kabul's market areas seemed much more common. On several occasions, I watched minor car accidents and incidents at police checkpoints quickly escalate into fistfights. Especially after car accidents in Kabul, it was not uncommon to see men threatening each other with tire irons. I never observed the equivalent in Istalif.

I was involved in only one accident, when the minibus I was riding in hit and injured a young goat being watched by a small nomad boy, just outside the town. The boy ran after the minibus with his staff; soon, a dozen of his relatives appeared. The minibus stopped and the men got out. At first, the atmosphere was tense, with passengers and nomads milling around, looking at the injured goat. The eldest man from the minibus quickly took charge, identified the oldest nomad, and began negotiating a settlement. With occasional interjections by the passengers or nomads, they discussed the recent market price of an adult male goat, adjusted it for the young age of the injured goat, and considered the fact that the goat might survive. Finally, the group agreed that 1000 afghanis ($20) was a fair payment. The minibus driver claimed not to have that much money with him, so the eldest passenger provided it. Both groups left the scene, the men in the minibus appearing relieved.

The contrast in the tendency toward violence in Kabul and Istalif was created by the social and political relationships between the various actors. In a traffic accident in Kabul, the participants were likely strangers; their acts probably would have no future repercussions, especially if the police remained uninvolved. In Istalif, on the other hand, in the bazaar, everyone knew everyone, at least by reputation. Because of business ties, kinship, and political alliances, any incident had lasting implications. In the case above, even though the minibus passengers did not personally know the nomads, the same group passed through town twice a year and often grazed their animals in the area. For the most part, settled Istalifis spoke disparagingly of the nomads, but there was also a desire not to engage with them—they could become more of a nuisance by disrupting the informal agreements about land use in the area. As a result, the elder in the minibus was willing to negotiate with the nomads even if it cost him financially. In this case of masterly inactivity, because the goat was already injured, there was no opportunity to try to undermine the opposing side. Instead, the best strategy was to act as quickly as possible to restore the balance, and then behave as if the incident had never occurred.

THE POLITICS OF OWNERSHIP

Shopkeepers made up what could be considered Istalif's middle class, and shopkeeping was generally more lucrative than day labor. Several grocers and pharmacy owners were well off by Istalifi standards, while others, such as the man who bought used sweaters in Kabul and then unraveled them to resell the yarn, were considered poorer than average. In contrast, the men who owned the stores, collecting monthly rents from the shopkeepers, were almost all very well off by Istalifi standards. In addition, building owners often owned land or other businesses, frequently in Kabul. Although owning the buildings that housed the shops required significantly more economic capital and provided a higher return, this group followed a similar pattern of masterly inactivity and conflict avoidance.

The 217 shops I surveyed in the bazaar were owned by 46 men. There were some concentrated holdings—six men owned more than ten shops each (with the maximum being 25). Only 11 men owned a single shop each, and 18 men owned between three and ten shops each.[18] No pottery shop was owned by its shopkeeper. In fact, there were few cases in which a shopkeeper owned his shop. For example, one pharmacy at the far end of the bazaar was owned by the same family that ran it. This is not entirely surprising; pharmacies tended to be more profitable than other businesses, but they also required more expertise and more working capital to purchase the stock. Most people who owned three or more shops were either from the new merchant class or were commanders—or they were closely associated with one of these groups. The carpet seller mentioned above (the first to take the name Istalifi), along with a business partner and two relatives, owned 19 shops on the southern side of the east-west road, where many of the pottery shops were located. The men had purchased gardens below the bazaar and collected rent from the shops in front of their gardens. Commanders were more likely to own shops on different parts of the street; their shops were not necessarily tied to a specific area of the bazaar.

The pattern of merchants and commanders owning property in and around the bazaar was not surprising; these were the two political groups in town with the greatest access to economic capital in recent decades. What is surprising is that there was not more competition within or between these groups, when it came to owning property within the bazaar. The three commanders usually referred to as the most important in town all owned shops or had close associates who owned shops, but there was no visible conflict among them in the division of rents for buildings located close together. It was remarkable, too, that the government did not interfere more actively in property ownership within the bazaar. While it did not own any of the bazaar's buildings, the road and the open land below the bazaar were government properties. In this area were several carts whose wheels had been removed to create semi-permanent stalls. One was run by a butcher; two others close to the taxi and minibus stand offered tire repair services. Though on public land, all three carts paid rent to a commander who was feuding with the district governor. People generally regarded the commander as the "owner" of that land. The commander claimed that the government had granted him the right to use the land, although he gave no real explanation for why the government would have done this or what ministry had granted him this right.

Not only was there no overt struggle over property rights, there was also little direct economic competition. My in-depth interviews with shopkeepers indicated that rents were fixed between 500 and 1500 afghanis per month ($10 to

$30) for each shop unit. (For shops with two units, whose dividing wall had been knocked down, the rate was about double.) While I discussed many economic issues with shopkeepers, they rarely discussed rental rates, and most did not complain about the cost of rent as a major variable in their daily business. However, several young potters who owned craft shops expressed the desire to open shops on Chicken Street in Kabul, but pointed to high rental rates as the major obstacle to opening a shop in that area. Somewhat surprisingly, there seemed to be little location-based variation in rent in the Istalif bazaar; the only significant variables were the size of the shop and the extent of recent renovations, such as a concrete floor, which most of the shops had. Despite the higher rent the renovations would bring, however, most owners were reluctant to invest in their shops. Several shopkeepers complained about the lack of maintenance, and the owners' expectation that shopkeepers were responsible for renovations. In one case, when a barbershop moved down the street because of the expansion of a neighboring shop, the barber and his relatives took every piece of wood out of the shop, leaving only the brick and concrete shell.

Several potters near the mosque, at the far end of the east-west road, complained about the rental price structure. Although they paid as much in rent as the pottery shops closer to the high school paid, they felt that proximity to the high school attracted international customers, because most visitors approached from the west. In the area near the mosque, there were also far more vacant shops or shops being used for storage, whereas all the shops near the high school had occupants. Since most shopkeepers in prime spaces were unwilling to move, those closer to the mosque were generally blocked from the best locations. (In their complaints about location, however, the shopkeepers near the mosque did not mention that the mosque was commonly visited by Kabulis who had come to Istalif for the day.)

It was clear that the owners of the buildings in the bazaar probably did not charge as much rent as the market could bear. With so many shops rented simply for storage by potters and other shopkeepers, visitors to Istalif often remarked on how empty the bazaar seemed. I never heard of a building owner being frustrated by his inability to rent a shop. For the owners, the guarantee of a steady income was more important than optimizing income, especially with the risk of confrontation with other owners in town, or the risk of losing income if a shopkeeper chose to move rather than pay a higher price.

Contributing to this inactivity was the fact that most building owners were important political and economic actors who did not collect rent themselves, sending young male relatives or employees instead. These men had less to gain from raising rents, and more to lose because of their weaker political positions. They had little interest in maximizing profit, and were more interested in making the collection process painless, to avoid conflict with other actors in town.

It is worth noting that at least some building owners took the time to maintain shops that brought in only $20 each month, a relatively small amount of money for them. This was particularly true for the commander Mohammad Zaher, who owned only four shops and probably collected no more than $80 in monthly rent. He also owned a car dealership in Kabul, so it was clear that he was maintaining his shops for more than economic reasons. (The same was true for several other merchants with more lucrative businesses in Kabul.) For such men, giving up shops was not so much about losing economic capital as about maintaining their political influence and, more importantly, keeping their rivals from gaining political influence. By collecting a small amount of rent from a few stores, these powerful individuals ensured that they had allies in the bazaar who would work to remain in their favor. This relationship was an easy, inexpensive way to create and maintain social and political alliances in an important public area of Istalif.

Thus, while the bazaar represented economic opportunity and flux more than anywhere else in town, shopkeepers and building owners alike worked to minimize both change and overt competition. Each group had been allotted an economic share of business in the bazaar, and most were unwilling to pursue growth strategies if it meant risking the loss of economic and political capital. Among shopkeepers and building owners, there was a sense of conservatism, a desire to avoid conflict (especially public conflict), and a general pattern of masterly inactivity.

LAND DISPUTES

One of the greatest sources of political tension in Afghanistan following the fall of the Taliban was land disputes. The five million refugees who had fled the country, along with many other internally displaced people and a general lack of legal documentation before the fighting began, all contributed to the confusion. In many ways, Istalif's situation was worse than that of other areas. The town had been completely abandoned after the second round of Taliban attacks in 1997, and Istalifis, for the most part, did not return as a group, meaning there were plenty of opportunities to usurp the land of those who returned later. Many people had land titles in Istalif, but such documents lacked uniformity. Older deeds were handwritten, and amendments were usually made by a set of signatures of various witnesses on the back. Deeds had been issued and reissued under a series of different governments. Because these were such important documents and many Istalifis were not convinced peace would last in Afghanistan, some owners had left the titles to their land with relatives in Pakistan. And despite the value of these documents, community consensus was often far more important, because ultimately that consensus would determine a deed's validity.

Even when documentation was not disputed, boundaries were. The damage to structures in town, from buildings to boundary walls, was augmented by years of neglect from the time the town had been abandoned. Mud boundary walls had crumbled and were beginning to wash away in the rain. Recent returnees, desperate for building materials, had contributed to the decay by using rocks from fallen walls to rebuild their homes. The remains of boundary walls gave a sense for where lines had been, but there was plenty of room for interpretation and dispute in Istalif's fertile vineyards and orchards. In addition, most Istalifis claimed that more land was being bought and sold than was the historic norm, because nonresident Istalifis sold plots to those who had returned.

There were few taboos on selling and purchasing land, and in several cases, families from one gozar bought land in another gozar dominated by a different qaum. In most cases, that land was on the edge of the gozar, but I occasionally heard complaints about new families moving into certain areas. It seemed that this practice had been less common in earlier eras, but there was enough diversity in more central gozars to suggest that areas had never been strictly homogenous. Despite these transactions, I could not find any cases of Istalifis selling their land to people outside of Istalif. Complicating matters were the many variables that determined land value. Flat, well-irrigated land was valuable in Istalif, but nearby plots were steep, rocky, and worth little. Land above the town's irrigation system was deemed worthless, and it was often difficult to determine whether it had a private owner.[19]

I arrived in Istalif believing land disputes would be interesting demonstrations of local political activity, and this was true in a few cases. The longer I stayed, though, the more I realized that the really remarkable fact was the *absence* of land disputes—and how quickly and quietly Istalifis resolved them. As early as 2002, the UNHCR reported that in the district of Istalif, landownership was "well defined. No problems reported."[20] There was a reluctance to discuss property disputes in formal interviews, and even when they gossiped, the young men in the bazaar rarely brought up land disputes. This was even more perplexing after a land dispute between two families in the town east of Istalif ended in a battle with assault rifles; however, I heard of no such instances in Istalif during my research. The lack of property disputes stemmed not from clarity of ownership and property boundaries (which were often ambiguous), but from the town's collective understanding that land disputes were disruptive conflicts that could upset delicate political balances. I realized this early on.

My realization came when I tried to rent a building near the bazaar. This was not entirely out of place—several NGOs had already rented plots, so I was not the first Westerner to go to the town and negotiate rent. I approached a weaver who had a large house close to the bazaar, but enough removed from other buildings that I would not be intruding on others. He had family nearby and planned to move in with them. His house was situated in a gozar where Sayeds owned most of the land, but the area was not as densely populated as other gozars. It was a typical walled Istalifi compound with the building in a U shape around a central courtyard. The garden in the back of the house was fairly well maintained and had numerous mulberry trees. The garden in front had a few small fruit trees in poor condition; the weaver allowed grass to grow around these trees so his cows could graze there, something that was rarely done in better-maintained orchards. The path to the bazaar from the front of the house led through this garden. After agreeing on rent, the weaver said he would move out of the house by the end of the month. At the end of the month, however, he was still there. I waited another week. Each time I went to speak to him, he gave some vague excuse about not being ready to leave. Eventually, I told him I would need to rent another house. The weaver said he understood, and eventually I rented the house next door.

What I did not realize at the time was that the weaver, who was from further up the valley, had purchased the house near the bazaar about forty years before from a member of the Sayed qaum. The front garden, where the path to the bazaar was located, was a separate plot he had purchased later from another member of the Sayeds. The date he had purchased this garden was not as clear. The weaver said he had purchased it long ago, but some other men I interviewed claimed the transaction had been more recent. The weaver did not have very good relationships with his Sayed neighbors, who said they were offended by his poverty and lack of manners, but they agreed that he had formally purchased the house. Some in the community, however, questioned whether he had actually fully paid for the garden in front of the house. The weaver claimed the deed to the land was in Pakistan, and everyone agreed that the man who had previously owned the land was now a rich man living abroad.

The land was in dispute before my arrival, but the dispute had arrived at something of a stalemate. The weaver's neighbors were not concerned enough to intervene, because they were not claiming the land and because the other previous owner had clearly lost interest in the property. At the same time, the weaver was obviously aware he could lose the land at some future point. For that reason, he had made few property improvements. He had not restored the boundary wall, did not plant high-investment crops such as grapes or new fruit trees, and allowed his animals to graze there, further damaging the trees.

My presence disturbed this calm. The weaver's neighbors had suddenly seen how much he could earn by renting the house to me, and they did not want to see the man advance. I later heard a rumor that the neighbors had contacted their relatives in Pakistan, trying to locate the owner of the land, a much more distant relative. The weaver seemed to believe there was some truth to this story, and decided that the financial gain of renting the house to me was not worth the risk of losing the land in front of his house. At the same time, he refused to acknowledge—to me or to anyone else—that he was staying in his house because of the property dispute. To acknowledge this would have meant also acknowledging that he feared the political strength of his neighbors, and would give credence to their claims that he did not have full rights to the garden in front of the house.

All the political actors in the neighborhood had been using strategies that were in response to the current political situation, leading them to favor masterly inactivity. The possibility of renting the property to a foreigner disrupted this balance by increasing the potential value of the land, and gave the neighbors an opportunity to undermine the weaver's attempts to gain economic capital. The weaver's refusal to invest in the land with new crops can also be understood as an attempt to keep the value of the land low, to avoid conflict. The perception that the value of the land had increased threatened to make political mobilization a more attractive strategy. At the same time, his neighbors worked to ensure that the deal fell through by making it subtly known that the conflict would escalate if he decided to move out. None of these attacks was ever public, and all were difficult to verify—for me, the weaver, or anyone else in the community.

The man I ended up renting from was a generally well-respected member of the dominant Sayed qaum in the neighborhood, who had recently returned from the hajj. He was only distantly related to the men who had been feuding with the weaver, so renting from him did not really threaten the weaver's honor, and renting from the Sayed did less to upset the neighborhood's political balance.

QAUMS AND LAND

Land disputes did not occur solely between individuals. As recounted in the previous chapter, the tract of land near the graveyard above the shrine was contested by both the pottery qaum and the Sayed qaum. As in the land dispute described above, this one involved passage rights more than ownership. Neither the potters nor the Sayeds were entirely pleased with the compromise, but elders from both sides came to an agreement that was generally accepted. The Sayeds, who were marginally more influential in town politics, retained control of the shrine, and the potters gained the right to maintain a path through the graveyard behind the shrine. In this case, both sides had little to gain by continuing the dispute.[21] Because the potters at least managed to secure passage rights, they had not lost much prestige in the town. (Most Istalifis also would have claimed that, in general, the Sayed qaum was stronger than the potters, though no potter would ever admit this.)

If the potters had continued the dispute and not secured control over the shrinekeeper position—and it was unlikely the Sayeds would forfeit such a position—they would have lost respect in town. Because the potters and the Sayeds were two of the more powerful qaums in Istalif, by continuing the dispute and failing to secure the land, the qaum elders would have risked losing the land and a significant amount of honor. Instead of admitting defeat, some potters continued to support a historic precedent for dividing the shrinekeeper position between the potters and the Sayeds, and the hope that in the future, the shrinekeeper might again be a potter. This seemed unlikely, but such statements enabled them to undermine the Sayed qaum's claims without directly confronting them.

In the meantime, young men continued to agitate quietly. Their reputations were less tied to the qaum leaders' ability to negotiate and to the reputation of the qaum in general. A few other potters complained about the situation, but these were generally men with poorer relations with Malik Abdul Hamid. In complaining about the outcome of the dispute, they were not complaining about the Sayed qaum as much as they were complaining about the inability of the Malik and his allies to maintain a resource they believed was historically theirs.

The young men would probably not risk displeasing the qaum leaders, who were their fathers and potential fathers-in-law, unless they thought their odds of success were very high. Though the dispute was not resolved to everyone's satisfaction, both sides had more to lose by continuing—and thus they both observed a strategy of masterly inactivity.

The relative absence of confrontation over property rights reflected the community's general reluctance to engage in disputes with potentially deeper repercussions. Thus, even if a man or family was not satisfied with a particular claim, there was significant pressure to accept the status quo. Land disputes were not simply about ownership; they were about the community's acceptance of certain political balances. Even during more formalized periods before the war, the system was based on a similar value system, in which ownership was based upon social recognition. When a land title was modified, even the most formal deeds were witnessed by community leaders, such as mullahs or maliks, who signed the back of the document. Parcels of land that had been sold numerous times were often represented by deeds with confusing layers of writing on the back, describing each transaction. Signatures by local leaders proved that the community had accepted the land claim and the transaction; the people signing could serve as witnesses in any disputes. During the less stable period following the fall of the Taliban, because the political balance in town was so tenuous, land disputes became increasingly dangerous. This led community leaders to practice and encourage a strategy of masterly inactivity, which made land disputes less noticeable and decreased direct confrontation over property.

WATER SHARING

Though political discord and violence are difficult to quantify in any setting, and measuring changes in political tension in Istalif was challenging, most Istalifis described earlier periods as more full of violent struggles between lineages, maliks, and gozars than recent periods had been. These narratives suggest, at least in the political understanding of most Istalifis, that recent political strategies, particularly what I have been calling masterly inactivity, created a situation that decreased direct confrontation and competition for resources. One such resource was water.[22]

Water remained valuable over different periods time, but it was treated differently during each period. The allocation of water in various orchards and fields was a sensitive political issue. In earlier periods a powerful man, called the *mir aw*,[23] had been in charge of water allotment, but since the fall of the Taliban, the role had lost much of its political import. The following account is based on interviews with several orchard owners who relied on a number of mir aws for their water. It focuses on Mohammad Daud, the mir aw who controlled the irrigation channel that brought water to the potters' neighborhood, the shrine, and most of the area north of the bazaar. Though most of my data comes from recollections that may have shifted over time, the emphasis on the discord of earlier periods demonstrates the degree to which Istalifis understood masterly inactivity as an effective strategy for dealing with a resource such as water in the post-Taliban constellation of political power.

In the era before the jihad, the mir aws' authority was similar to that of maliks. Like maliks, mir aws relied on their reputations to manage resources in certain regions, and each mir aw was influential in an area that received water from one main irrigation channel. In the center of Istalif there were originally five irrigation channels, each with its own mir aw, but one of the channels had been redirected to the hydroelectric plant, so during my time there, only four mir aws were active in the center of town.[24] Each mir aw was said to need to live near the source of the irrigation channel, where it split off from the Istalif River, above town, though in practice this did not always seem to be the case.

As with maliks, the mir aw's son was expected to inherit the position, though this could be disputed. People often stated that if the mir aw's son lacked the personal qualities necessary to be a mir aw—respect from community members, piety, and the ability to mediate between people—they would select a different mir aw. Mohammad Daud was rather adamant that he had not simply inherited this position; he also possessed the qualities necessary to perform the duties well.

Financially, mir aws have some other similarities to maliks. The mir aw was one of the few community members who could successfully and regularly collect money from Istalifis. Much of this money, however, was distributed back to laborers who helped the mir aw maintain the waterway (often from the very family that had paid the mir aw to begin with). According to most accounts, the mir aw seemed to earn little more than a day laborer, and needed additional sources of income.

The mir aw's job was necessary because irrigation channels passed through multiple gozars in which the members of several qaums lived. The mir aw was expected to be impartial. (This contributed to the image some Istalifis had of the mir aw as living alone at the entrance to the channel, high above the town, not within any of the gozars.) The most important skills attributed to the mir aw were honesty and fairness. Istalifis claimed it was necessary for mir aws to be morally strong, so they could resist bribes. This moral authority gave them the power to resolve disputes between maliks without threatening the qaum-based power structures.

In addition to piety, mir aws were expected to have extensive social networks in the area. Mohammad Daud claimed he had been chosen primarily because of his connections with people in different political groups. In earlier times, he had often solved smaller disputes simply by speaking with the people involved. When there was a larger problem, he invited the maliks and other elders, whether they were involved in the dispute or not, to his house for a *mehmani* (gathering), where they ate and then discussed the situation. By inviting these political actors into his house, he made each of them a *mehman* (guest), which decreased each one's power and put them all on equal footing. This arrangement enabled the group to come to a solution that might not have been possible elsewhere. The setting gave the mir aw authority as the host, and allowed maliks, who rarely accepted invitations except for formal occasions (such as weddings or funerals), to set aside the burden of hosting others without forfeiting any honor.

Other disputes were settled at meetings at the mosque, another neutral site. This was not always an ideal solution, because such a gathering involving more than one group would need to take place at the town mosque, not in any individual gozar's mosque, making the issue highly visible and potentially heightening the political tension. The town mosque was generally used as a gathering place only to discuss issues that affected the whole district, such as the upcoming elections. When the district governor was involved, he held meetings in the government building where his offices were. Mohammad Daud told me that the government only involved itself in larger water disputes, such as between towns. In these cases, he said, the district governors did not mediate the dispute themselves; they instructed the mir aws or maliks to resolve the situation instead.

Disputes of that size, Mohammed Daud told me, had rarely happened before the Soviet era. During the jihad against the communist government, the position of mir aw had apparently become increasingly politicized. As political parties became more important, if a mir aw was a member of one political party, he would generally refuse to allocate water to members of other parties. Mohammad Daud said that aside from their involvement in issues such as water allotment, joining political parties was generally *be-fawydah* (without benefit). Increasingly during this period, water distribution became an instrument political parties used for attracting followers. Mohammad Daud claimed that people were arming themselves more, and that quarrels escalated easily without the threat of government intervention. He continued to have mehmanis to resolve disputes, but it was only because of his numerous connections that he was able to continue as a mediator. This conforms to the general explanation Istalifis gave, that during the jihad, ideological differences between groups were unclear, but quarrels still tended to escalate quickly. Support for one commander over another tended to favor the resources he provided, rather than his political agenda. With so much at stake, the battles over resources were intense.

In some cases, commanders took control of irrigation channels and forced taxes on garden owners who used them. This continued after 2001, and while I was in Istalif people discussed similar practices in neighboring towns, but reported that it had ceased in Istalif. Water distribution was still a sensitive subject, however, and young men joked uneasily that Istalifis should cut off the water to the towns downstream. By the time I arrived, Mohammad Daud was retired as mir aw, and the authority of the mir aw position seemed to have declined throughout Istalif. Each spring, orchard owners typically paid the new mir aw about 400 afghanis ($8) for a year of his services; in return, the mir aw's main job was to ensure that the irrigation channel stayed clean and unblocked. When more maintenance was required, he hired several laborers to help him. Orchard owners usually opened smaller gates off the main channel to water their gardens. During the two springs I was there rain was plentiful, and I heard no serious complaints about one garden receiving more water than another.

In the years immediately following the fall of the Taliban there had been severe droughts, but most orchard owners who were concerned about water during this period of rebuilding seemed to complain about the irrigation channels that had fallen into disrepair, more than about the actual lack of water. Political and economic power during this period was derived from the ability to mobilize funds from the government or international agencies to repair damaged channels, rather than from increasing the amount of water received in a garden relative to one's neighbors. Istalif was aided by the fact that its irrigation system was not seriously damaged, and most repairs were straightforward. When a Korean NGO in town built the dam that diverted water to the hydroelectric plant, it also repaired and expanded the entrance to one of the main channels on the opposite side of the river, increasing the amount of water flowing toward the northern side of town. The National Solidarity Program (NSP) repaired several of the channels below the shrine and had much larger irrigation projects west of town. Although the NSP's council included representatives from many groups, including a mullah, maliks, and a commander's representatives, it did not include the mir aw.

These additional public works projects, run by the Afghan government and international organizations, made it clear that the most effective way to increase the water a gardener received was to have an outside group build or repair channels. In another context this might have encouraged cooperation between neighbors advocating for additional funds for projects, but the economic and political structures governing development funds actually discouraged cooperation. Had neighbors worked together to repair the channels around their homes, they would have missed out on aid from NGOs that targeted communities most in need. Similarly, as in the case of paving the road to Istalif, if one community leader advocated for funds from the government or an NGO, he often faced opposition, or at least reluctance, from rival groups, which limited his ability to convince groups to conduct public works projects in the area. With aid money continuing to flow into Istalif, even at a slower pace than in the years immediately after the fall of the Taliban, the best individual strategy for most garden owners was simply to keep the existing channels clean and hope someone would repair the other channels. With less incentive to cooperate and less tension between neighboring garden owners struggling for a scarce resource, the position of the mir aw declined in significance.

Many people reported a decrease in direct feuding between gozars over water, probably because of the violence of such disputes during the war. People saw how systems of taxation on water placed by commanders hurt all those involved and often led to serious violence. The avoidance of open and direct conflict that was part of the Istalifi strategy of masterly inactivity becomes clearer when we consider the issue of water in relation to land disputes, social alliances and feuds, and the distribution of other resources. To feud with a neighbor over water could easily lead to a discussion of property boundaries, whether one individual had received more than a fair share of aid, and retribution for wrongs committed during decades of fighting in and around Istalif. It was in the best interest of very few people to bring such issues to light.

At a higher level, disputes between gozars and towns were dampened because community leaders, such as maliks and mullahs, often had a vested interest in maintaining their authority by settling disputes quietly. Maliks feared challenges from community members with whom they were potentially feud-

ing, and commanders, who had previously taken advantage of political upheaval to tax water distribution, found that avoiding confrontation—with the
government and community members—was more valuable than the amount
of tax they could collect.

All these factors led to fewer open disputes over water distribution, even if
people were still not thoroughly satisfied with their allocations. The decline in
disputes meant that the job of the mir aw became both less necessary and less
prestigious. Some men received money for cleaning the channels, but this job
was very different than the mediation role the mir aws had held before the beginning of the jihad. In the post-Taliban period, the need for mir aws had been
replaced by masterly inactivity.

MASTERLY INACTIVITY AND PRESERVING THE STATUS QUO

As the discussion above demonstrates, there was not simply a lack of political mobilization in Istalif. In many cases, mobilization was rather common.
Within families, qaums, and gozars, there was regular economic cooperation
and a tendency to work together to resolve disputes before they became serious
enough to attract the attention of government officials. In the potters' dispute
with the Sayeds over the shrine, a peaceful resolution meant that because neither side was particularly happy with the outcome, there was the possibility the
dispute would recur. However, to have escalated the dispute under the political
conditions at the time would have required involving other parties (such as the
district governor) in time-consuming meetings, potential bribes, and a loss of
control over the outcome. Avoiding these things created a strong incentive for
quiet cooperation.

Similarly, while there was still considerable enmity between the two main
commanders, there was no direct conflict during my stay. Any serious struggle
would have potentially led to government intervention and sanctions on both
parties. Inaction was also politically convenient for the district government, because any confrontation with these commanders would have publicly tested the
shaky resolve of the local government. Even more devastating, an open struggle between the two could have finally turned the community, which had been
quietly tolerating the commanders, against them. As a result, the commanders
studiously avoided each other; I never observed them in the same place at the
same time, even though they visited the town with some regularity.

As the examples above illustrate, these strategies made it remarkably difficult to mobilize on a larger scale. Despite the fact that paving the road and sup-

porting one parliamentary candidate would have had tangible benefits for all residents of Istalif, the success of any of these ventures would have necessarily increased political capital for some parties. Since any increase in power would have threatened the tenuous balance the town achieved, most political actors found it in their best interest to act conservatively instead of promoting intergroup or townwide mobilization, and in some cases, they worked to ensure that such projects failed.

In addition, the system of international aid distribution in the country, as well as the lack of funds the district government distributed, created a political climate dominated by what might best be called a windfall effect. Funds, projects, and political influence did not increase and decrease incrementally in Istalif. Instead, they came in very large packages (in the shape of a dam, a road, or a new mosque). Orchard owners did not feud over an extra half-hour of water a day, because they were hoping to receive an entire new irrigation channel to their homes. The result of this windfall effect was a system that deincentivized investment in the community and cooperation that would build up enough political capital to incrementally alter the status quo. As a consequence, community members invested only in projects they felt the international community and the government were highly unlikely to support (building a new mosque in the center of town, refurbishing the shrine) or that were economically insignificant (minor irrigation channel repairs, rebuilding boundary walls), and avoiding contributions to projects they felt would receive funding (local schools, the new district government offices).

Compounding this situation was the stated goal of many NGOs: to target "vulnerable populations." In practice, this meant that communities judged to be "in need" by the international community received the most support. Istalifis were effective at shaping their narratives to this rhetoric. Malik Abdul Hamid seemed to have two personas for Western visitors. If he assumed the visitor was tied with an NGO that might be interested in working in the community, he would lament at length about how poor the potters were. If he thought the visitor was a journalist, he would talk about the long and noble history of the potters and how they had helped save Afghanistan from the Taliban. Having received aid from the international community for decades, the Istalifis, like many Afghans, had become aware of the best strategies for encouraging aid to the town—and to their groups in town.

On several occasions, I observed meetings between NGOs and the local *shura* (council). The shura members acted as if the shura was a formal institution in Istalif, with an established tradition of representing the people. In reality, the shura rarely met formally. The most important political meetings in town were much less formal, between a group of individuals in private homes or, occasionally, at the mosque. These gatherings looked very different from the shuras produced for the benefit of international groups, but Istalifis knew well that international groups were more comfortable dealing with groups of elders they felt were representative of the community.

Finally, the tenuous political balance between different categories of political actors meant that real status was unclear and untested. Since there was no direct confrontation, there was no real way to gauge the political might of a group or its ability (or inability) to mobilize a substantial number of people in the town. No one was sure how strong the commanders were, and although people tended to avoid the government, they were not convinced it could really impose its will in town. This instability meant that Istalifis could imagine circumstances that would enable any of the major groups to come completely to power in the next five years. A withdrawal of international troops could lead to a return of the former militias, the Taliban's return could mean increased power for the religious establishment, and a decade of stability and growth could potentially lead to the solidification of government power.

Because the future seemed so unclear, there was a strong incentive for each group to avoid compromise in its interactions with others. Individuals feared being associated with commanders and being perceived as opposing the commanders. For political leaders, sacrificing any political or economic power only meant having less political power in the chaos that might ensue. This shaped the way individuals and groups related to the Afghan state. Because of the uncertainty of both the power and the potential resources that could be extracted from the state, the traditional Afghan antagonism between the state and the periphery was replaced by an elaborate charade, in which individuals acted as if the state had power—even when they assumed it did not. The next chapter discusses the implications of this relationship.

The Director of Intelligence

People in Istalif called Zabiullah the "director of intelligence." What this meant, however, was never clear.

He dressed in plain clothes or in green fatigues with no insignia on the lapel. He sometimes sat in one of the police outposts, sometimes simply appeared in the bazaar or another place in town, and had a tendency to gaze up to the sky as if he were looking at one of the drones from the base, which people frequently talked about.

As an outsider living in town, he checked on me regularly, but not in any systematic or predictable fashion. Several times he claimed not to know me when I met him, but then someone else nearby introduced me, and he acted as if he had simply forgotten who I was.

One evening I was sitting at home, drinking tea and playing cards with a couple of friends, when Zabiullah stuck his head into the room. This was a little odd, but not unprecedented. He came in with three police officers, all in uniform. The three men stopped and took off their shoes, as typically done by anyone entering an Istalifi guestroom, but Zabiullah strode in and sat down without removing his. One of my friends glared at him, but he seemed not to notice.

We poured some more tea for the men, made a little small talk, and then went back to our game. Zabiullah looked out the window into the night as he sipped his tea. He then reached over, took the police radio from one of the officers, and began to listen intently to a conversation between two other men. With the static on the radio, I had trouble hearing what was being said, but Zabiullah seemed focused. He began to speak into the radio, but without pushing the send button. Unsurprisingly, the conversation between the men on the radio did not stop, and Zabiullah began to raise his voice. A couple of my friends glanced at him, but continued playing cards. After a few long seconds, one of the policemen leaned over and tried to help him, telling him to push down the talk button. Zabiullah harshly told him to leave him alone. He continued fiddling with the radio for some time, then casually handed it back to one of the officers.

He looked at my friend, pointed at me, and asked, "Where is he from?"

"He's from America, but speaks Dari, you can ask him," my friend replied.

Zabiullah seemed amazed that I spoke Dari, even though we had spoken together, in Dari, on several occasions. He began to make small talk with me, but after a couple of minutes began speaking Pashto.

"I don't speak any Pashto," I said, "but I am hoping to study it once my Dari is better." He went back to speaking Dari, but again switched to Pashto after a brief time, as if testing how much Pashto I understood. I tried to get him to switch back to Dari by asking him how long he had worked in Istalif.

"I have always lived in Istalif," he replied.

One of my friends thought he had misunderstood the question and tried to correct him.

"Well, really for the past 14 years," he clarified, staring at my friend before moving on to another topic.

My friend looked somewhat confused. Finally, Zabiullah got up with almost no warning and walked out with his men hurrying after him. My friends and I were left rather perplexed and slightly offended by the visit.

Later, I asked a few people how long Zabiullah had been in Istalif. None of them thought he had patrolled the town for more than a couple of years, and most thought he was originally from Jalalabad. Compared to how much Istalifis knew about everyone else, people had remarkably little information about Zabiullah.

I saw him the next day in the bazaar, leaning on my friend's car. He ignored me. Sometime later that month, I met him in the bazaar again, and he greeted me warmly, "Hello, my French friend!"

A shopkeeper standing next to him shrugged at me, and the conversation continued.

8 THE AFGHAN STATE AS A USEFUL FICTION

GOVERNMENT OFFICIALS, LIKE ZABIULLAH, had limited powers, and yet the state was still a constant topic of conversation among Istalifis. What was interesting about many of these conversations was how Istalifis emphasized the state as a rational, bounded entity, even when the actions of people in town implied that the state had no such clear limits. This public, fictional divide presented a contrast with the categories of local merchants, qaum leaders, commanders, and others that represented real differences in how power was created and used, but which Istalifis discussed much less frequently. Both Istalifis and government officials reinforced this fiction precisely because it allowed political actors to take advantage of the masterly inactivity that masked the true tensions in the area and contributed to the continued flow of aid.

Much had shifted since the pre-Soviet period, when analysts primarily described Afghanistan's political situation as an antagonistic relationship between tribes and the state, even if this was an oversimplification. Academic and popular accounts from this period portray this general pattern.[1] Old men in Istalif described their fear of being seized and conscripted when they went into Kabul, at that time a full day's journey away. Similarly, they described paying taxes, in the form of wheat, to government soldiers each year, and how those attempting to evade the tax were visited by soldiers, whom they were forced to feed and put up for the night.

Since then, a series of regimes seized and lost power, and as transportation improved, Istalif grew politically more integrated with the rest of the country. This was partly because Istalifis increasingly traveled back and forth from Kabul for economic reasons, but also because the fighting on the Shomali Plain, first with the Soviets, and especially with the Taliban, brought national political issues into Istalif and the surrounding countryside. As a result, perceptions of the state's responsibilities, powers, and boundaries had shifted.

In the meantime, anthropologists and political scientists have complicated the divide between Weberian models of the patrimonial and the rationalized, bureaucratic state that pervaded earlier analyses of the Afghan state. These new models often focused on what has been described as the flexible boundaries of the state and on an increasingly nuanced understanding of the way the state functions—in particular, how sovereignty is contested in response to Michel Foucault's notion of governmentality.[2]

Anthropologists have shown how states must use ritual and performance to demonstrate their authority, and also how citizens question claims of the state's monopoly on certain types of power. Literature from South Asia and Africa, in particular, argued that in conceptualizing the state, one must study the way political and economic authority seeps out of the "porous" boundaries of the formal state, into the quasi-official realm of what several writers have referred to as the "shadow state."[3] Despite this, many trying to solidify the hegemony of the state continue to rely on very Weberian rhetoric to describe roles and boundaries. As Thomas Blom Hansen and Finn Stepputat argue, international relations "has for decades assumed states to be both normal, that is, with *de facto* legitimate control of their populations and territory, and identical, that is, with similar interests, strategies, and expected patterns of action." While, in fact, "what is at stake is *de facto* recognition of sovereign power by a local and discerning 'audience' who often pay their dues to several authorities at the same time."[4]

What was remarkable about the role of the state in Istalif was that while the notion of sovereignty was similarly mired in a series of notions of power (see Chapter 6), and boundaries between state and non-state powers blurred, Istalifis and government officials continued to emphasize that the state–society divide was real. This is similar to James Ferguson and Akhil Gupta's argument that many "continue to rely on images of vertically encompassing states, even as the empirical situations being described are becoming ever less amenable to being captured in such terms."[5] What is interesting in the Istalif case is (to use Ferguson and Gupta's terms) that spatially there were real questions about the verticality of the Afghan state, which had a limited ability to encompass the various political actors in town, yet it was in the best interest of all involved to ignore this reality. Questions of sovereignty and power had the potential to raise real conflict, so instead they were left unanswered, with all participants promoting the fiction of clearly defined realms of authority. In Istalif, local actors had also decided it was in their best interest to use rhetoric and symbols that reinforced the image of a vertically encompassing state, even while privately denying its existence.

Instead, the state was a constant, though ambiguous, presence in daily politics. Local officials, who interacted with community leaders using the language of a rationalized state bureaucracy, still relied primarily on personal connections to establish political power. Similarly, local commanders acted as if they were independent of the state, yet maintained active relationships with individuals and state institutions in Kabul. Istalifis, through their interactions with the international community in Afghanistan, and with the more bureaucratic Pakistani state as refugees, also realized that this appearance of rationalization contributed to stability and to the continued flow of development funds to the area.

In the post-Taliban period in Istalif, the idea of the state as rational-legal, bounded, centrally located, and bureaucratically authoritative was a useful fiction that disguised the government's failure to establish a hegemonic power. This fiction dressed the state in formal clothes, allowing local actors to assert their authority within specific areas without publicly defining or testing the state's limits. In an era of relative stability and increasing wealth derived from international aid, government projects, and remittances, testing the state's limits would have, at best, disrupted the growth of prosperity; at worst, it would have revived old feuds, leading to violence and intervention by international forces.

Although all states, to some extent, attempt to disguise the degree to which state and society are intertwined, in the politically uncertain conditions of Istalif, the construction and maintenance of a symbolic state–society division became a useful fiction, created by the economic and political conditions of the times; it helped preserve the peaceful political balance established through masterly inactivity. Evidence from Istalif, however, suggests that while Weberian approaches are clearly less accurate than the descriptions of sovereignty as contested and existing outside the state by writers (including Hansen and Stepputat), there is still a clear incentive to describe the state as legal and bounded, while acting as if it were indeed a rational, authoritative presence.[6]

THE STATE IN ISTALIF

Set against Weber's rational-legal model, the state in Istalif was severely limited. There was a government bureaucracy, headed by the district governor, but governmental structures were weak and far from rationalized. The Afghan government had built a rather impressive bureaucracy in Kabul under Zahir Shah and Daud Khan, but it had never experienced a colonial era that established the much larger state bureaucracies in South Asia and Central Asia. Most of Afghanistan's government apparatus was confined to the major urban centers of Kabul, Jalalabad, and Herat. Following the fall of the Taliban regime, these centers saw the most rapid return of state bureaucracy, often with international financial and military backing.

In Istalif, however, the state's bureaucracy was small, and positions in the bureaucracy did not have the rational-legal authority posited in Weberian models of bureaucracies. Instead, the people within the bureaucracy endowed it with limited power, making dealing with the state in Istalif highly personalized and more similar to Weber's model of traditional, patrimonial forms of governance. For example, arranging a meeting with the district governor was not a simple task for someone without political influence. The key was often the district governor's deputy, a quiet, efficient man who controlled the governor's schedule. When a man without significant political authority needed to petition the government, he almost always brought a local malik, mullah, or another influential elder with him. Coming alone would have meant a longer wait, a less sympathetic ear, and perhaps no audience at all.

Beyond the formal bureaucracy of the government in Istalif there was minimal state penetration into daily life or governmentality in the Foucauldian sense. The few ways the government did try to structure power were highly personalized; for example, local maliks endorsed identity cards before they could be brought to the district governor's office. Whenever I saw Malik Abdul Hamid endorse one of these documents for an unfamiliar petitioner, he asked the person, "*Bach-e kee asteed?*" ("Whose son are you?"). If he did not recognize the name, he would ask for the grandfather's name, reinforcing the degree to which such a document was based on personal and kinship ties and underscoring the lack of rationalization in the system. This pattern fit into wider Afghan trends in which the periphery strove to avoid subjugation to the center, while the center attempted to increase its reach by relying on patronage networks.

The state was particularly ineffective as a redistributive force, collecting few taxes in Istalif and providing minimal services. NGOs supported the delivery of the few services the town received, and Istalifis, like many Afghans historically, had minimal expectations when it came to the delivery of services.[7] Even the services the government paid for were often delivered by individuals working in Kabul, who paid out of their pockets when they visited Istalif—further solidifying personal patronage networks.[8] At the same time, Istalifis still perceived the state as an important force in town politics, and though people sometimes disparaged them, the state and national politics were a common topic of conversation. The state had no monopoly on violence, political legitimacy, or the distribution of goods, but community leaders made no attempt to publicly question the state's claims to power, and the state's presence was constantly visible. Part of this visibility was due to the fact that clear symbols were used to mark the power and boundaries of the state in Istalif.

SYMBOLS AND THE STATE

In Istalif, the state was symbolically set off from the people. This was not an even divide between the state and society; instead, the state was portrayed as the source of reason and legality, surrounded by chaotic personal relations, tradition, and irrationality.

All the state buildings were clearly separated from living spaces, and even the public space of the bazaar and central mosque. The main government building, in a semi-destroyed hotel on the top of the southern ridge, housed the offices of both the district governor and the chief of police. It sat, rather dramatically, on the edge of the ridge looking east over the Shomali Plain and the Bagram Airfield, and north toward the ridge that made up the rest of the center of town. The north and south ridges were divided by the Istalif River, which ran steadily most of the year but raged for several months each spring. The river divided the town in two, with the government headquarters on the south and most other landmarks, such as the town mosque and the bazaar, on the north. Most Istalifis did not live on these two central ridges, but in neighborhoods and villages scattered above and below the center of town. Most of these neighborhoods were self-contained and separate from the neighborhoods in the center.

Creating a symbolic symmetry between the state and society, the Eshan Sahib shrine was on the north ridge, almost directly opposite the district offices. To reach the shrine or the district offices, one had to climb the steep paths that isolated these buildings from the rest of the town. Both were built near irrigation channels where large poplar trees grew, a location that made them pleasant places to sit in the hot summer months. The key difference was that the shrine was a public space integrated into two residential neighborhoods, surrounded by several houses and a small graveyard, whereas the district office was not as close to private space. The public nature of the government space was reinforced by the fact that the French military and visitors from Kabul often parked there. Furthermore, the shrine had been recently renovated by the community, but the government building was still heavily damaged from the years it had served as a military installation.

The few other buildings associated with the government were similarly, if less dramatically, separated from the town's main gozars. The clinic stood just behind the district government building, and most of the police outposts were set back from other buildings. None of these buildings abutted any other buildings, despite the fact that it was common for residential buildings, workshops, and even mosques to be built against each other, particularly in the hilly sections of town. Istalifis often summed up this separation between government and society with the common expression *eenja zindagee na me-kunad*, meaning the state "does not live here." They meant this metaphorically, but there was literal truth to it; all the district officials lived in Kabul and commuted to Istalif each day (as did many, though not all, of the Afghan employees of NGOs in town). Driving from Istalif to Kabul at around 7:00 in the morning, as many laborers did, one could watch the cars of the district governor,

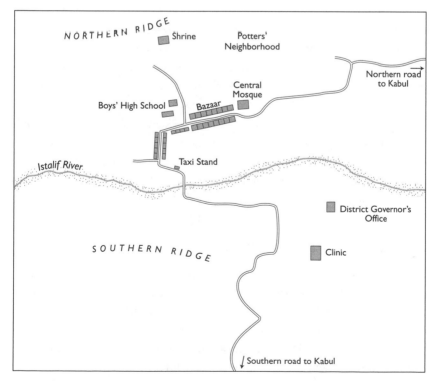

Map 2. The center of Istalif.

police chief, and other officials as they passed by in the opposite direction, on their way into Istalif.

The state was set off geographically from the people in Istalif, but those who worked for the state also used symbols to differentiate themselves from others who simply lived in Istalif. As discussed previously, certain hats marked a man as a state employee. Administrators favored the karakul lambskin hat, which was not worn by any other group in Istalif. The policemen, even when they were off-duty, usually wore their uniforms, which included the distinctive kepi hats. This meant that even when a police officer was off-duty and strolling through the bazaar, he was symbolically separate from the other men he walked past. Policemen drove around in conspicuous green Ford Ranger pickup trucks, which also marked them, even from a distance.

Clothing set off the district governor and the principal of the boys' high school, who were two of the only men in town to wear Western suits on most days. Some Istalifi businessmen who lived in Kabul also occasionally wore Western suits, but when visiting Istalif they often donned their *shalwar kameez*, the traditional robes most Afghan men wore, to blend in with the rest of the Istalifi community. There were other typical symbols marking the power of the state, such as the Afghan flags that hung at police posts and the map of Istalif that hung on the wall directly behind the district governor's desk. These nationalistic symbols were rarely visible outside of government offices.

The images the symbols promoted—the district governor in his Western suit, sitting in his office, in strict contrast with the malik, in his shalwar kameez, holding court on the opposite side of the town—created not an exemplary center so much as an exemplary boundary line that separated the state, assigning certain powers to the realm of the state and others to the realm of society. The state was not absent in Istalif as it was in many other parts of the country, but it was removed, sitting on the hill above town, looking down upon daily political life.

DEFINING STATE AUTHORITY

Political actors may have acted as if the symbols that delineated the boundaries between state and society were significant, but these boundaries would not have been effective if they had been purely symbolic, without material consequences. The fiction was effective because, in many cases, it did produce meaning and defined political authority that was respected by political actors in town, while hiding the ways power was continuously being renegotiated. Just as each part of the town was defined symbolically as state space or people's space, both groups acted as if there were a similar lack of ambiguity on many political issues. In conversations, especially when discussing theoretical issues, it was common for people to conclude, "that is the work of the government," even when concrete examples displayed considerably more uncertainty.

At one formal gathering several elders, including the mawlawi and a malik, were drinking tea after a rather large meal, when the group began to discuss a recent incident in a village west of Istalif. A local man had killed his wife and then committed suicide. The men in the room wanted to know what the mawlawi thought of this, particularly whether the husband's family should be forced to pay compensation to the woman's family, a matter that apparently had come before the district governor. The mawlawi resisted addressing the matter. At first he simply tried to avoid the question. However, once they asked him more directly, he explained that what the man had done was a sin (*guhnah*) against Islam, but the state was involved and the matter of compensation should be decided by the law (*qanoon*). Now that it had passed from his realm of authority to the realm of the state, the mawlawi publicly professed not even to have an opinion on the matter.

Whether the mawlawi actually had a personal opinion or not, acting as if he had no point of view was a wise political choice. Stating an opinion on an issue that was now before the district governor could have had dangerous repercussions for both himself and the government official's projection of his power. Disagreeing with the district governor could have elicited a response that would have revealed the weakness of both sides, but agreeing with the district governor directly would have further legitimized the governor's power and made the mawlawi seem beholden to the state. Instead, the mawlawi's use of masterly inactivity minimized conflict, cost him little, and preserved the useful fiction of the state–society divide.

State officials often acted in a similar manner. Partway through my time in Istalif, when the new police chief was struggling to define his powers, he emphasized his connection to the state in Kabul and declared that it was his duty to bring stability and order to Istalif. Notably, in conversations with me he emphasized his connection with the Ministry of the Interior, rather than his personal relationships with specific officials (as was more typical). When I met with him in his office for the first time, I was accompanied by an employee of a local NGO, who had dealt with him before, and the son of Malik Abdul Hamid. The police chief sat at a large desk, and visitors sat on couches lining the wall of the large room, making conversations awkward. There was a small

Afghan flag on his desk and a heavy nameplate with the chief's name spelled out in Roman letters.

After we entered and began to talk, he paused and dismissed the Malik's son rather rudely. At no point had I seen the Malik's son treated so brusquely, except perhaps by his own father. The police chief explained that because I was a foreigner and my security was his main concern, only those directly associated with my security should be involved. Because the NGO employee worked for an international organization—and was upper class and from Kabul—the police chief did not see him as a threat to my security and allowed him to stay. Probably more importantly, the police chief saw the NGO as on the side of the state and the international community as opposed to the threatening, local society. After the Malik's son departed, the chief rang a bell on his desk to have one of the policemen outside shut the door, emphasizing that such matters should be treated with some secrecy. The policeman outside the office did not seem accustomed to being told to shut the door, and did not respond immediately. The chief rang the bell again impatiently. The confused officer put his head in the door and had to be told directly to shut it. Under these conditions, the police chief was ready to begin discussing my security in Istalif.

The police chief made the environment symbolically secure by removing the Malik's son, whom he portrayed as a threat because he was from Istalif and not part of the formal state order. These actions suggested that the Malik's son and, by extension, all of the Malik's connections, had nothing to do with the town's security. The police chief was symbolically proclaiming the state's monopoly on violence and its ability to provide security.

The varied perceptions of my security in Istalif by different actors were revealing. Most government officials told me the biggest danger to me was local Istalifis, particularly those who were not wealthy and had few connections to Kabul. On the other hand, almost all Istalifis thought the biggest threat to me came from outside Istalif. This threat was often labeled as the Taliban, though they seemed to mean any outsiders at all. In particular, they pointed to criminals from Kabul, many of whom had ties to corrupt government officials. Though most Istalifis did not think government officials were a direct threat to my security, they made it clear that they saw them as corrupt and incompetent, and that if I was not protected by the community, the state would do little help to me. In this case, the responsibility for my security was a contested political issue, but one the Malik's son was willing to concede by leaving the room to avoid conflict with the chief of police.

A STATE WITH NO BOUNDARIES

As this case suggests, attempts to demarcate the state ignored the deep political and economic relationships involving the government in every aspect of local society. Security in Istalif depended on the actions and attitudes of state officials and a variety of other actors, including Taliban members, often working with local criminal groups, and the tacit support of the corrupt government officials. At the national level, the difficulty in defining the state's boundaries was perhaps most apparent in the corruption that took advantage of the complex networks of government officials and local leaders that are typical in patrimonial states. Afghanistan had several high-value industries—mining, logging, and construction—over which government officials had influence. Government officials penetrated even completely illegal industries, such as the opium economy, to the extent that, over a six-month period, each police chief position in drug-rich areas was allegedly being sold for $100,000.[9]

Customs revenue was another area of difficulty in attempts to separate the formal and informal economies. Corrupt officials and complicated procedures caused long waits and incurred heavy costs. In 2005 importation required ten documents with fifty seven separate signatures, and caused, on average, an eight-day delay.[10] These regulations created a space in which officials could demand large bribes in exchange for reducing delays. One Istalifi carpet merchant complained that to export a $3000 rug, it was necessary to pay almost $3000 in bribes. Despite the money lost to corruption, customs revenues still accounted for 55 percent of Afghanistan's total revenue in 2006 and 2007, and had increased from $50 million to $399 million between 2004 and 2009, according to the World Bank. Thus, customs was a national political issue of increasing importance and a point of tension between Karzai and local leaders who controlled customs posts, such as Ismael Khan in Herat and Gul Agha Sherzai in Jalalabad.

In Istalif, illegal rents did not appear to be as important as the political and social capital gained by political figures as they demonstrated their ability to exploit government funds and connections, while remaining independent of state control. When the local commander collected rent from pushcarts parked on what was technically public land, the rent of less than $100 a year was not economically significant, but collecting from these shopkeepers expanded the commander's patronage network and ensured he maintained a presence in the politics of the bazaar. The fact that government officials had not confronted him about collecting these rents quietly suggested that the commander had government connections that were protecting him.

Some cases were less ambiguous; for example, the mawlawi was an officially approved position with a salary from the government. Other cases were more vague. It was never clear how much the state directly acquiesced to the continued presence of certain commanders and their militias in the town. Both the police and the commanders adamantly asserted that they were personally responsible for security in Istalif. A few years before, the main commander had even shared offices with the district governor, but that governor, perceived as too close to the people by authorities in Kabul, had been reassigned to a district closer to Kabul. When I questioned people about the role of these two men and how power had been divided during that period, their answers were vague, reflecting the difficulty in distinguishing between the two, beyond the simple rhetoric that one worked for the government and the other was a commander.

Later, after I left town, I heard rumors that the commander had returned to favor with the Ministry of the Interior and had reopened an office in Istalif. When I inquired further, some people responded that he was working for the intelligence department in the Ministry of the Interior, reporting from Istalif. Others said he was assigned to gather intelligence in Paghman, a district west of Kabul, but was allowed to reside in Istalif. Still others said he continued to have no formal position at all. During this period, instability had increased in the area, with attacks in neighboring districts and in the town. As a result, there was increased anxiety about his position, and such ambiguity made it hard to know how much power he actually had. At the same time, the commander had a clear incentive for maintaining the ambiguity. Because people were unsure of the commander's position, they were unenthusiastic about discussing the issue and only talked about it when I inquired directly.

Illicit figures, such as commanders, contributed to the unclear definition of the state's role, but development aid and the presence of international groups also played a part. Many studies of NGOs focus on the creation of parallel states, and Ferguson and Gupta argue that such "outsourcing of the functions of the state to NGOs" has become central to what they refer to as the "emerging system of transnational governmentality."[11] In Istalif, this created increased ambiguity about what precisely the state was, but this ambiguity did little to change the way people made choices. The common perception was that NGOs were simply an alternative form of providing services that tended to be more effective than the state, but they were not entirely separate from the state. If, for example, a young man wanted to raise capital to start a business, he had several options. He could raise money from relatives and other members of his qaum, he could seek a private loan from a merchant, or he could approach the local NGO about a microloan. Young men usually weighed all these options carefully, perhaps using a combination to raise funds. While I was in Istalif, the unpopularity of the microloan option had nothing to do with local opposition to NGOs. It was based on the amount on time needed to secure a loan and the small amount of money generally available.

The ways NGOs operated in the community further contributed to the ambiguity of the relationship between state and society. Following the fall of the Taliban, the Afghan state did not have the capacity to facilitate or organize the delivery of aid to Istalif and other areas. Similarly, international governments seeking to deliver large amounts of aid relied on subcontracting out this work to an increasing number of thriving NGOs, quasi-NGOs, and private companies based in Kabul. NGOs usually hired Afghans who had been educated abroad, former government officials, or those who had direct connections with government officials. Many of these organizations approached local leaders in Istalif, particularly maliks, and attempted to work through them to deliver aid. One NGO worked directly with a merchant in town to help reconstruct the bazaar.

Further complicating the divide between NGOs and the state, the National Solidarity Program was designed to disperse World Bank funds throughout Afghanistan, but it was also a means of building up local, grass-roots governance. Each community elected a Community Development Council (CDC), which was in charge of determining where funding should be distributed. The CDCs were designed to "emphasise community participation, empowerment, local contributions, and the development of community capacity."[12] In reality, the CDC in the center of Istalif simply reinforced the power of local political actors, who took advantage of the government funds the NSP provided, using funds to create more patronage for themselves, and studiously ignoring the district government. The CDC was composed of a mix of local actors, including Malik Abdul Hamid, a mullah, and a representative of the central commander, each acting independently.

Members used the CDC to increase their individual patronage networks, rather than to gain political capital for the group itself. Residents complained quietly that the CDC tended to spend money only on projects that benefited members of the council and their close allies, but the amount of money being spent by the CDC, once divided, was not enough to cause individuals to complain too loudly. Even though in a village further up the valley from Istalif, the CDC had taken on a more active role in local politics, it was unlikely that the council in Istalif would take on much more of a political role; given the competition of state and non-state actors for political influence, there was little space for a new system to emerge without causing conflict.

Even as the Afghan government became stronger, NGOs' perception of the government as another level of corruption and bureaucracy led many international groups to continue operating through local authorities. While limited, the services and political authority NGOs produced continued to erode the institutional power of the state, thereby increasing the ambiguity of the state's role and adding to the strength of local actors who had access to development funds.

A USEFUL FICTION

Though there was an inherent contradiction in the understanding of political power in Istalif, actors on both sides of the invented state–society divide continued to promote the useful fiction of the clear boundary between the two. Government officials promoted state symbols because they suggested the state was a bastion of rationality and legal authority. Istalifis also supported these symbols primarily because they presented the state as a bounded entity that did not intrude on many daily political matters.

In many ways, the state in Istalif fit the Middle Eastern historical pattern of the state with minimal local purchase or legitimacy,[13] but this did not necessarily limit the impact of the concept of the state on local politics. In Istalif, the state shaped the local landscape, not through direct or tyrannical rule, but through the possibility of intervention. The presence of the state limited the ability local commanders and other actors to expand their authority without risk. Istalifis still felt the government officials had access to outside forces that could disrupt politics in town, whether through personal networks with national political figures or through bureaucracy (the police and the Ministry of the Interior). Direct engagement between government officials and local commanders would have led to serious conflict, but by maintaining only the threat of intervention through its local presence, the government encouraged local political actors to limit actions that exceeded the bounds of their authority. The result was tacit acceptance of the fiction created by these symbols, because it helped preserve stability. Most Istalifis did not use the Arabic term *fitna*, which is used elsewhere to refer to political upheaval, but the concept of social chaos that would occur with a collapse of authority was clearly on many people's minds.

In other cases, actors used the ambiguous definitions of power and political roles to promote the fiction of the state–society divide in ways that solidified their own authority. Traditionally, it was said, the district governor had to recognize the malik of each gozar. Malik Abdul Hamid spoke of having been presented to the district governor by the elders of his qaum, with a formal ceremony that accompanied his installation as malik. More recent accounts stated that there was no longer a ceremony, but made it clear that it was still necessary for the district governor to "accept" each new malik. The malik used this position to reinforce the separation of qaum and state power, claiming he had the exclusive ability to access the power of the state. Of course, others from the qaum could approach the district governor, but the malik tried to be involved in most cases, and the district governor also seemed to prefer to work in this way, because it let him avoid internal qaum politics. Others in the qaum worked to undermine this connection, and on more than one occasion I saw the Malik hurrying off to the district offices after hearing there was some meeting in progress which he felt he should attend.

On the government side, the district governor relied on the maliks to provide information and perform such tasks as announcing new government policies, even though the governor went out of his way to avoid making this interdependence apparent. The state demonstrated its mastery of Istalifi society by reinforcing the idea that the district governor had to approve a malik, though in fact the state had no real recourse if it disapproved. In principle, the state could forcefully remove a malik from office, but such a practice was unheard of. If the state had replaced a malik, it is difficult to imagine how the appointed malik could acquire the political capital to lead the qaum in a meaningful manner.

Similarly, although documents such as land titles were considered official government documents, they were rarely endorsed by government officials. Instead, when a deed was transferred, several maliks, mullahs, or other local notable figures signed it. When government officials did rule on such a document, they recognized the signatures, despite the unclear relationship between these local leaders and the state. Thus, in almost all land rights disputes, the state continued to grant local leaders power to shape the outcomes, even when the district governor seemed to be officially resolving them.

International intervention also revealed the ambiguity of the state's power, even as government officials acted as though the state's powers were not distinctly demarcated. This was most obvious in the presence of international troops. Although their presence prevented a state monopoly on violence, the police chief went out of his way to demonstrate his partnership with the troops, insinuating collaboration even when there was clearly none. On the other side of the supposed division, local leaders took advantage of government funds through programs such as the NSP, while deemphasizing that this money actually came through government channels and instead focusing on the fact that NGOs (not the state) delivered the funds.

The more ambiguous a figure's political position, the more important it was to promote the fiction of the state as a bounded entity. Local leaders gained the most legitimacy when they could argue that the state was removed and ineffective. As a result, leaders argued, it was their duty (wazeefah) to use NSP funds without consulting the local authorities. Simultaneously, they gained influence by proving they could extract funds and other resources from the state and additional places. Privately these figures could tell their allies they were delivering funds for their group without being tainted with the corruption that most people associated with the government. In the meantime, the fiction of the bounded state allowed them to publicly accuse rivals of corruption whenever they accessed government funds the same way. This is one of the reasons the malik who had brought the engineers to Istalif could not plead his case more directly in the public setting of the district governor's office. To have done so would have revealed the extent to which his connections were built on personal, possibly corrupt, links. He, like other local leaders, could privately take advantage of the unbounded nature of the state, but could not publicly expose that nature.

EXPLOITING THE LACK OF BOUNDARIES

The absence of clear boundaries between the state and civil society, and the resulting ambiguities, created opportunities that individual actors could exploit. Poorly defined central power allowed these individuals to take advantage of the moments when power was not clearly demarcated, or when the powers of government officials and local leaders were untested. Using such a strategy was risky, and there were only a few notable figures brave enough to threaten upsetting the town's delicate balance in public spaces.

One of the most mysterious figures who succeeded in exploiting the ambiguous boundaries of the state was Zabiullah, whom I introduced in the interlude that precedes this chapter. Zabiullah claimed to work for the intelligence branch of the Ministry of the Interior; he did not report to the district governor or the chief of police. Sometimes I saw him several times a week; other times he disappeared from town for weeks at a time. His position was never entirely clear. Some Istalifis told me with conviction that he reported directly to the president, while others claimed with the same conviction that he worked for the Afghan military. Some even referred to him as a *jasus* (spy), and others said he worked for the head commander in town. Finding information about him was difficult; people seemed more afraid of him than they were of the police chief, even though Zabiullah only occasionally traveled with armed policemen and usually only carried a sidearm. Most of their fear came from the fact that he deliberately cultivated an aura of mystery.

It was never clear to me, or to most people in Istalif, exactly what information Zabiullah was gathering or what his role was, and he used that lack of clarity to his advantage. More than the district governor or the chief of police, people gave him wide berth in the bazaar. When he asked questions, people responded quickly, hoping he would move along. As a result, my friends tried to ignore his rather rude visits and inquires, something they would not have done with someone's whose power was more clearly defined.

Zabiullah's power did have limits. Because his power was largely based on the ambiguous nature of his authority, if he committed any act that truly tested his power he would have to reveal its limits, thereby eliminating his greatest advantage. I never formally interviewed Zabiullah; like everyone else, I felt intimidated and thought it best to avoid him, not to mention the fact that I would hesitate to believe anything that emerged from the interview. I am not sure whether he was aware of the limits to his power, but while I was in Istalif he never involved himself in a major dispute or town issue that might have brought his role into question. Because he worked to keep others in uncomfortable positions and cultivated a mysterious persona, people did not know how to respond him. This caused considerable anxiety in those who interacted with him, and made them less likely to challenge him. People did not fear that Zabiullah would directly involve himself in a dispute as much as they feared his connections to the Ministry of the Interior or a local commander would cause problems, or that he would do something completely unexpected.

Thus, while the lack of a true state–society divide allowed murky figures like Zabiullah to exist in an ambivalent position both inside and outside the system, giving them power, that ambivalence also limited their power. Such a position was only effective if the actor used it very occasionally. Repeatedly crossing the line led to negative consequences, as we will see next.

THE FICTION EXPOSED

Why did actors in the government and the community go to such lengths to affirm the division between the community and the state? In other accounts of the shadow state, there is often complicity: Everyone knows the state is corrupt, but one must work within the system. While everyone in Istalif believed that the state was corrupt, public acknowledgements were rarely made, and actors worked diligently to maintain the fiction. When the fiction was exposed, there were often serious consequences, as actors were forced to confront the tensions between political groups and the inherently unsettled nature of power in Istalif.

In one case, a conflict between a government official and an ambiguous figure took place on the main highway just east of Istalif. (The individual had previously been part of the formal government.) Though the dispute involved national political figures—the attorney general, Abdul Jabar Sabet, and Panjshiri General Din Mohammad Jurat—its proximity to Istalif and the fact that it involved a prominent regional leader made it a topic of discussion for several days. People spoke of the episode as a lesson about what could happen when disputes were allowed to escalate.

As people discussed the confrontation, everyone agreed there had been a fight between Abdul Jabar Sabet and Din Mohammad Jurat, but they debated the details. This local account is mainly from Istalifis, but it includes reports from some informants in Qara Bagh and Kabul, and one informant who claimed to have actually watched the initial incident. All my informants agreed on the initial details: On Friday, June 8, 2007, the attorney general Abdul Jabar Sabet, a Pashtun, was on the road from Kabul, headed north toward Charikar, for a picnic with several government officials from the area. As was typical on Fridays, there was a serious traffic jam on the main highway. While traffic in one lane slowed, large four-wheel-drive vehicles owned by rich Kabulis, international organizations, and high-ranking government officials often drove along the shoulder or in the opposite lane—into oncoming traffic.

Such road violations were common in and around Kabul, and policemen rarely stopped vehicles, in order to avoid the risk of interacting with passengers who were government officials, commanders, or employees of international security firms. Istalifis who regularly traveled between Kabul and Istalif generally did little more than curse them as they sped by. This avoidance behavior by the police demonstrated the useful fiction of the rational and bounded state. Acting as if anyone in expensive vehicles was a government official or had government sanction, police officers avoided the inevitable conflict from challenging the drivers, most of whom did not have any official mandate to violate traffic laws. Particularly on a Friday, all these factors could lead to complete gridlock, as traffic using the opposite lane ran up against oncoming traffic, forcing a standoff.

On the day in question, Sabet was said to have been so angered by the traffic and the disorder that he got out of his convoy and started directing traffic himself, forcing all the cars driving into oncoming traffic back into the proper lane. Most people considered this an audacious and somewhat undignified thing for the attorney general to do. At one point, however, a convoy of police vehicles came speeding up the now partially cleared lane, screeching to a halt right in front of Sabet. The convoy belonged to General Mohammad Jurat.

There were contradicting accounts among my Istalifi informants as to who Jurat was, reflecting the ambiguity of certain figures in Afghanistan and the lack of clarity between commanders and government officials. Everyone called Jurat a general, but most agreed he was no longer a general or even an official government employee. Most described him as a commander who had been high up in the Ministry of the Interior, but had been forced out as Karzai consolidated power. Jurat was a Tajik from the Panjshir; after being removed from his position at the ministry, he had started a security firm, some said with American partners. No one was clear why he had a police escort, but this was common for quasi-government officials.

According to most accounts, Sabet did not know it was Jurat's convoy when it stopped (though this contradicts most of the stories in the international press, and many Istalifis could quickly identify local figures in convoys as they sped past). The first vehicle in the convoy did not have a license plate, and Sabet began berating the driver for this and for driving in the wrong lane. General Jurat, who was riding several cars back, stormed out of his car and began screaming at Sabet for stopping his convoy. Sabet evidently hit Jurat with a water bottle.[14] Immediately, guards from both sides started exchanging blows and the two men were pulled apart. Guns were drawn, and the parties took positions on either side of the road.

Here, accounts begin to differ. Shots were apparently fired, but no one was killed. At this point, most Istalifis claimed that a local commander with a compound nearby, who was allied with Jurat, intervened and took Jurat and his men into his home. Eventually, Sabet and his men returned to Kabul. The next day, Sabet sent police to arrest Jurat at the commander's house (some accounts said this took place after Jurat had returned to Kabul). Another firefight broke out, in which six police and security men were killed, but Jurat escaped back to the Panjshir.

Later, Sabet used the national and international press to attack Jurat. Claiming to have been unarmed, he said it was a deliberate kidnapping attempt.

Interestingly, Jurat never spoke with the international press but did give an interview to Tolo, a local television station, several days after the event. Karzai initially seemed to support Sabet in the affair, but over the next couple of days there were rumors that groups of men from the Panjshir were coming to Kabul to protest Jurat's treatment, and such protests could turn violent. Some of the most extreme rumors claimed that the Panjshiris were preparing to attack the capital, though most people I spoke with did not really believe this. Karzai apparently met with some elders from the Panjshir to defuse the situation. The next day, Sabet publicly declared that the entire episode had been a misunderstanding, implausibly stating that he and Jurat were, and always had been, friends.

In telling the story, Istalifis generally sympathized with Jurat, partially because he was a Panjshiri who had been removed from his post at the Ministry of the Interior at the same time that the main commander in Istalif had been forced out of town in what was perceived as an effort to crack down on Tajik, and specifically Panjshiri, influence in the national government. More importantly, Istalifis were critical of Sabet's actions during the episode. Even those who noted Jurat's corruption argued that he had been an important figure during the jihad, and that government officials should respect such figures. This defense of former mujahideen was common, and the national government often went out of its way to accommodate former fighters. Sabet's actions were seen as a violation of this informal truce.

My informants also described Sabet's actions as ill-advised and lacking in dignity. By stepping out of his car and attempting to direct traffic, he was doing what a strong leader would have simply ordered his men to do. Sabet had spent a good deal of time in Canada in the past years, and people clearly felt that he had been too influenced by foreign ideas. Who was he to get out of his car and direct traffic? Why would he hit another man with a water bottle? Why did he attack Jurat's house, instead of negotiating first, as most elders would? Clearly, he had forgotten how Afghan politics worked. Moreover, Sabet's public apology made him appear weak and unsupported by the president. While there was also some criticism of Jurat, the Istalifis generally defended even his most extreme actions. In his attack he expressed his disdain for Sabet, his refusal to acknowledge his authority, and Jurat's own affirmation of his right to be violent, all without pulling out a gun, which could have caused countless casualties in the traffic, perhaps destroying the tentative truce between Pashtuns and Panjshiris in the national government.

The entire incident was fascinating. It was discussed at length by many Istalifis because, in that one moment, much of the carefully suppressed political tension in Afghan politics came to the surface. There were elements of Tajik against Pashtun, traditional leader against government bureaucrat, those who had left Afghanistan for the West against those who had stayed during the entire jihad, and Kabul against the provinces. All these were major issues in the national political landscape in the years following the fall of the Taliban, but leaders rarely discussed them in public. The local and national tensions that were normally obscured by the fictional divide between state and society were dangerously exposed. People feared violent repercussions and were relieved as the situation defused (though only after President Karzai expended a good deal of political capital). Ultimately because he had stepped out of the role state officials were expected to play, Sabet was the one that most Istalifis condemned, and most were unsurprised when Karzai forced him to apologize on national television.

More than anything else, the episode seemed to remind Istalifis how fragile the political balances in Afghanistan were and how easy it was for situations to escalate to violence. This situation convinced community members and government officials in Istalif that continuing to act as if the state were bounded, rational, and authoritative was a far better strategy than dealing with its ambiguities.

INTERNATIONAL PERCEPTIONS OF THE STATE IN AFGHANISTAN

International accounts of the conflict by the media and by policy makers were rather different from local accounts, reflecting the difference between Istalifi perceptions and the international community's understanding of the Afghan state. Although the incident was not a major news story, many of the major outlets with journalists in Kabul reported it. The way they framed the event told a very different story. Immediately following the episode on the highway, Attorney General Sabet gave an interview to national and the international media that became the basis for most accounts in the international press.[15] Voice of America, for example, claimed Sabet had been beaten with rifle butts and quoted him as saying it had been an orchestrated kidnapping attempt.[16] Some international analyses saw the event as "not isolated . . . strongmen, motivated by power and ethnic tensions, were acting congruently against the Karzai Presidency."[17] No one I spoke to in Istalif described the incident as a kidnapping attempt, nor did they recount any other conspiracy theories. This is remarkable, because Istalifis often blamed deeply rooted conspiracies for shaping national and international politics.

Having had previous press coverage, both Sabet and Jurat had established reputations in the media. Most international accounts spoke of Attorney General Sabet, who had lived for many years in Canada, as the victim in the story. In 2006, when he was appointed attorney general and was widely praised in the Western media as a reformer who would rein in corruption. In the *Washington Post*, Pamela Constable wrote that he had "already earned a reputation as a fearless, even fanatical crusader. Blunt and impatient, he appears eager to shake up the status quo and indifferent to his growing list of enemies in high places."[18] His image was helped by the fact that he was a charismatic figure with a long white beard, who played to the Western media by declaring a "jihad" against corruption.

The international press portrayed Jurat, on the other hand, as the type of person who was responsible for the lack of stability in Afghanistan. The *Chicago Tribune* referred to him as a "stocky cop known for tough questioning of suspects" and implicated him in the assassination of Aviation Minister Rahman, suggesting that he was also plotting the murder of Interior Minister Wardak.[19] The article gave no evidence to support these claims, and most of the quotations came from allies of Jurat's chief rival in the Ministry of the Interior. The quotes mostly point to Jurat's questionable history, spent in Afghanistan instead of the West, and his involvement with a private American security firm.

Most international accounts described the event as reflecting the corruption and weakness of the state in Afghanistan. Barnett Rubin, a noted American analyst and advisor to diplomat Richard Holbrook, used the incident in his blog to counter charges that Afghanistan was becoming a "narco-state." He defended Sabet by pointing to the incident as an example of his commitment to rooting out corruption. Rubin's description made the event sound like an attempted arrest, claiming Jurat had "detained Sabet and disarmed and beat his men."[20] In these accounts, Sabet was praised as the reformer trying to create rule of law, and Jurat was depicted as the corrupt figure outside the state. These versions tended to push aside the other layers of the conflict—ethnicity, economics, and regionalism—reducing the event to a fight between a reformer and a commander.

Istalifi commentators were troubled by the incident, but their concern was not about threats to the state. They were generally concerned that the episode had been allowed to escalate, thus demonstrating the weakness of the state and the ambiguous role of commanders. In international accounts, Jurat was the villain because he threatened Western notions of what the state should look like; the international media assumed the major issue was the fragility of the Afghan state. According to Istalifis, Sabet was the primary offender because he did the most to publicly undermine the division between society and the state. The key difference was that the international community did not fully realize the ambiguity of the state's role in Afghanistan. Instead they acted as if Afghanistan followed the bounded, Westphalian model, with certain figures representing state institutions and all others threatening the state's power. In accounts that describe the state as Westphalian, complaints of corruption come from the idealistic notion that corruption resulted from government officials not performing their duties correctly, as opposed to the reality that corruption reflected the state's lack of clear borders and the ways local patronage networks connected to government officials. This difference reveals how different constructions of the state altered the conceptualization and enactment of politics, from the local to the international level.

HOW FICTION CREATES STABILITY

The masking of certain political realities, particularly the complex and tense ways sovereignty was contested, had clear benefits for most local political actors. The fictional divide between state and society helped maintain stability. For government officials, the independence of the state was a useful fiction because it concealed many weaknesses in the government bureaucracy, and hid the government's inability to assert authority over local commanders and maliks. By maintaining the fiction, government officials could act as if there were no warlords in town to threaten their power. The great number of political actors (described in Chapter 6) and the practice of masterly inactivity (Chapter 7) combined to create a high level of ambiguity and anxiety among individuals in town. With so much of the true power hidden from sight and impossible to gauge, the fiction of the strong, bounded, and rational state—as symbolized in its spatial distinctiveness—helped obscure much of this ambiguity. By creating a narrative of power with the state as absolute arbiter, Istalifis could avoid confrontations over the true allocation of resources and power.

Meanwhile, development funds were entering Istalif steadily, and residents and leaders alike were wealthier than they had been in years, so there was little incentive for local commanders to overtly oppose the government. Furthermore, as we have seen, most social groups in Istalif were precarious. The Malik had to constantly work to maintain cohesion among the potters, as did a wide array of other local leaders. The stability of the myth of a bounded state further stabilized other social units in town and encouraged young men not to look beyond the porous boundaries of their own groups.

At the same time, the international community used the fiction of a firm separation between state and society in several different ways. The international military was always eager to partner with the local power holders, whose authority was ratified by the state. The military rarely had local intelligence, and it was sometimes unclear whom they were expected to be protecting and whom they were fighting. Instead of attempting to unravel the complex relationships among local commanders, international forces treated the police chief as if he were the only significant military force in town. While this missed much of the actual threat of violence, it made the work of international troops much simpler.[21]

NGOs, on the other hand, often emphasized how the state, separate from society, was weak and corrupt. This enabled them to justify working outside the state apparatus, setting up their own methods of delivering services. This occurred on a small scale when, for example, the school principal worked to get new textbooks from the international military. It also operated on a much larger scale, such as when the NSP and other programs completely bypassed the district governor's office. Administrators in development organizations always worried where next year's funding would come from, but as long as there was the threat of Afghanistan failing, grant money continued to pour in, thereby preserving jobs. For NGOs, the international military, and other international political actors, all of whom were accustomed to operating in a political paradigm that conceptualized the state using the Westphalian model, thinking about the Afghan state in different terms was simply impossible. In a globalized world where trade flows and diplomacy all demand certain norms enforced by states, entities that function differently present a serious threat. As a result, it was also essential for international actors to think of the Afghan state in rationalized, bureaucratic terms, even when strong evidence revealed the flaws in this type of thinking.

For Istalifis, the fiction of the state as bounded was useful because it lowered instances of violence between the state and the groups that threatened the state's supposed monopoly on violence. The difference between local and international actors was that local actors understood the ambiguity of the state, while international actors relied expressly on the assumption that the state was bounded. Even if the state was ineffective and unbounded, for local actors this was something that could mean additional external aid programs—a "failed state" could even lead to more international aid—whereas if the international community admitted the ambiguous role of the state, it would have been necessary to completely rethink paradigms of international aid and intervention. Simultaneously, the fiction of the boundary of between state and society allowed individuals such as Malik Abdul Hamid and the district governor to constantly renegotiate who had decision-making authority. This allowed the district governor to delegate authority to local leaders, who were more familiar with local political issues, without acknowledging that he was conceding power.

Could Istalifis have more actively resisted the state, which was ineffective, corrupt, and generally treated with disdain? Perhaps. But while I was in Istalif, the alternatives were unclear. Commanders could have re-exerted their power, mullahs could have regained some of the respect they had had during the Taliban era, the international military could have increased its presence in the area—or all of these groups could have clashed simultaneously. In the end, Istalifis were not afraid of being incapable of throwing off the state; they were concerned by the potential violence and uncertainty that accompanied the alternatives.

Paktya—Eighteen Months Later

The explosion was not strong enough to knock me down. It felt like a strong push against my shoulders, making me stumble forward. I turned in time to see sections of the roof of the building across the street ripple upwards and then fly apart in the air.

A few minutes later, pieces of paper, some still burning, began fluttering down from the sky.

I was attending a youth peace conference that brought young men together from the provinces of Paktya, Khost, and Nangarhar. A qari had led the group in prayer, and the program manager from the Afghan NGO that had planned the conference had welcomed everyone. Each delegation had selected a representative to voice its ideas about how to end violence in the troubled area. The first young man from Khost had risen and begun, in a clear, slightly nervous voice, to thank the organizers.

Then the explosion.

The windows behind us had blast film on them, so they cracked instead of shattering. One pane in the door teetered and then fell, almost lazily, to the ground. I stood with the young men, torn as to whether to move closer to the windows to get a better view, or to go to the back of the room in case there was a follow-up blast. For a few moments we simply stood in the middle of the room, undecided, watching the smoke billow up from the building across the street.

Our daze was broken when two policemen burst through the door, shouting angrily in Pashto. They pushed a few of the young men who were closest to the door around, looked under the table, and, deciding that we were not insurgents, rushed back out the door. They joined a growing crowd of police, military, and bodyguards from the nearby governor's office on the street, preparing an assault on the smoking building.

Several of the more recent attacks in Gardez had been coordinated with multiple bombers and shooters. The police officers' obvious fear was that there was another bomber or group of insurgents in the area. As the young men craned to get a view of what was happening in the street, people were first convinced that the governor's office had been attacked. The office, however, was several blocks from where we were, and the blast had been just across the street. Later, someone came in and told us the building was the office of an American contractor working on setting up small businesses for the U.S. Agency for International Development. The person said five people had been killed; he had seen the body parts.

Another man claimed twelve.

Another said three.

Ten minutes later another group of policemen entered the room, led by a man more obviously in charge, who said we needed to evacuate the premises immediately. The police had set up a cordon in the middle of the street—they directed us to run through it. As the only foreigner in the room, I was told to go first.

So we ran.

About 200 yards away, a boy stood in the middle of the road with a rocket-propelled grenade launcher slung lazily over his shoulder. The boy, who looked about 15, waved at us to stop. We joined the mass of shopkeepers and shoppers in the bazaar, watching the smoke billow up from the remains of the building to the west.

Already some of the spectators had begun to turn away, returning to work.

9 THINKING ABOUT VIOLENCE, SOCIAL ORGANIZATION, AND INTERNATIONAL INTERVENTION

POLITICAL LIFE IN ISTALIF was fraught with tension. Within the family, brothers competed for capital to start businesses and for women to marry. Between families, there was tension over the selling of wares. Qaums struggled against each other for the control of water, religious sites, and connections with international groups. Commanders still owned arms, and a long history of feuding and collapsed boundary walls made land disputes common. Yet with all these tensions, the most interesting aspect of life in Istalif was that it never turned violent. Why were bombings and other attacks so common in Paktya and places much closer to Kabul, but so rare in Istalif? At the center of this ethnography have been questions relating to how group organization shapes decision making, and why individuals might or might not turn to violence as a political tool, especially in a setting with limited state intervention. Violence has long been an important aspect of studies in political anthropology, but even in a town that had recently witnessed decades of war, it remained a slippery concept.

Among social theorists all along the political spectrum, there is surprising agreement on the inevitability of violence. Emile Durkheim saw the march of societies from mechanical solidarity to organic solidarity and the disintegration of social relations as contributing to a rise in violence, particularly to the self. Karl Marx considered force to be "the midwife" to every revolution, interpreting violence not as the cause of change, but as a necessary condition for it. Max Weber, on the other hand, saw the monopolization of legitimate violence as a necessary step toward the modern state. For Weber, part of the process of rationalization and bureaucratization was the struggle to end the arbitrary violence that plagued societies in which power was based on traditional, more personal authority.

One of the problems of theorizing about violence is the difficulty of defining the concept. As political thinker John Keane pointed out, the definition of violence changes over time and space.[1] Structural elements and cultural understandings reshape violence in different settings. Events considered to be violent today were not necessarily considered violent in earlier periods, and the acceptability of phenomena such as domestic violence is continually being redefined. Weber's classic understanding of state authority as the legitimate use of violence leaves many questions, even in the modern state: Is violence within the family acceptable? What about violence in sports and depictions of violence in the media? Surely political violence should be controlled by the state, but how, then, do we explain its incredible persistence in the world today, particularly in Afghanistan?

Hannah Arendt addressed some of the confusion among such political terms as violence, power, strength, and authority, which are at the heart of understanding politics in Istalif. Arendt argued that violence is entirely instrumental. Power, on the other hand, "belongs to the group" and "corresponds to the human ability not just to act but to act in concert."[2] This makes political power the inverse of violence, with violence only occurring "where power is in jeopardy."[3] During uncertain political times in Istalif, power was almost always in jeopardy, and there were numerous social forces acting to suppress violence. Keane, revisiting Arendt's work on violence, addressed some of these concerns by arguing that violence and power are sometimes positively related, and that Arendt's structural understanding of violence oversimplifies the individual's decision to choose violence as a political tool. Violence "can indeed destroy power relationships . . . just as power relationships can sometimes stop violence in its tracks; but out of the barrel of a gun violence can also *create* bonds of solidarity, power relationships in Arendt's sense, where none had existed before."[4]

This is especially true in settings where the state is weak and its monopoly on legitimate violence is uncertain, such as Afghanistan when armed political groups from the jihad period continued to exert political influence and served as a means for political organization on the national level. In such cases, violence can reinforce the power of figures outside the state, and the failure of the state to use violence can erode its power. Instead of a negative linear correlation, violence and power have a continuously shifting relationship; one cannot exist without redefining a culture's understanding of the other. This was certainly the situation in Istalif

To understand and explain violence in its cultural and social setting in Istalif, I have focused on the incentives that shape an individual's decision to act violently or refrain from violence. In his reflections, Keane relied on a narrower definition of violence, as "any uninvited but intentional or half-intentional act of physically violating the body of a person who previously had lived 'in peace.'"[5] This definition is useful for our understanding of politics in Istalif because it emphasizes the way violence implies a change in the status quo—from what is understood to be peace to what is understood to be violence. Violence is a sharp break in social relationships. A slap on the back between friends may not be considered violent, but the same gesture with a stranger is violent because it constitutes a break in the formality and social distance required of strangers. Once violence is introduced, the relationship is forever changed.

Many political scientists have tried using game theory models to explain the individual's choice to engage, or not to engage, in political confrontation and violence. While it is true that individual actors in Istalif made decisions within commonly agreed-upon social bounds, overly deterministic, economic models are problematic when it comes to questions of violence. Individuals are never the purely rational actors game theorists would like. Instead, as Fredrik Barth argued in his attempt to keep studies of individual decision making at the center of anthropology, "cultural stock" and the "accretions of experience— modeled by premises, tacit assumptions, and cultural imagery variably shared by the group" combine to shape the individual's decision-making process.[6] While many of the potters in Istalif lived under similar social constraints and economic conditions, their own experiences made their political decisions unique. Individual experience and knowledge ensured that decision making, even in social and cultural contexts that could shape the process and the outcomes, was still, inherently, individual.

Further complicating the matter for game theorists, violence, unlike many economic decisions, represents a change that tends to be unpredictable. As Arendt pointed out, "violence harbors within itself an additional element of arbitrariness; nowhere does Fortuna, good or ill luck, play a more fateful role in human affairs than on the battlefield."[7] This element of unpredictability and ambiguity is important. In Istalif, violence was not feared so much for the physical injury it might cause; the people of the town were more concerned about its unpredictability and the political chaos that could grow out of a single violent act. This creates a problem for social scientists attempting to formulate a model that explains decision making and violence, because the potential outcomes are often unknown to those making the decisions. Game theory models are generally unsuccessful when it comes to violence because violence and its unpredictability often threaten to end the game completely.

To a certain degree, this is true of all forms of violence—from Arendt's description of the nuclear arms race, in which violence threatens to destroy all life, to Istalif, where any violence threatened to reignite old feuds or involve international military forces, thus destroying the tenuous local political balance. This also suggests that, while there is a spectrum of small-scale to large-scale violence, violence is difficult to control, and even the most minor incidents can escalate violence. It is for this reason that government and social structures are often so concerned with regulating violence.

SOCIAL ORGANIZATION AND VIOLENCE IN ISTALIF

Conducting research in Istalif and, later, in other parts of Afghanistan, I was constantly confronted with questions about violence. The country had been at war for thirty years. During that time, Istalifis had witnessed an incredible array of violence, from aerial bombardment by outsiders to civil war between neighboring villages, culminating in the complete razing of the town by the Taliban. The partially reconstructed buildings around town and the ruins of the old bazaar mosque were not the only reminders that violence was always a possibility; police, international troops, and members of former local militias moved around town, heavily and conspicuously armed. Even local men with no such ties often carried shotguns at night. The high number of amputees showed the physical scars of war; psychological scars were less obvious, but still apparent in the cases of post-traumatic stress disorder. People pointed at young men who had been imprisoned and tortured by the Taliban, often saying simply that they were "not right." War continued to predominate the town's collective memory. Even when I was conducting interviews about purely economic aspects of life, it was rare for a speaker not to mention the years of war at some point during our talk. In almost every life history I collected, the destruction of the town and the resulting years of displacement were the central points of the narrative.

Internationally and throughout Afghanistan, there was constant debate about the continued fighting between international coalition forces and the Taliban. Civilian causalities from Taliban suicide bombers and coalition air strikes demonstrated to ordinary Afghans that there was no clear line between terrorist violence and legitimate, state-sponsored violence. The entire premise of the escalation of international troops during my time in Istalif was that internationally sanctioned violence could halt the illegitimate violence of the Taliban. But who defines whether violence is legitimate or not? The state? The international community? The Afghan people? Civil society?

In reflections on violence, there is a tendency to focus on the way society is centrally organized and governed. For Hobbes, the state controlled violence; for Thomas Paine, the monarchy led to violence; for Arendt, totalitarian dictatorships chiefly created violence; for Marx, violence resulted from the need to throw off repressive forms of domination. Each approach argued that certain social and economic configurations lead to increased instances of violence within a society. In a world where most continue to use the Westphalian model of the sovereign, clearly bounded nation-state to describe the current world order, many rely on Weber's classic definition of the state—an entity with a monopoly on violence—to explain the distribution and regulation of violence. But, while states continue to discuss relationships using rhetoric based on the Westphalian model, our notions of the state and sovereignty have become much more nuanced. Foucault's conception of governmentality and the ways it has been expanded to ask how sovereignty is both manifested and enacted demonstrates that the state rarely actually has a monopoly on violence and highlights the importance of state performance of violence in order to enact sovereignty.[8]

Other writers have emphasized the ways in which the state, particularly in places with significant international presence, has become increasingly complicated by a series of international and extra-state actors, ranging from the United Nations and NGOs to terrorist organizations.[9] Such international groups clearly did play a role in Istalif, especially NGOs, and there was considerable competition over international funds. Since concluding my research in Istalif, I have spent much more time in Kabul, examining elections and working more closely within international groups; as a result it is tempting to focus on how these groups are influencing the political life of Afghanistan on a national level. Doing this, however, threatens to overstate the importance of the international community on a local level. NGOs did contribute funds to the local economy, and in some cases created perverse incentives that limited economic cooperation, but in general, daily life in Istalif was rarely interrupted by international groups. There has been a trend in the anthropology world over the past decades to focus on the ways NGOs reshape social structures.[10] This literature, however, if applied to the Istalif case, exaggerates the ability of NGOs to influence politics and economics and understates the resilience of local structures.

Funds from NGOs increased the economic stakes in the town, but the financial support rarely altered the way business was done. Similarly, the international military threatened to intervene if the area became violent, but it did very little on a daily basis. While it is tempting to argue that the international community is to blame for all of Afghanistan's current ills (and they are guilty of much), analyses that center specifically on these international groups detract from the focus on local actors, who continue to be the true decision makers in the community. In Istalif, NGOs and the international military were political forces, but they were generally not as influential as other actors, such as local elders, mullahs, and commanders.

At the end of the twentieth century and beginning of the twenty-first, the relationship between state and sovereignty has become increasingly problematic, while violence and wars appeared to be less concerned with national boundaries. The central conflicts in the world today involve violent revolutions, civil strife, and terrorism—in the Balkans, Somalia, Sudan, Yemen, the frontier region between Pakistan and Afghanistan. Even strong states, such as Saudi Arabia and the United Kingdom, seem to have a tendency to promote certain forms of political violence despite their ostensible monopoly on legitimate forms of violence. It seems that violence is not as linked to governmental forms, as many social thinkers would have us believe. The case of Istalif specifically demonstrates that stability is not a consequence of state institutions, and forces us to rethink what is it that makes groups choose—or not choose—violence as a political tool.

Social scientists seem drawn to the ends of the spectrum: On one side, states control most forms of violence; on the other side are stateless societies where violence must be regulated through other means. Weber's bureaucratic, state-based analysis of violence is unhelpful in Afghanistan, where the state has limited reach and many other groups have access to violence, legitimate or otherwise. In opposition to this analysis, many classic anthropology studies, such as E. E. Evans-Pritchard's work on the Nuer, examined the organization and management of conflict and power in acephalous societies.[11] This may help us understand many tribal feuds in Afghanistan, but classic works that rely on structural concepts such as segmentary opposition do not accurately describe political life in Istalif.

Tribal algebra in Istalif broke down in the face of friendships, business relationships, and marriage alliances that crossed traditional patrilineal lines. In addition, even when local issues did not include the national or international military, the Afghan state and international forces were a constant presence in daily politics, though they rarely intervened. With the country's main U.S. airfield and a key detention facility for captured Taliban just down the road in Bagram, it was clear to Istalifis that they were implicated in a series of decisions that had global ramifications. Without state or "tribal" controls on violence, the central fear of many Istalifis was that small-scale violence, such as a feud over land or marriage, would spiral upward, involving an increasing number of actors, including the government and local warlords. With the memory of the Taliban's brutality still fresh, the vision of local political or social violence leading to full-scale war was never far from people's minds.

The lack of violence in Istalif coincided with a high degree of political tension, generated in part by a strong belief in the equality of all Muslim men, as well as the male resistance to domination by any other man with a long history in the region.[12] Politics in Istalif were shaped by what Charles Lindholm calls "competitive egalitarian individualism."[13] Lindholm sees this tendency across the Islamic Middle East as a consequence of ecological and historical conditions that created a political environment similar to the one Alexis de Tocqueville reported in the early United States.[14] In his work, Tocqueville warns of the dangers of democracy and the potential excesses caused by the tyranny of the majority that could arise from a system that allowed for such individualism. Majoritarianism was particularly dangerous in the legislative branch of the government and needed to be closely controlled by other structures, such as judicial review, that were not as vulnerable to the whims of the masses.

In the world of competitive egalitarianism, what prevents a tyranny of the majority or a Hobbesian war of all against all? Tocqueville saw two potential solutions: either despotism or an active civil society. In the first, a strong center controls and manages violence, preventing widespread chaos; in the second, society regulates itself through a series of civic organizations. In post-2001 Afghanistan, a weak (but not entirely impotent) state created a unique balance in which the state was not strong enough to have an absolute monopoly on violence, but was strong enough to prevent former warlords from exerting power as forcefully as they had in the past. The state was not strong enough to be despotic, yet it was able to prevent despotic local leaders from emerging from among the local commanders or traditional elders in most parts of the country.

While claims of direct ties between democracy and nonviolence are oversimplified, and in certain cases outright wrong, some more recent considerations of violence in anthropology have emerged from the brief, lively debate about civil society at the end of the 1990s and early 2000s, especially in the Middle East and South Asia. In these conversations, civil society is often understood as an ideal type, regulated by a transparent, democratic state that facilitates open debate and political discussion and eliminates violence within a society. This model tends to be overly theoretical. In reality, we see numerous accounts of active, vibrant societies that turn violent, from ethnic violence in India to sectarian violence in the Middle East. As Keane pointed out:

> Violence is . . . prima facie incompatible with the civil society rules of solidarity, liberty and equality of citizens . . . [yet] *all known forms of civil society are plagued by endogenous sources of incivility,* so much so that one can propose the empirical-analytic thesis that incivility is a chronic feature of civil societies, one of their typical conditions, and, hence, normatively speaking, a perennial barrier to the actualization of a fully "civilized" civil society.[15]

Several studies from the region demonstrate why the relationship between violence and civil society is not as simple as the democratic peace paradigm tends to assume. Just as the relationships among political groups in Istalif were rarely simple, the way civil society and the state interact often shapes the role of violence in politics. Robert Hefner's recent study of Islam and democratization in Indonesia, for example, leads us to think beyond narrow definitions of civil society and consider what actually drives processes of democratization. He describes how Islamic civic groups can instigate violence, but he argues that this does not mean that Islam and democracy are necessarily incompatible. Instead, democratization depends on formal institutions, such as elections, and on a public culture that encourages "universal habits of participation and tolerance" overseen by a "civilized and self-limiting state." He concludes, "civil society is not opposed to the state but deeply dependent on its *civilization.*"[16]

But if civil society is deeply dependent on the state, political violence depends on how individuals make choices within these political frameworks and how social groups shape the way these choices are determined. Violence in post-Taliban Afghanistan is based on numerous variables, from access to weapons to economic opportunities. As I examined how these variables interacted, it became clear that approaches which studied the way individuals and groups acted toward each other, such as Ashutosh Varshney's investigation of ethnic violence in India[17] and Hefner's analysis of the role of the state and public culture, provided a framework for starting to answer some of my questions about why certain areas were violent and others were not. Though civil society is not a phenomenon commonly discussed in Afghan politics, many of the groups in Istalif—largely based on kinship, but also on profession, business arrangements, loyalty to a common leader, and friendships—raise very similar questions about group organization and violence, particularly since these groups created "a buffer between state and citizens."[18]

These questions were more important in Istalif than in many other parts of Afghanistan due to the quasi-guild system that organized craft production in the area. As Lindholm points out, such forms of economic and social organization have a long history, in the Middle East, of furthering "the peculiar moral stance typical of people who live by trade—an attitude that is individualistic, calculating, risk-taking, and adaptive to circumstances."[19] The result in Istalif was a social system dominated by groups, based on professions that were prone to disintegration due to the fierce individualism and adaptability they promoted. With these groups, and in any study of groups and violence, it was essential to ask exactly what relationships and attitudes were being created and how they played out in everyday life.

While many of the groups were based on kinship ties, boundaries were not fixed, and individuals could potentially leave one group for another. This was especially true of young men; for older men, the political cost of leaving a group and establishing new ties became prohibitively expensive. This made boundary maintenance, in the sense defined by Barth in his reflections on ethnicity, an essential aspect of political life.[20] While the boundaries appeared permanent, their flexibility threatened group coherence. In response, leaders often worked hard to disguise the groups' truly porous nature—something Istalifis often blamed on city life in Kabul, but which was also an important part of political life in Istalif.

Competition is an important aspect of any democratic system. Groups and associations compete for power and attempt to translate political capital into other resources, from economic capital to increased political leverage. In most cases, what generates stability is the fact that competition is regulated by the shared understanding of members of society that, while they may be defeated on one political issue, the system guarantees them the ability to return the next day and compete for other resources. As Hefner points out, however, this regulation depends on a benevolent state with effective institutions and certain democratic values. In Istalif, without a strong state or a consistent international presence in the town, the fear was that unregulated group competition would eventually lead to violence. So although there was inherent competition, it was often muted, taking place only behind closed doors and in whispered conversations.

Istalif's political structures prevented violence, not through direct competition in a public forum, but through the tacit agreement to avoid public confrontation and the understanding that an outbreak of violence threatened the well-being of the entire community. Importantly, this was not a pre-modern or pre–civil society form of political organization. Many Istalifis, especially those who had lived in Pakistan, had been members of active political parties, and international governments and organizations had worked to "grow" civil society, often through NGOs and by promoting elections. Political decisions in Istalif were a product of the available resources and incentives, which often encouraged individual actors to avoid public and potentially violent political forums.

Such a system created a high level of tension, but it was generally in everyone's best interest to suppress competition that could have led to violence. The system appeared harmonious, but that harmony was little more than political theater to mask the strain that underlay political relations in Istalif. The fact that there were numerous groups in town, with membership to each involving a negotiable set of rights and obligations, made group cohesion unstable. Leaders attempted to mobilize politically, but not in a way forceful enough to threaten breaking the group apart. The result of the fragile boundaries was an emphasis on a rhetoric reinforcing the sense that the groups were stronger than they were, while individuals were strongly encouraged not to take drastic political action that would reveal the true group weakness.

Violence, of course, was one such galvanizing act. An individual's resorting to violence would test the boundaries of the various groups, because others would have to decide to support or turn away from the violent person. Thus, there was an immense amount of pressure on individuals to avoid violence at all costs. Such a situation tended to make political actors highly conservative, since any shift in incentive structures in town threatened to realign interests, awaken old feuds, and end the peace that had tenuously reigned in the area since the fall of the Taliban.

This suggests that social scientists need to be careful when drawing conclusions about the presence or absence of violence in certain political settings, and about the interrelationship of violence, group organization, and government institutions. The fact that Istalif was peaceful during my period of study does not mean it will remain that way. The absence of violence should not lead to the assumption that the state had found traction in Istalif which it had not found elsewhere in the country. Istalifis adopted a series of practices that discouraged state penetration into society and temporarily regulated violence. As a result, the lack of violence in Istalif was not a product of a strong state, democratic competition, or even its residents' attempts to avoid state control; it came from a complex political situation based on a temporary arrangement of incentives and the ways that groups organized socially.

VIOLENCE AND INTERNATIONAL INTERVENTION

All the political debates in Istalif took place in the context of an intensifying insurgency in the southern part of the country. There was a growing realization that the international community's attempts at state-building in Afghanistan had run into serious problems. The situation in Istalif illustrates the fundamental flaws in many assumptions that have guided the international intervention—particularly about violence, stability, and state-building in the twenty-first century. This was not simply a case of the international community misunderstanding unruly Afghan tribes. Much of our current thinking about violence, political tension, and instability relies on the assumption that violence is the result of linear political processes: People interact with each other in a society with limited resources; they disagree on the distribution of those resources, which leads to tension; tensions led to disputes; and disputes, unchecked by the state or some other force, lead to violence.

Other paradigms, such as Marxist approaches, may see different causes for violence, but they still regard violence as a phenomenon that occurs toward the end of a series of political processes—in the Marxist case, the inevitable overthrow of the bourgeois. Even Arendt's reflections on the role of violence in politics, which took seriously some of the "arbitrariness" that violence creates, still approached violence in a linear fashion, calling violence "the final arbiter,"[21] growing directly out of the failure of authority. These understandings are deeply embedded in many of the more recent interpretations of civil society and democratization. As Keane pointed out about much of the civil society literature, "civilization was normally understood as a project charged with resolving the permanent problem of discharging, defusing and sublimating violence; incivility was the permanent enemy of civilization."[22] The conclusion by many, especially in places with recent international interventions, is that by "growing" civil society and promoting democratic processes, such as elections, violence can be reduced.

What these approaches assume is that violence is something of a last resort; it occurs when other alternatives have failed and when there are no other options. For those of us living in predictable political worlds where processes and motives tend to be transparent, that is a logical conclusion. Unfortunately, it is not the situation in places like Istalif, where groups are less stable and politics far from transparent. Following the fall of the Taliban, the international community and especially the U.S. government based much of their initial programs on the assumption that political enfranchisement ends violence. This approach argues that by providing political alternatives, particularly in processes such as elections, individuals will not choose violent strategies. As a result, the international community prioritized holding presidential and parliamentary elections in Afghanistan, and even before these elections, both the Bonn Conference and the Constitutional Loya Jirga were meant to give the transition government the aura of democratic legitimacy.

Rooted in many of these conclusions and the programs that grow out of them, however, is the assumption that violence, or even a lack of cooperation, is the failure of a political process, not a strategic decision. What political life in Istalif suggests, instead, is that treating violence as a last resort or as the product only of a failed process ignores the fact that violence is simply one of many political tools available to actors in certain settings. This is especially true in Afghanistan, where the state does not have a monopoly on violence. Accordingly, academics and policy makers should consider the conditions and incentives that lead individuals to select one strategy over another. Political enfranchisement may reduce violence in some contexts, but this is not inevitable. Enfranchisement is often effective strictly because it gives the individual more political alternatives—and yet these alternatives must be more appealing than the option of turning toward political violence. In Istalif, political actors chose not to act violently—not because democratization had somehow let them participate in a civil democratic system, but because violence was a temporarily unappealing choice, given the economic and political incentives in the town.

Instead of a linear model for understanding violence in Afghanistan, I believe we must focus on the most remarkable aspect of political violence: the way the decision to act violently creates a social and political break. When an individual turns violent, an element of unpredictability enters the picture. In Istalif, the political and social conditions had caused a situation in which political power was defined and distributed in such a way that individuals were invested in the preservation of the fragile balance between relatively equivalent competitors. The unpredictable nature of violence, combined with the high levels of political and social tension, could have destroyed that precarious balance. One individual's decision to become violent would put the entire system in jeopardy.

The corollary, of course, is that in a political system where certain actors want to cause serious disruption, violence is an effective tool. We see this in the case of Paktya, where several dominant Pashtun tribes had achieved a relative political balance early in the post-Taliban period. As the insurgency spread into the southeast, however, the Taliban targeted tribes that had been marginalized by the provincial government and international community. These groups were more willing to turn to violence against the government and other groups in the area, because they believed that upending the entire political situation would give them greater access to resources in the chaos and rearrangement of resources that would ensue. The Taliban has made use of this pattern by encouraging marginalized groups to join the insurgency and by directing their attacks at those few who are highly invested in the current political system. The result in Kandahar was a growing number of insurgents from tribes traditionally opposed to Hamid Karzai, his brother Ahmed Wali Karzai, the head of the Provincial Council, and their Popalzai allies, who have monopolized economic resources in the area since 2001, combined with a series of targeted assassinations.

What this analysis of Istalif also implies is that the lack of violence should in no way be considered permanent. Any change in the structures of power or incentives (a weakening of the government, an influx of external funds, an increased insurgent presence, etc.) could quickly make violence a much more appealing option for individuals in town. The reason this possibility is of such concern is that the current political system does not resolve tensions or disputes; it simply suppresses them. As described earlier, ambiguity is a central element in town politics and in the local understanding of the state. Actors who benefit from the poor definition of power and the uncertain allocation of resources may see violence as one of their only political tools if these ambiguities are exposed. If violence becomes a viable political option, it is likely that many suppressed tensions will quickly return to the surface.

Finally, this study suggests that the way we analyze political situations and the likelihood of violence is flawed. The political categories often discussed by international actors are not always the most important for understanding the local political situation. The common approach—that one must first ask whether the state has a monopoly on violence—suggests that the relevant political divide is between society and state. As discussed, this paradigm drives the current international intervention in Afghanistan. In fact, in Istalif, and in much of Afghanistan there are political incentives "to act as if" this divide exists and "as if" the state is a bounded, rational entity. Political categories and actions are not defined by the line between state and non-state actors; instead, power coalesced around political actors operating as religious figures, government officials, and commanders. This is also true among national figures in

Afghanistan; the parliament is an odd collection of warlords, religious leaders, party leaders, and Afghans returned from abroad. To understand politics and the potential for violence in Afghanistan, one must analyze the meaning of the categories in which these powerful figures operate and the local cultural definitions of power, as opposed to focusing on the fictitious state–society divide.

Unfortunately, by concentrating on the state–society divide and neglecting to analyze the role of violence and its changing place in the world, policy makers and academics often assume that violence results solely from the failure of government institutions or supporting elements, such as civil society, democracy, and good governance. As a result, the international community in Afghanistan has, for example, supported voter education during recent elections, but it has not developed many programs to address the way elections have increased political tension and violence in certain areas. These fairly uniform state-building programs ignore the local political landscape and the way cultural contexts shape the nature of violence, particularly its unpredictability.

This unpredictability has important negative and positive consequences for those hoping to understand violence in our world. Asymmetrical warfare in Afghanistan, and elsewhere, gains much of its power from its unpredictability. Conventional warfare takes place on a battlefield, with clear lines and armies making a series of somewhat predictable choices. Insurgents, terrorists, and other unconventional combatants gain their advantage by striking anywhere, at any time. In addition, most security measures in Afghanistan are based on an expectation of predictability—an armed guard in front of a compound will stop an attacker, because that attacker does not want to be shot. The increase in suicide bombers, a tactic that was unheard of in Afghanistan until recently, weakens these security measures by undermining the fundamental assumption—that the attacker does not want to die—behind them.

In many cases, unpredictability leads to increased levels of violence, but it is important to note that it can also *decrease* violence, because it creates a situation in which the consequences of violence are potentially so serious and destabilizing that even enemies agree to work to contain conflict. In Istalif, though the commanders and the chief of police had access to violence, they never used it as a political tool. Local violence would have had immediate repercussions, including decreasing aid and government funds and encouraging the presence of the international military. The fact that international efforts to stabilize Afghanistan have focused on violent areas means that local tensions, land disputes, and political ambiguities in places like Istalif have not been addressed by the Afghan government or the international community. These flawed approaches have potentially serious implications; a lack of violence today does not guarantee a lack of violence in the future.

At the same time, this conclusion has a more positive corollary. If political and economic incentives shift and insurgents cease seeing disruption of the system as their most effective strategy, violence could end as quickly as it began. For example, a decrease in the amount of money being spent in the country, and a drawdown of international troops, seem likely to reduce violence because these measures will remove a significant source of political tension.

CONSIDERING THE FUTURE OF VIOLENCE IN AFGHANISTAN

This study suggests that political agendas that attempt to stabilize Afghanistan over the long term without dealing with the realities of local political conditions, the peculiarities of the Afghan state, and the country's troubled past are also likely to fail. As we have seen in Istalif, Afghanistan's tumultuous history has resulted in a wide range of political actors, forms of power, and residual tensions that the current domestic and international political system does not address. Commanders guilty of war crimes have not been tried. Some of them continue to control local militias. International and Afghan officials have attempted to marginalize local elders, but have not replaced them with a reliable government. Religious leaders, the upper-class elite, and international organizations all continue to have ambiguous, though influential, roles in Afghan politics. As Istalif demonstrates, it is possible for these tensions to be suppressed or alleviated through what I have called masterly inactivity, but it is also possible that some small incident will trigger widespread violence in a community, as historical tensions again come to the surface.

In the political life of the bazaar in Istalif and elsewhere across Afghanistan, countless local actors, local elites, and government officials benefit from how military and development resources have entered the country. Development and stabilization programs alike are being used by local actors for their own ends. The result is that violence has much less to do with the current international intervention (though the resources provided by international groups can increase the stakes in a conflict and make violence more likely) and more to do with local political realities and how groups organize themselves. While instability can increase the likelihood of violence, it can also decrease it if violence would be so destabilizing that it threatened to destroy the entire system. In parts of Afghanistan where individuals and groups have decided they stand more to gain from threatening the entire system than working within it, groups have turned to violence as a regular political tool.

For Istalif, and much of the north of the country during this period, most political actors agreed they had more to lose than to gain from disrupting the current system. To understand violence in Afghanistan and elsewhere we must begin by using approaches that ask how groups organize and individuals make political decisions within shifting systems that the unpredictability of violence constantly threatens to undermine. This allows us to move away from approaches that dismiss Afghans as unruly tribes to be conquered and frustrating institution-building models that dismiss local political realities. Focusing on the potters in Istalif and how they fit into town politics demonstrates the ways that individuals are constantly making choices on a local level about violence and the future of Afghanistan. It is only with this type of approach—looking at the rich political and cultural contexts in which we all make decisions—that we can begin to understand the causes of political violence.

NOTES

If an entry has two dates, the date in brackets is the original date of publication.

Chapter 1

1. Maliks are local elders usually chosen by the community to represent them to government officials. There is some tension between the way certain maliks describe themselves (often the leaders of the community) and the way community members describe them (often as representatives). The term is often used as an honorific (e.g., Malik Farid), much the way Hajji is used for those having completed the hajj (pilgrimmage to Mecca). In this book, I capitalize the term when referring to a specific individual, and lowercase it when referring to the position generically.

2. The term "warlord" is highly problematic and is not used critically enough in most discussions of Afghanistan. The different types and roles of warlords in the area, who were simultaneously feared and respected, are discussed more fully in Chapter 5. For a thorough analysis of the term, see Giustozzi 2009 (particularly 5–9), which provides a framework for understanding the place of such non-state actors in Afghan politics. In contrast with Giustozzi, however, Istalifis generally used the term "commander" to refer to these men, a name that allows much more ambiguity. Throughout most of this book, I follow their lead.

3. While Barth's most influential work on ethnic groups has done much to shape how ethnicity is understood in anthropology (Barth 1988), this study draws more on his thoughts on decision making through a series of premises based on "cultural stock," knowledge, and experience, which leads to actions with their various intentions and interpretations (particularly in Barth 1993, 157–74).

4. As Colonel Haughton, a British officer stationed in the Shomali during the first Anglo-Afghan war, drily noted, it is difficult to precisely define the limits of Kohistan, which means land of the mountains, since most of Afghanistan is mountainous (Haughton 1879, 2).

5. In published works, Istalif is mentioned only in passing in a few historical studies of Afghanistan (e.g., Noelle 1997) and in studies of crafts in Afghanistan (e.g., Olesen

1994). The only substantial work on the town was an architectural study conducted by students at Kabul University, published in Barfield and Szabo (1991). This work provides some beautiful and detailed pictures of the architecture and landscape in the area during the 1970s, but no social or political data.

6. Newby 1958, 94.

7. In Thackson ed. 1996, 162.

8. Masson 1844, vol. III, 120.

9. Burnes 2001 [1842], 146-7.

10. Burnes 2001 [1842], 149–50.

11. Masson 1844, vol. III, 122.

12. Haughton 1879, 2.

13. Haughton 1879, 28.

14. Fortes 2005 [1892], 44.

15. In Tanner 2009, 2.

16. Fortes 2005 [1892], 46.

17. Most accounts ignore the fact that numerous Indian soldiers did survive the retreat. There are many romantic descriptions of the British retreat from Kabul, and in the late 1840s British readers were captivated by a series of best-selling memoirs and studies of the doomed march. Among the best firsthand accounts are Eyre 1843 and Sale 1843 (reprinted 2002). Early histories of the retreat and aftermath include Fortes 1892 (reprinted 2005) and Kaye 1851. For more recent reevaluations, see Hopkirk 1992 and Meyer and Brysac 1999. Fictional accounts from the period include George MacDonald Fraser's Flashman Chronicles and Maud Diver's romance, *The Hero of Herat*, 1912 (reprinted 1913), whose main character is based on Eldred Pottinger.

18. Low 1873, 410–1.

19. Greenwood 1844, 239.

20. Pottinger 1983, 196.

21. Because Istalif was never at the center of the fight between the Afghans and the British (or, later, the Taliban and the Northern Alliance), I gathered most of the information in this section from brief mentions of the town in various memoirs, letters, and dispatches.

22. Stacy 1848, 333.

23. Stocqueler ed., vol. II, 1854, 157.

24. One account puts the number of women and children captured as high as 4,000, but most report it as 400 or 500. See Greenwood 1844, 23.

25. Hansard 1843, vol. 66, 767.

26. Broadfoot et al. 1888, 364–5.

27. Greenwood 1844, 239–40.

28. Hall 1848, 389–90.

29. Low 1873, 482.

30. Hansard 1843, vol. 66, 767.

31. Muhammad 1999 [1929], 123.

32. Muhammad 1999 [1929], 104.

33. Dupree, L. 1980 [1973], 459–60.

34. Jihad is often translated as "struggle" in Islamic studies, and in more popular media as "holy war." In Istalif the term was actually used most often simply to refer to the period of fighting against Soviet troops.

35. In contrast, the town was united in its opposition to the Taliban, and people readily discussed these terrible, but much less contested, political narratives.

36. This account of the Taliban in Istalif comes primarily from Istalifi informants; it also incorporates the accounts of several commanders who fought with Ahmad Shah Massoud. I was not able to locate any Taliban who claimed to have been in Istalif during this period; most of the higher level commanders were active fighting Massoud to the north, so the account is primarily based on Istalifi versions of events. A few Western texts confirm Istalifi accounts (e.g., Tanner 2009; Johnson and Leslie 2004), but even the best academic accounts of the height of the Taliban period include a limited amount of detail about the tragedies that befell the Shomali Plain.

37. Johnson and Leslie 2004, 71.

Interlude

1. Louis Dupree expressed a similar skepticism about economic surveys three decades before, noting that the fear of taxation clouded most economic numbers in Afghanistan (Dupree, L. 1980 [1973], 148).

Chapter 2

1. Masson 1844, vol. III, 122.

2. UNHCR Sub-Office, 2002.

3. Istalif was emptied in 1997, so the population was clearly not 75,000. It seems likely that the report meant to claim that the population had been at this level before 1997, and that this is simply an error in UNHCR recording.

4. UNHCR Sub-Office, 2002, 1.

5. Coburn and Larson 2009a, 3.

6. Central Statistics Office 2006.

7. Elphinstone 1815, 132.

8. Elphinstone 1815, 407.

9. Elphinstone and others during this period used the term Afghan to refer to Pashtuns.

10. Elphinstone 1815, 407.

11. This is not to imply that Pashtun tribal identity is simple; it is often complicated by marriage ties, locality, business relationships, and friendships. These complications are

often masked, however, by the rather straightforward nature of tribal divisions among the Pashtuns in Afghanistan.

12. Elphinstone 1815, 408.

13. Elphinstone 1815, 408–12.

14. Qaum, occasionally transliterated as qwam, quom, or qawm, comes from Arabic, but is also used in Dari, Pashto, and Urdu.

15. Edwards 1996, 50.

16. Olesen 1994, 45.

17. Klimburg 1999, 62.

18. Barth 1959, 16.

19. Olesen 1994, 46.

20. Centlivres 1972.

21. Olesen 1994, 45.

22. Noelle 1997, 107.

23. Barth 1988 [1969], 14.

24. Rubin 2002, 25.

25. This is clearest in the distribution of aid. In Istalif, several aid groups directly approached certain qaums and most worked closely with qaum leaders, further solidifying the qaums' power. In areas of more active insurgency, where "tribal mapping" has become a popular military tool, the labeling of groups by the international military as "friend" or "foe" has led to a similar process.

26. Part of what made Istalif unique was the presence of its remarkable craft industries—primarily pottery, various forms of weaving, and jewelry, but also some rarer crafts such as gun-making and the only domestic production of car filters in Afghanistan. According to the UNHCR, 80 percent of Istalif's economy was craft-based (UNHCR Sub-Office, 2002, 2), although this estimate seems exaggerated because agriculture was still such an important part of economic life in the area.

27. Azoy 2003, 28–9.

Chapter 3

1. As Mohammad Seddiq liked to joke, during the winter the older men of Kulalan sat under their *sandale*, a raised wooden table with embers under it that kept the lower half of the body warm. When I asked what else they did, he would laugh and say "Nothing! We just sit under our sandales all winter!"

2. Most glazes were lead-based, and this stage in the process was probably the most detrimental to the potters' health. Several NGOs had worked briefly with the potters to try to convince them to move away from lead-based glazes. A Pakistani woman had worked with the potters for several months before my arrival. She had been sent by an American NGO to train the potters in using lead-free glazes and in marketing techniques. The potters were aware of the potential harm, but lead-free glazes were expensive

and tended to crack more than lead-based glazes. Since no organization had presented a truly viable economic alternative to the lead glazes, the potters continued to rely on them.

3. Eleven out of twenty-four wheels that I surveyed were donated by this group, but most of the workshops that owned multiple wheels tended to rely first on the more recently made ones from the NGO. Multiple NGOs worked at different stages with the potters, and it was surprisingly difficult to determine which groups had provided what aid—a partially political phenomenon discussed in the next chapter. These groups included the Polish Humanitarian Organization, Aid to Artisans, Agence d'Aide à la Coopération Technique et au Développement, Turquoise Mountain, the Aga Khan Trust for Culture, and the Eurasia Foundation. Other international aid groups worked in the town, but never specifically in the potters' neighborhood.

4. The difficulty of building residential compounds on the steep land in Istalif contributed to the great diversity in their size and shape.

5. Dupree, N.H. 1967, 2.

6. The other economic opportunity that young men commonly discussed was setting up a small shop in the bazaar, which had both lower start-up costs and significantly less risk, because many shops kept a minimal stock that could be sold to neighboring shops at only a slight loss if the business failed.

7. Evans and Rye 1976.

8. This NGO had already established a health and education center in town that was considered a women-only space, something the potters regarded with a great deal of suspicion.

Chapter 4

1. Dupree, L. 1980 [1973], 132.

2. These numbers are based on 21 days of surveying in June and July 2007.

3. As was true in many bazaars in Afghanistan, it was considered shameful for a family to send women to do the shopping, because this indicated that the men were too poor and busy to fulfill their duties. There was, however, a complex network of paths and alleys around the edges of the bazaar that allowed women to move about town and visit other areas without being observed in the bazaar.

4. In general, Sayeds and potters did not have very good relationships (see Chapter 7). This Sayed's relationship with the potters was at least partly due to the fact that he was a small orchard owner and not as well-off as many other Sayeds in town.

5. Pottery shops along this stretch of road in Qalah Murad Beg and Qara Bagh existed during the 1960s, according to a guidebook produced by the Afghan Tourist Organization (Dupree, N.H. 1967, 2–3).

6. There is some variety in these numbers, because of the way kilns were loaded. Most kiln loads, however, were a mix of different-sized objects; the estimates represent this type of balanced kiln load.

7. All of these prices are based on observations of numerous transactions, and they reflect the prices shopkeepers reasonably expected from each category of customer, but there was variety in the pricing system. A seller would often try to get more than $1.00 per pot from Afghan visitors, but might sell for less to a persistent customer.

8. One problem with these estimates and the surveys I conducted was that the number of Kabuli and international visitors varied widely according to security, weather, and time of year. Most potters sold more than 30 percent of their goods to internationals in the spring and summer, and almost none during the winter months. Merchants were more reliable as customers.

9. This practice was not new; in N. H. Dupree, 1967 (facing p. 2), there is a photo of similar pottery trinkets made in Istalif in the 1960s.

10. *Pustin*, which translates as "skin," was used primarily to refer to leather jackets, but could be used for hats, carpets, and a range of leather products. A *patoo* is a long woolen shawl that all Afghan men wear during the winter. Higher-quality patoos usually had a colorful band woven into each end.

11. Afghanistan Institute for Rural Development 2006.

Interlude

1. Emperor Babur recounted visiting Istalif more than 500 years ago (Thackson ed., 1996). Malik Abdul Hamid could mean that Kulalan, the neighborhood the potters lived in, was founded 300 years ago, but he tended to leave this statement ambiguous, suggesting that it was the potters who originally founded the town.

2. Kulal means potter.

3. This tale is a wonderful distortion of the history of the founding of the Naqshabandi Sufi order. Bahodean Naqshabandi Bukhari was head of the Naqshabandi order in the fourteenth century, not the seventeenth. His teacher was Sayed Amir Kulal, but he was famed for being a wrestler, not a potter, and is said to be buried in his village of origin outside of Bukhara. (For more on the two figures, see Kabbani 1995.) How much this history had actually evolved over many years and how much was a rewriting of other histories by Istalifi elders who had traveled to Bukhara was never clear to me.

4. Again, it is interesting to note that the potters had no written *risala*, or text laying out the rules and regulations of the group, as other guilds in Afghanistan and Central Asia do. The fact that the Malik diligently maintained the group's mythology, and that there were some clear moral beliefs associated with group membership, suggests that, perhaps at one point, the group did have such a text, which the group lost. It is also possible, of course, that they had acquired some of these practices through diffusion from other groups, particularly while living in Pakistan.

5. Duad Khan was prime minister from 1953 to 1963 and president from 1973 until his assassination in 1978; Malik Abdul Hamid is referring to Daud Khan's time as president.

Chapter 5

1. The Malik's intermediary position meant he also had to maintain good relationships with government officials, especially the district governor. Due to the relative weakness of the state at this point in Istalif, however, the Malik's obligations to his qaum were much stronger than his obligations to the district governor, who would only consider removing a malik under the most extreme conditions.

2. During my interviews of Provincial Council candidates running in the August 2009 elections, they told a similar story of being thrust forward by the community before declaring their candidacy (Coburn and Larson 2009b).

3. Dupree, L. 1980 [1973], 332–4; Ewans 2001, 32–3.

4. It was not always easy to get a visa to go on the hajj. Securing one suggested connections within the Ministry of the Hajj and Religious Affairs or some related government ministry. By the end of President Hamid Karzai's first full term, there were rumors of so much corruption in the Ministry of Hajj and Religious Affairs that the minister of hajj was not renominated.

5. I have reservations about the potters' claim to have been in Istalif for three hundred years. Many nineteenth-century accounts provide descriptions of the village, some considering economic and political aspects, but none mentions the potters as a group (e.g., Burnes 2001 [1842], Vigne 1843, and Wood 1976 [1872]). Such exaggerations in group mythology are unsurprising, however, given the tensions, in this ethnically heterogeneous area, over land and the "true" original inhabitants of the area.

6. As with the selling of pots in the bazaar, currency was easily convertible. In fact, Istalifis often used Pakistani rupees when discussing bride-price, a practice remaining from the jihad and civil war periods when the afghani was unstable. Informants did, however, also use dollars, and I keep the prices here in dollars for the reader's convenience.

7. Young men relished describing to me the elaborate tricks they used to surreptitiously listen to their cassettes. Early in my stay I asked a young man about the Taliban's ban on girls' education in Istalif. He sighed deeply and said, "Noah, that was a truly terrible time; we were not even allowed to have music at weddings!"

8. Masson 1844, vol. III, 122.

Chapter 6

1. Particularly Rubin 2002, Johnson and Leslie 2004.

2. Barth 1959.

3. Giustozzi 2009.

4. Bourdieu 1986, Bourdieu 1990.

5. Barfield and Szabo 1991, 197.

6. Especially in areas where gozars were not clearly defined, a malik sometimes represented multiple gozars. In Qara Bagh, the district to the east, some gozars had multiple maliks or multiple individuals claiming to be malik. The political system in Qara Bagh

was generally more fractured; this allowed for an ambiguity that was not present in any Istalif gozars during my time there.

7. For a similar model of honor and respect in Swat, see Barth 1985, 174–5.

8. Alexander Burnes, on his trip to Istalif in 1837, noted that the town was decorated for the visiting dignitaries in what appears to be a similar manner (Burnes 2001 [1842], 148).

9. This game had symbolic relevance. Taking more than one's allotted amount of water, and thus denying those below their share, had resounding political implications. Access to water in the winter was less important, so in these games there was an element of symbolic release from the political tensions.

10. See Pedersen 1994.

11. Barth 1959, 100–1.

12. UNHCR Sub-Office, 2002.

13. Many Istalifis reported this same story to me, though it seems more likely that the American was a CIA official, not Madeline Albright, who was Secretary of State at the time.

14. While the shrinekeeper was adamant that he was not a malang, he dressed more like a malang than anyone else in Istalif. His hair was matted and he wore elaborate, old robes. There may have been a strong economic advantage to dressing the part. Most the visitors to the shrine who donated generously were from outside of Istalif, and many expected to see a malang at this type of shrine. This acting may also help explain why other Sayeds, who prided themselves on dressing in newer and cleaner robes than other Istalifis, allowed one man to assume the responsibility of shrinekeeper.

15. While the DDR did have some nationwide success collecting arms, it struggled to integrate former fighters into the Afghan Army (ANA). Only 2.3 percent of former militia fighters chose to join the ANA (AREU 2008; for a further assessment, see also Giustozzi and Rossi, 2006). I spoke with several people in Istalif who had turned in their arms, but could not find any who had been "re-integrated" and joined the ANA.

16. The commander was forced out of town after a shakeup at the Ministry of the Interior attempted to dislodge many of the Tajiks who had gained political and economic power in the upheaval following the fall of the Taliban. At this point, the district governor, who was from Istalif and a close ally of the commander, was replaced by a man from outside the community. This resulted in increasing the divide of power in the town. Not long after my time there concluded, the local police chief was replaced, and this political shift allowed Mohammad Zaher to return to town more regularly.

17. This is the man mentioned in Chapter 3, who had earned his initial reputation by killing many men during a blood feud triggered by a failed marriage arrangement.

18. About a year after the conclusion of my research, his office was moved to the new district government building on a barren tract of land to the north. Security concerns dictated a stronger police presence dug in around the building. This formally set the

government farther apart from the rest of the community, and on the occasions I visited the new office, there were always fewer people there; most of them were police lounging in their vehicles.

19. In most of the other districts where I subsequently conducted research, district governors tended to have more influence and were drawn more actively into dispute resolution in the community (see Coburn and Larson, 2009b). The limited influence of the district governor in Istalif seems to derive from a combination of personality and the robust alternative layers of local political actors.

20. In the cases studied by Hamish Nixon (2008), he found that, on average, district governors had been in office for only 8 months and district police chiefs only 7.5 months.

21. For similar accounts, see The Asia Foundation 2007 and Johnson and Leslie 2004. One study estimated that two-thirds of all international aid in the post-Taliban period completely bypassed the Afghan government (Waldman 2008, 5).

22. The positive opinion about the previous district governor could have been a result of the time he had served in his position. During the early years following the collapse of the Taliban government, state interference was minimal while large amounts of aid poured into the area.

23. The Asia Foundation 2007, 13.

24. Beginning his second full term as president, Hamid Karzai called for district council elections in 2010, with many in the international community continuing to oppose them. At the time of writing, it was still unclear when these elections would occur.

25. This fits many historical trends in both Afghanistan and the Middle East. For more on these trends in Afghanistan, see Tapper, ed. 1983, and for more on the Middle East in general, see Tapper 1990.

26. For a deeper analysis of Afghan perspectives of democracy that raises some similar issues, see Larson 2009.

27. This failure of cooperation between the police chief and the district governor has been reported in other districts as well (Giustozzi 2007, 175). However, I later conducted research in other areas where the two did have a strong working relationship.

28. In considering the Istalifi perception of international military presence, it should be added that from its location in the hills above the Shomali Plain, Istalif had a good view of the Bagram Airfield, the main U.S. airfield in the north of the country and the home of the major American detention facility. As a result, the planes and helicopters taking off and landing were a fairly common sight and a constant reminder of the international presence.

29. Translators were usually not from the same region in which the forces were operating. I later spent a rather awkward hour with some troops outside a base in the southeast. They were trying to communicate with a group of elders who only spoke Pashto, using a Tajik translator who only spoke Dari.

Interlude

1. The presidential and provincial council elections in August 2009 described here did not occur during my period of study in Istalif; they happened while I was conducting research on the election process for the Afghanistan Research and Evaluation Unit (see Coburn 2009, Coburn and Larson 2009a, Coburn and Larson 2009b). However, I continued to track many of the key political players discussed in this work during that period.

Chapter 7

1. There is some overlap here with James Scott's concept of "weapons of the weak," which are often "symbolic sanctions: slander, gossip, character assignation" (Scott 1987, 25). But there are some important differences. In Istalif, these weapons were not used only by the lower class and they were not directly linked with resistance. They were a means of reducing an opponent's political capital, which was more than symbolic.

2. In addition to being associated with the medical idea of watchful waiting, this phrase was used to describe the British Empire's policy towards Afghanistan and other frontier areas of South Asia in the second half of the nineteenth century. The British found it had more to lose by engaging with the Afghans than it had to gain. During this period, they did not actively meddle in Afghan politics, but worked to ensure that Afghanistan did not directly engage other powers. The British used the term differently, particularly since for them it was a deliberate political strategy, while for Istalifis it was the result of the way political power and economic resources were distributed. The end result, however, was the same, and political actors in both periods primarily worked to limit the power of their opponents, creating a tension-filled, temporary stability.

3. The highway between Kabul and Charikar was also the road that linked Bagram Airfield with Kabul. It was one of the best-paved roads in the country.

4. Almost a full term later, this prediction proved true: Provincial Councils continued to be weak and had minimal influence in national and regional politics, while the Wolesi Jirga, though it struggled to reach consensus at times, became one of the only counterpoints to executive power within the national government. In the Provincial Council elections of 2009, some incumbents did not stand for reelection because they were preparing to run for Parliament in 2010, instead.

5. See, for example, Coburn and Larson 2009b, Kippen 2008, Wilder 2005.

6. In the 2009 Provincial Council elections, there were more than 500 candidates.

7. Coburn and Larson 2009b.

8. The difficulties of winning through primarily illegal means seemed to have lessened by the 2009 and 2010 elections, when it was increasingly apparent to voters and candidates alike that fraud was an effective means of winning the election (see Coburn and Larson 2009b).

9. For a complete breakdown of parliamentary seats, see Wilder 2005, 5. However,

political parties remained weak in Afghanistan and alliances within Parliament broke down quickly, meaning that party affiliation was not always politically meaningful.

10. Kippen 2008, 7.

11. The title "wakil" was used to refer to elected parliamentary representatives and other representatives who were appointed directly by the government. People disagreed about whether Agha Mohammad's father had been elected or not.

12. Because votes were not tallied by polling station, the numbers are impossible to confirm. However, in the elections of 2009, Istalifis in certain neighborhoods voted with startling conformity, suggesting the same pattern in 2005.

13. Studies by Wilder and others suggest that fraud was lower in the province of Kabul than in many other provinces, though this was not the case in 2009 (see, for example, Wilder 2005, 26–38). One informant showed me stacks of voting tally sheets a commander had given him (Coburn and Larson 2009b).

14. Wilder 2005, 33.

15. Several travelers made photograph collections in the 1960s and 1970s. Of those that are accessible on the Internet, one of the best is by Dr. William Podlich (Esterson, Afghanistan: Gallery 1). The Norwegian linguist Georg Morgenstierne also provides some interesting examples (National Library of Norway, Georg Morgenstierne).

16. Public space in Istalif was not a simple concept; moreover, public space in Central Asia is not as important to political life as it is in other regions. In Istalif's factional political system, political realms were often well defined. This did not make public space irrelevant; rather, it made the few public areas, especially the bazaar, even more complicated, because authority was so poorly defined outside of such spaces as the mosque or the gozar, where boundaries were clearly delineated.

17. This practice was widespread in Kabul among groups from other regions without tribal names, such as Panjshiri and Kalakani. Normally no one used last names in Istalif.

18. I believe these numbers to be fairly accurate, although gathering economic data in Istalif presented several issues, as discussed previously (see Chapter 4). In addition, 32 of the shops were being used for either storage or some other purpose, and I could not determine ownership of those buildings during the time of the survey.

19. For such land, the default answer to the ownership question from most Istalifis was simply "the government." In the town to the east, where some rain-fed wheat was grown on unirrigated hills, there was a significant conflict when the government tried to exert control over land it had left for several decades.

20. UNHCR Sub-Office 2002.

21. Demonstrating the collective nature of many disputes in Istalif, the path was only used by a group of pottery families who lived in one section of the neighborhood. Despite this, Istalifis almost always described the dispute as being between the entire pottery qaum and the entire Sayed qaum.

22. The struggle over water in the area around the Shomali Plain has likely been continuous for centuries. Emperor Babur described water channels in Istalif that he constructed, and the defeat of the British at Charikar in 1841 that proceeded the disastrous retreat from Kabul resulted in part from the fact that the water channels leading to their fortification were all diverted, forcing the British to abandon the fort (Haughton 1879, 59).

23. "Aw" is the local pronunciation of *ab* (water).

24. Above the village there were also numerous irrigation channels, but I found no mir aws in this area. It is possible that because the population was less dense in that location, there were fewer disputes over the distribution of water. It is also possible that families were more closely related in this area through kinship and marriage ties and did not need an outside mediator, such as a mir aw, to resolve their disputes.

Chapter 8

1. See Dorronsoro 2005 for examples of the integration between tribes and the state before 1979.

2. Foucault 1991.

3. Harris-White 2002, 80.

4. Hansen and Stepputat 2005, 3–4. In addition, there is extensive literature on the role of NGOs in reshaping and, in many cases, eroding the functions of the state and sovereignty. See especially Ferguson and Gupta 2002, and examples from Inda and Rosaldo, eds. 2002. As discussed in Chapters 6–7, however, NGOs had done very little to alter the structure of town politics or the role of the state. Sometimes they did provide resources, but due to the disorganized nature of most of the international programs during this period, these were primarily opportunities for local political actors to increase their own networks, rather than creating new nodes of power independent from those structures already in place. It remains to be seen if the long-term effect of international aid in Afghanistan reshapes this, but during my research period, in Istalif, NGO resources were simply not predictable or significant enough to cause real change.

5. Ferguson and Gupta 2002, 991.

6. In her case study of propaganda supporting the cult of President Asad in Syria, Lisa Wedeen described the politics of "acting as if" in which "citizens in Syria are not required to believe the cult's flagrantly fictitious statements and, as a rule, they do not. But they are required to act *as if* they do" (Wedeen 1998, 506). This comparison with a very different authoritarian case is instructive. President Asad's regime is supported by a large cadre of secret police who coerce citizens into the politics of "acting as if." In contrast, in Istalif the state had limited coercive powers, but political conditions created incentives such that people still believed it was in their best interest to "act as if" the state was a rational, authoritative, and bounded body.

7. Andrew Wilder was helpful in my thinking about service delivery in Afghanistan, personal communication.

8. This image was particularly meaningful in Istalif; *jeeb*, or pocket, was also used as a general term for wealth, as in "his pockets are empty" to describe a poor man or "the money went into his pocket" to describe corruption.

9. See, for example, Filkins 2009.

10. World Bank 2005.

11. Ferguson and Gupta 2002, 990.

12. Nixon 2008, 34.

13. Lindholm 2002, 264.

14. Another account claims that Sabet first put his head into Jurat's car and spoke rudely to all those inside, including Jurat's wife. According to several people, Sabet had hit people with water bottles before when they had upset him, though in an interview on an Afghan television station a few days later, Jurat claimed that Sabet had hit his driver with the water bottle, insinuating that he was mentally unbalanced (Gardesh 2007). None of my informants in Istalif said he had hit his driver.

15. This brings up an issue rarely addressed in analyses of Afghan affairs—the fact that certain Afghan leaders, particularly those who had resided in the West, were adept at accessing and getting their message to the small group of Western journalists assigned to Kabul. Others—in this case, Jurat—were noticeably less comfortable dealing with this group.

16. Voice of America 2007.

17. Chan 2008, 199.

18. Constable 2006.

19. Torriero 2002.

20. Rubin 2008.

21. As it became clear that dealing only with local police was ineffective and often missed the true power brokers in the area, the U.S. military began developing programs that relied on local militias. These programs, however, attempted to formalize the military groups and make them a part of the formal state, as opposed to treating them as the informal networks they were.

Chapter 9

1. Keane 1996, 65.

2. Arendt 1969, 44.

3. Arendt 1969, 56.

4. Keane 1996, 79.

5. Keane 1996, 6.

6. Barth 1993, 160.

7. Arendt 1969, 6.

8. See, for example, Hansen and Stepputat 2005.

9. See Ferguson and Gupta 2002.

10. See especially Inda and Rosaldo, eds. 2002.

11. See especially Evans-Pritchard 1960 [1940].

12. This moral tension was similar to the conflict described by David Edwards between this fierce individualism, Islam, and the state (see Edwards 1996).

13. Lindholm 2002, 262.

14. Tocqueville 2003 [1835, 1840].

15. Keane 1996, 63, 68.

16. Hefner 2000, 215.

17. Varshney 2002.

18. Norton, ed. 1995, 7.

19. Lindholm 2002, 31.

20. See especially Barth 1967 and Barth 1988 [1969].

21. Arendt 1969, 5.

22. Keane 1996, 19.

BIBLIOGRAPHY

If an entry has two dates, the date in brackets is the original date of publication.

Afghanistan Institute for Rural Development, Ministry of Rural Rehabilitation and Development. 2006. "Literacy Rates and Primary School Enrollment." www.mrrd.gov .af/aird.

AREU: Afghanistan Research and Evaluation Unit. February 2008. "A to Z Guide to Afghanistan Assistance." 6th ed Kabul: AREU.

The Asia Foundation. April 2007. "An Assessment of Sub-National Governance in Afghanistan." San Francisco.

Arendt, Hannah. 1969. *On Violence.* New York: Harcourt, Brace & World.

Azoy, G. Whitney. 2003. *Buzkashı: Game and Power in Afghanistan,* 2nd ed. Prospect Heights, IL: Waveland Press.

Barfield, Thomas J. 1981. *The Central Asian Arabs of Afghanistan: Pastoral Nomadism in Transition.* Austin: University of Texas Press.

———. 2005. "An Islamic State Is a State Run by Good Muslims: Religion as a Way of Life and Not an Ideology in Afghanistan." In *Remaking Muslim Politics: Pluralism, Contestation, Democratization,* edited by Robert Hefner. Princeton, NJ: Princeton University Press.

———. 2010. *Afghanistan: A Cultural and Political History.* Princeton, NJ: Princeton University Press.

Barfield, Thomas J., and Albert Szabo. 1991. *Afghanistan: An Atlas of Indigenous Domestic Architectiture.* Austin: University of Texas Press.

Barth, Fredrik. 1959. *Political Leadership Among Swat Pathans.* London: Athlone Press.

———. 1967. "Economic Spheres in Darfur." In *Themes in Economic Anthropology,* edited by Raymond Firth. London: Tavistock Publications.

———. 1985. *The Last Wali of Swat: An Autobiography as Told to Fredrik Barth.* New York: Columbia University Press.

———. 1988 [1969]. "Introduction" and "Pathan Identity and Its Maintenance." In *Ethnic Groups and Boundaries: The Social Organization of Cultural Difference,* edited by Fredrik Barth. Long Grove, IL: Waveland Press.

———.1993. *Balinese Worlds.* Chicago: University of Chicago Press.

Bayart, Jean-Francios. 1993. *The State in Africa: The Politics of the Belly*. New York: Longman.

Bourdieu, Pierre. 1977. *Outline of a Theory of Practice*. Cambridge, England: Cambridge University Press.

———. 1986. "The Forms of Capital." In *Handbook of Theory and Research for the Sociology of Education*, edited by John Richardson. New York: Greenwood Press.

———. 1990. *The Logic of Practice*. Stanford, CA: Stanford University Press.

Broadfoot, George, William Broadfoot, Edward Ellenborough, and Henry Hardinge. 1888. *The Career of Major George Broadfoot C.B.: In Afghanistan and the Punjab*. London: Murray.

Burnes, Alexander. 2001 [1842]. *Cabool: Being a Personal Narrative of a Journey to, and Residence in that City, in the Years 1836, 7 and 8*. New Delhi: Munshiram Manoharlal Publishers Pvt. Ltd.

Canfield, Robert L. 1973. *Faction and Conversion in a Plural Society: Religious Alignments in the Hindu Kush*, Anthropological Papers, no 50. Ann Arbor: University of Michigan Press.

———. 1984. "Islamic Coalitions in Bamyan: A Problem in Translating Afghan Political Culture." In *Revolutions and Rebellions in Afghanistan: Anthropological Perspectives*, edited by Robert L. Canfield and M. N. Shahrani. Berkeley, CA: Institute of International Studies.

Centlivres, Pierre. 1972. *Un Bazar d'Asie Centrale: Forme et organization du bazaar de Tashqurghan*. Wiesbaden: Reichert Verlag.

Central Statistics Office (CSO), Afghanistan. 2006. "Settled Population by Civil Divisions (Urban and Rural) and Sex." www.cso.af.gov.

Chan, Samuel. 2008. "Breaking the Impasse in Afghanistan: Problems with Neighbors, Brothers and Guests." *China and Eurasia Forum Quarterly*, vol. 6, no. 4.

Charpentier, C-J. 1972. *Bazaar-e Tashqurghan: Ethnographical Studies in an Afghan Traditional Bazaar*. Uppsala: Almqvist & Wiksell Informationsindustri AB.

Coburn, Noah. 2009. "Losing Legitimacy?: Some Afghan Views on the Government, the International Community, and the 2009 Elections." Kabul: AREU.

Coburn, Noah, and Anna Larson. 2009a. "Patronage, Posturing, Duty, Demographics: Why Afghans Voted in 2009." Kabul: AREU.

———. 2009b. "Voting Together: Why Afghanistan's 2009 Elections Were (and Were Not) a Disaster." Kabul: AREU.

Constable, Pamela. November 23, 2006. "Top Prosecutor Targets Afghanistan's Once-Untouchable Bosses." *Washington Post*. www.washingtonpost.com.

Diver, Maud. 1913 [1912]. *The Hero of Herat: A Frontier Romance*. New York: G. P. Putnam's Sons.

Dorronsoro, Gilles. 2005. *Revolution Unending: Afghanistan, 1979 to the Present*. New York: Columbia University Press.

Dupree, Louis. 1980 [1973]. *Afghanistan.* Princeton, NJ: Princeton University Press.

Dupree, Nancy Hatch. 1967. *The Road to Balkh.* Kabul: Afghan Tourist Organization.

Durkheim, Emile. 1984 [1893]. *The Division of Labor in Society,* translated by W. D. Hall. New York: Free Press.

———. 1997 [1897]. *Suicide: A Study in Sociology,* translated by John Spaulding and George Simpson. New York: Free Press.

Edwards, David B. 1996. *Heroes of the Age: Moral Fault Lines on the Afghan Frontier.* Berkeley: University of California Press.

———. 2002. *Before the Taliban: Genealogies of the Afghan Jihad.* Berkeley: University of California Press.

Eickelman, Dale F. 1985. *Knowledge and Power in Morocco: The Education of a Twentieth-Century Notable.* Princeton, NJ: Princeton University Press.

Elphinstone, Mountstuart. 1815. *An Account of the Kingdom of Caubul, and its Dependences in Persia, Tartary, and India; Comprising a View of the Afghaun Nation and a History of the Dooraunee Monarchy.* London: Longman, Hurst, Rees, Orme and Brown, Paternoster-Row and Murray.

Esterson, Clay. 2010. "Afghanistan: Gallery 1." Restored photographs by Dr. William Podlich. www.pbase.com/qleap/afghan_1.

Evans, Clifford, and Owen Rye. 1976. *Traditional Pottery Techniques of Pakistan: Field and Laboratory Studies,* Smithsonian Contributions to Anthropology, no. 21. Washington: Smithsonian Institution Press.

Evans-Pritchard, E. E. 1960 [1940]. *The Nuer: A Description of the Modes of Livelihood and Political Institutions of a Nilotic People.* New York: Oxford University Press.

Ewans, Martin. 2001. *Afghanistan: A Short History of Its People and Politics.* London: Curzon Press.

Eyre, Vincent. 1843. *The Military Operations at Cabul which Ended in the Retreat and Destruction of the British Army in January 1842 with a Journal of Imprisonment in Afghanistan.* London: Murray.

Ferguson, James, and Akhil Gupta. 2002. "Spatializing States: Toward an Ethnography of Neoliberal Governmentality." *American Ethnologist,* 29(4):981–1002.

Filkins, Dexter. January 1, 2009. "Bribes Corrode Afghans' Trust in Government." *New York Times.*

Fortes, Archibald. 2005 [1892]. *The Afghan Wars: 1839–42 and 1878–80.* London: Elibron Classics Facsimile of Seeley & Co.

Foucault, Michel. 1991. "Governmentality." In *The Foucault Effect: Studies in Governmentality,* edited by G. Burchell, C. Gordon, and P. Miller. Chicago: University of Chicago Press.

Gardesh, Hafizullah. June 27, 2007. "Afghan Government Divided Against Itself." Institute for War and Peace Reporting. www.e-Ariana.com.

Geertz, Clifford. 1980. *Negara: The Theatre State in Nineteenth-Century Bali*. Princeton, NJ: Princeton University Press.

Gellner, Ernest. 1994. *Conditions of Liberty: Civil Society and Its Rivals*. New York: Penguin Press.

Giustozzi, Antonio. 2007. *Koran, Kalashnikov and Laptop: The Neo-Taliban Insurgency in Afghanistan*. London: Hurst & Co.

———. 2009. *Empires of Mud: Wars and Warlords in Afghanistan*. New York: Columbia University Press.

Giustozzi, Antonio, and Simonetta Rossi. June 2006. "Disarmament, Demobilisation and Re-Integration of Ex-Combatants (DDR) in Afghanistan: Constraints and Limited Capabilities." Working Paper 2, Series 2. London: Crisis States Research Centre.

Greenwood, Lieutenant. 1844. *Narrative of the Late Victorious Campaign in Affghanistan; Under General Pollock; With Recollections of Seven Years' Service in India*. London: Henry Colburn Publisher.

Hall, J. H. W. 1848. *A Soldier's Life: Being a Connected Narrative of the Principal Military Events on Scinde, Beeloochistan and Affghanistan*. London: Longman.

Hansard House of Commons Debate. February 17, 1843. vol. 66.

Hansen, Thomas Blom, and Finn Stepputat. 2005. "Introduction." In *Sovereign Bodies: Citizens, Migrants and States in the Postcolonial World*, edited by Hansen and Stepputat. Princeton, NJ: Princeton University Press.

Harris-White, Barabara. 2002. *India Working: Essays on Society and Economy*. Cambridge, England: Cambridge University Press.

Haughton, J. Reprint: No date [1879, 2nd ed.]. *Char-ee-kar and Service There with the 4th Goorkha Regiment (Shah Shuja's Force) in 1841: An Episode of the First Afghan War*. Uckfield, England: Navy & Military Press.

Hefner, Robert, ed. 1998. *Market Cultures: Society and Morality in the New Asian Capitalisms*. Boulder, CO: Westview Press.

———. 2000. *Civil Islam: Muslims and Democratization in Indonesia*. Princeton, NJ: Princeton University Press

———. ed. 2005. *Remaking Muslim Politics: Pluralism, Contestation, Democratization*. Princeton, NJ: Princeton University Press.

Hopkirk, Peter. 1992. *The Great Game: The Struggle for Empire in Central Asia*. New York: Kodansha.

Inda, Jonathan Xavier, and Renato Rosaldo, eds. 2002. *The Anthropology of Globalization: A Reader*. Malden, MA: Blackwell.

Johnson, Chris, and Jolyon Leslie. 2004. *Afghanistan: The Mirage of Peace*. London: Zed Books.

Jones, Schuyler. 1974. *Men of Influence in Nuristan: A Study of Social Control and Dispute Settlement in Waigal Valley, Afghanistan*. London: Seminar Press.

Kabbani, Shaykh Muhammad Hisham. 1995. *The Naqshabandi Sufi Way: History and Guidebook of the Saints of the Golden Chain.* Chicago: Kazi Publishers.

Kaye, John William. 1851. *History of the War in Afghanistan from the Unpublished Letters and Journals of Political and Military Officers Employed in Afghanistan Throughout the Entire Period of British Connection with that Country.* 2 vols. London: Richard Bentley.

Keane, John. 1996. *Reflections on Violence.* London: Verso.

———. 2009. *The Life and Death of Democracy.* New York: Norton.

Keiser, Lincoln. 2001. *Friend by Day, Enemy by Night: Organized Vengeance in a Kohistani Community.* Belmont, CA: Wadsworth Group.

Kippen, Grant. 2008. "Elections in 2009 and 2010: Technical and Contextual Challenges to Building Democracy in Afghanistan." Kabul: AREU.

Klimburg, Max. 1999. *The Kafirs of the Hindu Kush: Art and Society of the Waigal and Ashkun Kafirs,* vol. I. Stuttgart: Franz Steiner.

Larson, Anna. 2009. "Toward an Afghan Democracy: Exploring Perceptions of Democratisation in Afghanistan." Kabul: AREU.

Lindholm, Charles. 1982. *Generosity and Jealousy: The Swat Pukhtun of Northern Pakistan.* New York: Columbia University Press.

———. 1988. "Kinship Structure and Political Authority: The Middle East and Central Asia." *Journal of Comparative History and Society,* 28:334–55.

———. 2002. *The Islamic Middle East: Tradition and Change,* revised edition. Malden, MA: Blackwell.

———. 2008. "Culture and Envy." In *Envy: Theory and Research,* edited by Richard Smith. New York: Oxford University Press.

Lister, Sarah, and Hamish Nixon. 2006. "Provincial Governance Structures in Afghanistan: From Confusion to Vision?" Kabul: AREU.

Low, Charles Rathbone. 1873. *The Life and Correspondence of Field-Marshal Sir George Pollock, Bart., G.C.B., G.C.S.I., (Constable of the Tower).* London: William H. Allen.

Masson, Charles. 1844. *Narrative of Various Journeys in Balochistan, Afghanistan and the Panjab, Including a Residence in Those Countries to Which Is Added an Account of the Insurrection at Kalat, and a Memoir on Eastern Balochistan.* 4 vols. London: Richard Bentley.

Meyer, Karl, and Shareen Brysac. 1999. *The Tournament of Shadows: The Great Game and the Race for Empire in Central Asia.* New York: Perseus.

Mills, Margaret Ann. 1991. *Rhetorics and Politics in Afghan Traditional Storytelling.* Philadelphia: University of Pennsylvania Press.

Monsutti, Alessandro. 2005. *War and Migration: Social Networks and Economic Strategies of the Hazaras of Afghanistan.* New York: Routledge.

Muhammad, Fayz. 1999 [1929]. *Kabul Under Siege: Fayz Muhammad's Account of the 1929 Uprising,* translated by Robert D. McChesney. Princeton, NJ: Markus Wiener.

National Solidarity Programme. January 2009. The Islamic Republic of Afghanistan Ministry of Rural Rehabiliation and Development. www.nspafghanistan.org.

Nelson, Soraya Sarhaddi. July 11, 2007. "Afghan Attorney General Criticized in Corruption Fight." National Public Radio, *All Things Considered*. www.npr.org.

Newby, Eric. 1958. *A Short Walk in the Hindu Kush*. London: Secker & Warburg.

Nixon, Hamish. 2008. "Subnational State-Building in Afghanistan." Kabul: AREU.

Noelle, Christine. 1997. *State and Tribe in Nineteenth-Century Afghanistan: The Reign of Amir Dost Muhammad Khan (1826–1863)*. Surrey, England: Curzon.

Norton, Augustus Richard, ed. 1995, 1996. *Civil Society in the Middle East*, vols. I and II. Leiden, Netherlands: E. J. Brill.

Olesen, Asta. 1994. *Afghan Craftsmen: The Cultures of Three Itinerant Communities*. New York: Thames & Hudson.

Pedersen, Gorm. 1994. *Nomads in Transition: A Century of Change among the Zala Khan Khel*. London: Thames & Hudson.

Pottinger, George. 1983. *The Afghan Connection: The Extraordinary Adventures of Major Eldred Pottinger*. Edinburgh: Scottish Academic Press.

Putnam, Robert D. 1993. *Making Democracy Work: Civic Traditions in Modern Italy*. Princeton, NJ: Princeton University Press.

———. 2000. *Bowling Alone: The Collapse and Revival of American Community*. New York: Simon & Schuster.

Reno, William. 1995. *Corruption and State Politics in Sierra Leone*. Cambridge, England: Cambridge University Press.

Roy, Olivier. 1990. *Islam and Resistance in Afghanistan*, 2nd ed. Cambridge, England: Cambridge University Press.

Rubin, Barnett. 2002. *The Fragmentation of Afghanistan*, 2nd ed. New Haven: Yale University Press.

———. July 25, 2008. "Schweich, ICG, etc.—Assume the Existence of a State in Afghanistan." *Informed Consent: Global Affairs—A Group Blog on Current Events*. www.icga. blogspot.com.

Sale, Lady Florentia. 2002 [1843]. *A Journal of the Disasters in Afghanistan: A Firsthand Account by One of the Few Survivors*. London: Waterlow Co.

Scott, James C. 1977. *The Moral Economy of the Peasant: Rebellion and Subsistence in Southeast Asia*. New Haven: Yale University Press.

———. 1987. *Weapons of the Weak: Everyday Forms of Peasant Resistance*. New Haven: Yale University Press.

———. 2009. *The Art of Not Being Governed: An Anarchist History of Upland Southeast Asia*. New Haven: Yale University Press.

Shah, Amir. June 8, 2007. "Afghan AG Accuses General of Kidnap Try." Associated Press. www.washingtonpost.com.

Shahrani, M. Nazif. 2002. *The Kirghiz and Wakhi of Afghanistan: Adaptation to Closed Frontiers and War.* Seattle: University of Washington Press.

Sorel, Georges. 1999 [1912]. *Reflections on Violence*, edited by Jeremy Jennings. Cambridge, England: Cambridge University Press.

Stacy, Lewis Robert. 1848. *Narrative of Services in Beloochistan and Affghanistan in the Years 1840, 1841, and 1842.* London: W. H. Allen.

Stocqueler, J. H. ed. 1854. *Memoirs and Correspondences of Major General Sir William Nott, G.C.B., Commander of the Army of Candahar and Envoy at the Court of the King of Oude.* London: Hurst & Blackett Publishers.

Strand, Richard F. 1984. "The Evolution of Anti-Communist Resistance in Eastern Nuristan." In *Revolutions and Rebellions in Afghanistan: Anthropological Perspectives*, edited by Robert L. Canfield and M. N. Shahrani. Berkeley, CA: Institute of International Studies.

Tanner, Stephen. 2009. *Afghanistan: A Military History from Alexander the Great to the War Against the Taliban*, rev. ed. Cambridge, MA: Da Capo Press.

Tapper, Richard, ed. 1983. *The Conflict of Tribe and State in Iran and Afghanistan.* New York: St. Martin's Press.

———. 1990. "Anthropologists, Historians, and Tribespeople on Tribe and State Formation in the Middle East." In *Tribes and State Formation in the Middle East*, edited by Philip Khoury and Joseph Kostiner. Berkeley: University of California Press.

Thackson, Wheeler, ed. and trans. 1996. *The Baburnama: Memoirs of Babur, Prince and Emperor.* New York: Modern Library.

Tocqueville, Alexis de. 2003 [1835, 1840]. *Democracy in America and Two Essays on America*, translated by Gerald Bevan. London: Penguin Books.

Torriero, E. A. September 27, 2002. "Afghan Lawman Knows He's Marked for Death." *Chicago Tribune.* www.e-Ariana.com.

Tucker, Robert C. ed. 1978. *The Marx-Engels Reader*, 2nd ed. New York: Norton.

UNHCR Sub-Office, Central Region. April 4, 2002. "Istalif District Profile."

Varshney, Ashutosh. 2002. *Ethnic Conflict and Civic Life: Hindus and Muslims in India.* New Haven: Yale University Press.

Vigne, G.T. 1843. *A Personal Narrative of a Visit to Ghuzni, Kabul, and Afghanistan, and of a Residence at the Court of Dost Mohammed with Notices of Runjit Sing, Khiva and the Russian Expedition*, 2nd ed. London: Routledge.

Voice of America. June 8, 2007. "Afghanistan's Attorney General Attacked in Kabul." www.voa.com.

Waldman, Matt. March 2008. "Falling Short: Aid Effectiveness in Afghanistan." Kabul: ACBAR Advocacy Series.

Wedeen, Lisa. 1998. "Acting 'As if': Symbolic Politics and Social Control in Syria." *Comparative Studies in Society and History*, vol. 40, no. 3, 503–23.

Wilder, Andrew. 2005. "A House Divided?: Analyzing the 2005 Afghan Elections." Kabul: AREU.

Wood, John. 1976 [1872]. *A Journey to the Source of the River Oxus with an Essay on the Geography of the Valley of the Oxus by John Yule.* New York: Oxford University Press.

World Bank. 2005. "The Investment Climate in Afghanistan: Exploiting Opportunities in an Uncertain Environment." Finance and Private Sector Development Unit, South Asia Region.

INDEX

Laura Bier, *Revolutionary Womanhood: Feminisms, Modernity, and the State in Nasser's Egypt*
2011

Joel Beinin and Frédéric Vairel, editors, *Social Movements, Mobilization, and Contestation in the Middle East and North Africa*
2011

Samer Soliman, *The Autumn of Dictatorship: Political Change in Egypt under Mubarak*
2011

Rochelle A. Davis, *Palestinian Village Histories: Geographies of the Displaced*
2010

Haggai Ram, *Iranophobia: The Logic of an Israeli Obsession*
2009

John Chalcraft, *The Invisible Cage: Syrian Migrant Workers in Lebanon*
2008

Rhoda Kanaaneh, *Surrounded: Palestinian Soldiers in the Israeli Military*
2008

Asef Bayat, *Making Islam Democratic: Social Movements and the Post-Islamist Turn*
2007

Robert Vitalis, *America's Kingdom: Mythmaking on the Saudi Oil Frontier*
2006

Jessica Winegar, *Creative Reckonings: The Politics of Art and Culture in Contemporary Egypt*
2006

Joel Beinin and Rebecca L. Stein, editors, *The Struggle for Sovereignty: Palestine and Israel, 1993–2005*
2006